LAW OF TORTS

Eighth Edition

Alan Pannett
LLB, Barrister
Director BPP Professional Development

M&E PITMAN PUBLISHING

London · Hong Kong · Johannesburg · Melbourne · Singapore · Washington DC

PITMAN PUBLISHING
128 Long Acre, London WC2E 9AN
Tel: 0171 447 2000 Fax: 0171 240 5771

A Division of Pearson Professional Limited

Eighth edition published in Great Britain 1997

© Pearson Professional Limited 1997

The right of Alan Pannett to be identified as author of this work
has been asserted by him in accordance with the Copyright,
Designs and Patents Act 1988

British Library Cataloguing in Publication Data
A CIP catalogue record for this book can be obtained from the British Library

ISBN 0 7121 1070 4

10 9 8 7 6 5 4 3 2 1

Typeset by WestKey Limited, Falmouth, Cornwall
Printed and bound in Great Britain by Bell and Bain Ltd, Glasgow

The Publisher's policy is to use paper manufactured from sustainable forests.

CONTENTS

Note: a reference in the text such as *see* **12** refers to numbered section 12 of that particular chapter; a reference such as *see* **6: 20** refers to section 20 of Chapter 6.

PREFACE

Law of Torts is designed as a comprehensive guide to the subject. I have endeavoured to set out the principles of the law of torts in a way which, in my experience as a lecturer and examiner, will make them readily understood by students.

The primary purpose is to help students pass their examinations and in doing so to stimulate interest in this common law subject. The book is designed for two categories of students: (a) candidates studying law at degree level and those taking a torts examination as part of the Common Professional Examination or the Diploma in Law, (b) students who are taking law as a subsidiary subject within the framework of a management studies, accountancy or company secretarial qualification. It is hoped that both categories of students will find the text stimulating and a useful guide to key topics within the particular syllabus which they are studying.

There have been many significant developments in the law of torts in recent years, a number of which have been in the area of negligence, not least the House of Lords decisions in *South Australia Asset Management Corporation* v. *York Montague* [1996], *White* v. *Jones* [1995], *Henderson* v. *Merrett Syndicates Ltd* [1994], *Page* v. *Smith* [1996] and *The Nicholas H.* [1996].

In order to provide a detailed and thorough coverage of this area of the law, the relevant chapters have been re-written and expanded.

I would like to thank my wife, Peta Sweet, for her help in the preparation of this eighth edition and particularly for her patience.

I take full responsibility for any errors, deficiencies, inaccuracies or omissions which may be in the text. The law stated in this volume is that which was in force on 1 December 1996.

Alan Pannett
Brighton, December 1996

TABLE OF CASES

TABLE OF STATUTES

1

THE NATURE OF TORTIOUS LIABILITY

INTRODUCTORY

A tort is a civil wrong. The commission of a tort will entitle the person suffering the wrong to seek redress in the civil courts. Torts is essentially a common law area of liability, based upon a bedrock of decided cases. Where statute operates in the law of torts, its function is usually to reform or to limit the common law, e.g. Occupiers' Liability Act 1984. In society it is inevitable that some people will suffer injury, loss, damage or annoyance due to the activities of others. The province of the law of torts is to determine whether such losses are actionable in the courts. Where actionable, a further function is to determine the remedy which the law will provide.

For what kind of losses does the law of torts provide? Needless to say *physical injury*, pain and suffering are covered, such loss now extending to nervous shock. *Economic loss* has more recently been recognised as a form of loss for which compensation is payable. Damage to one's *reputation* is covered through the tort of defamation. The scope of the law of torts is considerable, ranging from liability for negligent actions which cause physical injury or damage to property, to nuisance, trespass and liability for defamation of character. In all of these, and in many other situations, the law of torts governs the issue of liability. That is, whether or not the injured party (the plaintiff) has a right of action against the party responsible for his loss (the defendant). The purpose of such an action is to recover compensation for that which the plaintiff has suffered as a result of the defendant's act or omission.

It is sometimes said that the law of torts is concerned with the readjustment of those losses which are bound to occur in society. In other words, the function of the law is to allocate responsibility for injurious conduct. In this regard the law of torts is an imperfect system. There are some losses for which it is unable to compensate and these losses may well be ones for which we, as persons living in today's society, expect compensation or at least consider it appropriate. To this extent the law of torts is an incomplete compensation system. The law of torts only recognises loss in certain specific areas, it does *not* recognise a general right to compensation. This is a result of the piecemeal way in which this body of law has evolved through the common law.

THE GROUND RULES

1. Defining torts

It is common in textbooks for an author to offer some form of definition to outline the scope of the subject matter on which he or she is writing. The formulation of such a definition in the law of torts is most difficult. Professor Winfield states that: 'Tortious liability arises from the breach of a duty primarily *fixed by law*; this duty is towards *persons generally* and its breach is *redressible* by an action for *unliquidated damages.*' The learned authors of *Salmond and Heuston, On the Law of Torts*, offer this definition of a tort: '. . . a tort consists in some act done by the defendant whereby he has without just cause or excuse caused some form of harm to the plaintiff'.

The problem with defining torts is that some definitions are at too high a level of abstraction and others are too cumbersome to be a practical guide. One can, however, ascertain aspects of a tort which are fundamental to any definition:

(a) *Duty*. Tortious liability is based upon breach of duty. Such a breach is recognised by the law as actionable.

(b) *Tortious liability arises by operation of law*. It is said that tortious liability is 'fixed by law' and not by agreement of the parties. This is a point of contrast between tortious liability and liability imposed through contract.

(c) *A tortious duty is owed to persons generally*. If the wrong complained of arises exclusively from a breach of agreement between the parties it will not be a tort. Such a breach may however amount to a breach of contract, a breach of trust or a breach of some other equitable obligation.

(d) *A tort gives rise to a civil action for unliquidated damages*. Some other remedy, an injunction for example, may be claimed in a tort action, either jointly with or independent from damages; but the wrong complained of will not be a tort unless it is capable of giving rise to a claim for unliquidated damages. Damages are *unliquidated* when they are not for a fixed sum, but are set by the court at its discretion to compensate the plaintiff for the loss which he has sustained.

2. *Damnum sine injuria*

The law does not take account of all forms of harm. Damage which the law does not take account of is what is termed *damnum sine injuria*: for example, the law does not recognise damage where it is caused by a person authorised to act under statutory authority.

3. *Injuria sine damno*

This covers the situation where a person's conduct is actionable as a tort although it has *not* caused any damage at all. We call such a tort one which is *actionable per se*, since it is actionable without proof of damage to the plaintiff. A clear example of such a tort is trespass.

TORTS IN CONTEXT

4. Torts and other branches of the law

It is important to look at the way in which tort relates to other branches of the law as Lord Wilberforce pointed out in *Jobling* v. *Associated Dairies* [1981], where he states: 'We do not live in a world governed by the pure common law and its logical rules. We live in a mixed world where a man is protected against injury and misfortune by a whole web of rules and dispositions, with a number of timid legislative interventions. To attempt to compensate . . . upon the basis of selected rules without regard to the whole must lead either to logical inconsistencies, or to over- or under-compensation.'

It is important at this juncture to draw up the lines of demarcation between tortious and other forms of liability.

5. Tort and crime

Both tort and crime amount to wrongdoing. Both may arise out of the same facts.

For example, Rex is driving his car at high speed through a built-up area. He overtakes a car in the path of an oncoming vehicle driven by Jane. The car driven by Rex crashes into Jane's car, causing considerable damage to both vehicles. Jane sustains a broken arm, cuts to the face and bruising to the body.

In assessing Rex's driving, it may be considered that he was negligent, if his driving was not of the standard of a reasonable driver. It may also be the case that his driving was such that if prosecuted he could be convicted of a criminal offence under the Road Traffic Act 1988, e.g. driving without due care and attention or reckless driving.

The key difference between the two forms of liability, tortious and criminal, lies in the purpose of each of the respective areas of the law and the court in which each matter is heard:

(a) A crime is an offence against *society*, made punishable by the state. A tort is a wrong against a particular *individual*.

(b) The primary function of the criminal law is to *protect* the interests of the public. The primary function of the law of torts is to provide a method of *redress* for individuals who have suffered loss.

(c) Tort is a civil action. Civil actions are governed by civil procedure and are heard in the civil courts (County Court or the High Court of Justice); criminal prosecutions are governed by a different form of procedure and are tried in the criminal courts (the Magistrates' Court or Crown Court).

(d) The object of a criminal prosecution is to punish a person who has been duly tried and convicted of a criminal offence. The purpose of an action in the civil courts is to obtain compensation for the loss sustained by the plaintiff.

6. Tort and contract

The relationship between the law of torts and the law of contract is rather closer than that between torts and the criminal law. The recent trend has been to minimise the differences between tortious and contractual liability, and some academics write of a *law of obligations*. Lord Roskill took the view in *Junior Books Ltd* v. *Veitchi Co. Ltd* [1983] that: '. . . today the proper control lies not in asking whether the proper remedy should lie in contract . . . or tort, not in somewhat capricious judicial determination whether a particular case falls on one side of the line or the other . . . but in the first instance in establishing the relevant principles and then in deciding whether the particular case falls within or without those principles'.

There remain, however, a number of clear points of distinction between the respective areas of torts and contract:

(a) Differing rules on the commencement of limitation periods.

(b) Differing rules on quantum of damages.

(c) Varying tests on the issue of remoteness of damage.

(d) Separate approaches to the issue of pure economic loss.

It is particularly important to appreciate in this area that one incident may give rise both to contractual and tortious liability. Many examples of this phenomenon are to be found in the case law, e.g. where a property developer negligently built on unsuitable land (*Batty* v. *MPR Ltd* [1978]) or a solicitor fails to register a land charge (*Midland Bank Trust Co.* v. *Hett, Stubbs & Kemp* [1979]).

In the 1970s the courts took the view that the existence of a contract between the parties did not itself preclude an action in tort, where such an action would be advantageous to the plaintiff. A plaintiff could opt for the more advantageous form of action; this point can be seen in the case of *Esso Petroleum Co. Ltd* v. *Mardon* [1976] and *Midland Bank Trust Co.* v. *Hett, Stubbs and Kemp* [1979].

The above cases emphasise the overlap between contractual and tortious liability. Judicial attitudes subsequently changed, *see Leigh & Sullivan Ltd* v. *Aliakmon Shipping Co. Ltd* [1986]; and *Tai Hing Cotton Mill Ltd* v. *Liu Chong Hing Bank Ltd* [1985]. In the latter case it was stated that there was nothing 'to the advantage of the law's development in searching for liability in tort where the parties were in a contractual relationship'. It should, however, be noted that in *Tai Hing* the Court did not deal with the situation common in professional negligence claims of using tort to supplement the contractual obligation in order to obtain procedural advantage, in particular a longer limitation period. The Courts have expressed differing views of the acceptability of concurrent liability. By contrast see, for example, Lloyd L.J. in *Lee* v. *Thompson* (1990) who appeared to support the view that, following *Tai Hing*, concurrent liability had been fatally undermined and more recent dicta from the House of Lords in *Smith* v. *Eric S. Bush* [1990] and *Murphy* v. *Brentwood District Council* [1991]. In *Smith*, Lord Jauncey regarded a valuer's duty to a building society as being founded both in contract and tort. In *Henderson & Others* v. *Merrett Syndicates Ltd* [1994] the House of Lords held that Lloyds Names, having available to them concurrent remedies in contract and tort, were entitled to choose the advantageous; this obviously provides a procedural advantage to plaintiffs in terms of limitation. Lord Nolan in *White* v. *Jones* [1995] stated that:

> '*Henderson* v. *Merrett Syndicates Ltd* [1994] shows that a contractual duty of care owed by the defendant to A may perfectly well co-exist with an equivalent tortious duty of care to B. Both duties depend on an assumption of responsibility by the defendant. In the former case the responsibility is assumed by the making of the contract and is defined by its terms. In the latter the responsibility is assumed by the defendant embarking on a potentially harmful activity and is defined by the general law. If the defendant drives his car on the highway, he implicitly assumes a responsibility towards other road users, and they in turn implicitly rely on him to discharge that responsibility.'

Henderson v. *Merrett Syndicates* has now been applied in *Barclays Bank* v. *Fairclough Building Ltd* (1995).

The main points of distinction between tort and contract are traditionally stated to be:

(a) In tort the duty owed is fixed primarily by the law, whereas in contract the obligations are fixed by agreement between the parties to the contract.

(b) In tort the duty is one owed towards persons generally, whereas in contract the obligation is owed only to a specific person or person(s) who are privy to the contract.

In practice, professionals such as solicitors, surveyors and accountants will carefully draft standard terms of business with their clients. They will be mindful of the need to narrow the scope of their instructions in order to minimise the risk of a claim in tort or contract. In *South Australia Asset Management Corporation* v. *York Montague Ltd* [1996] the House of Lords set out the breadth of duty of care in negligence when a surveyor values a property.

TORT OR TORTS?

The learned authors of *Salmond and Heuston, On the Law of Torts*, outline the issue in this way: 'Does the law of torts consist of a fundamental general principle that it is wrongful to cause harm to other persons in the absence of some specific ground of justification or excuse, or does it consist of a number of specific rules prohibiting certain kinds of harmful activity, and leaving all the residue outside the sphere of legal responsibility?' The first school of thought takes the view that *all* actions are actionable unless they can be justified under the law. This school argues, therefore, for a unified principle of tortious liability. The second school of thought takes the view that there are a number of named torts which owe their origin to the various *forms of action*. Under the second school a plaintiff will have no remedy unless he can bring the facts of the case within an established form of tortious liability. Professor Salmond has argued in favour of the second school: 'Just as the criminal law consists of a body of rules establishing specific offences, so the law of torts consists of a body of rules establishing specific injuries. Neither in one case nor in the other is there any general principle of liability.' For Professor Salmond there is no English law of tort; there is a list of acts and omissions which, subject to certain conditions, are actionable.

It can be argued that the present trend is towards the former of the two schools, namely that liability exists unless the defendant's conduct can otherwise be justified. Notably, there appears to be no reported case in which an action was refused on the sole ground that it was novel. This is not to say that there exists a developed principle of general liability in tort. In many ways it simply counters the argument that Professor Salmond's view, if taken to its logical conclusion, means that the law of torts cannot develop, since any new form of liability is destined to be stillborn.

THE MENTAL ELEMENT IN TORT

One common element in both torts and criminal law is that both areas of liability may require that a mental element on the part of the defendant is present. In criminal law, it is vital to criminal liability that *mens rea*, the guilty mind (e.g. intention, recklessness, gross negligence), is proven. Without proof of *mens rea* a crime cannot be established (except in a very limited category of crimes known as absolute liability offences). The defendant's motive for committing the offence is irrelevant. In tort, what can be said with certainty is that the absence of a malicious motive will not make an otherwise unlawful act lawful. Similarly the presence of malicious motive will not normally make an otherwise lawful act unlawful. In *Bradford Corporation* v. *Pickles* [1895], this point was succinctly made by Lord McNaughten who states: 'It is the act not the motive for the act that must be regarded. If the act, apart from the motive, gives rise merely to damage without legal injury, the motive however reprehensible it may be will not supply that element.'

Intention is, however, another matter. Some torts specifically require an intention to be proven on the part of the wrongdoer. Intention here refers to the defendant's knowledge that the consequences of his action are inevitable, where the consequences, either desired or not desired, are foreseen as certain to result from the defendant's action. Certain areas of liability in tort are said to be *strict*, meaning that liability does not depend upon the wrongdoer's state of mind.

Tortious liability, with notable exceptions (e.g. trespass, which is a strict liability tort), requires proof of fault. Professor Salmond has argued strongly that tortious liability is necessarily fault based. Similarly one can say that tortious liability is based upon the concept of individual responsibility; a person is only liable for his own actions. Strict liability does not fall happily into this philosophy. Other writers have stated three major objections to Professor Salmond's view:

(a) Fault is not an essential aspect of certain torts: trespass, nuisance, defamation and the vicarious liability of an employer for the tort of an employee.

(b) Fault where it exists as an element should *not* be equated with guilty mind, *mens rea*, in the criminal law. Fault is a function of an objective standard of care which one is required to observe. An example of this can be seen in the case of *Nettleship* v. *Weston* [1971], where it was held that an inexperienced learner driver should be judged with reference to the standards of the 'reasonable driver', albeit that the learner driver lacked the experience of the reasonable driver.

(c) The object of the law of torts is to *compensate* rather than to *punish*. This assumes that finding fault on the part of the defendant is at most a side-issue, the principal issue is one of compensating the plaintiff's loss.

7. Loss of a chance

There has been much controversy as to whether or not in the law of tort, a person can sue for the 'loss of a chance'; this is conveniently considered in an article entitled 'A lost chance recovered' in the *Solicitors Journal* (1996, vol. 140, p. 534).

Progress test 1

1. Define tortious liability.
2. Differentiate between tortious and criminal liability.
3. How do tortious and contractual liability differ?
4. Is there a law of tort or a law of torts?
5. To what extent can it be said that fault is the basis of tortious liability?
6. How far is it true to say that a combination of *damnum* and *injuria* must be found in every tort?

2

NEGLIGENCE 1: DUTY OF CARE

INTRODUCTION

The tort of negligence has grown considerably in importance in recent years. The concept of negligence owes its origin to the case of *Donoghue* v. *Stevenson* [1932] and in particular to the famous dictum of Lord Atkin, which defines duty of care. In the following three chapters on negligence we will consider each of the primary elements of the tort of negligence: duty of care, standard of care/breach of duty, and causation and remoteness of damage. This chapter will examine in detail duty of care – how it has been defined, redefined and still further revised in recent years. The issue of public policy surrounding duty of care will be considered and specific areas of difficulty analysed: liability for economic loss, nervous shock, professional and medical negligence.

DEFINING NEGLIGENCE

The tort of negligence comprises three elements: duty of care, breach of that duty, and damage caused to the plaintiff by that breach.

Although a generalised concept of negligence is difficult to find we can look to established precedent for guidance. In *Blyth* v. *Birmingham Waterworks Co. Ltd* (1856) Alderson B defined negligence in the following terms: 'Negligence is the omission to do something which a reasonable man, guided upon those considerations which ordinarily regulate the conduct of human affairs, would do, or doing something which a prudent and reasonable man would not do.'

Negligence is therefore measured by the conduct of the defendant relative to that of a notional moral exemplar, 'the reasonable man'. Negligence does not require 'fault' on the part of the defendant, in the sense of moral blameworthiness, however it does require fault insofar as the defendant's conduct was not of the standard of a reasonable man. The most helpful analysis of negligence is to be found in the opinion of Lord Wright in *Lochgelly Iron and Coal Co. Ltd* v. *McMullan* [1934] where he states: '. . . negligence means more than heedless or careless conduct, whether in omission or commission: it properly connotes the complex concept of duty, breach and damage thereby suffered by the person to whom the duty was owing'.

The tort of negligence therefore comprises three elements:

(a) *Duty*: which determines whether the type of loss suffered by the plaintiff in all the circumstances of the case is actionable.

(b) *Breach*: which is concerned with the standard of care that ought to have been adopted in all the circumstances of the case, and assesses the extent to which the standard of care exercised by the defendant fell short of that expected.

(c) *Damage*: which covers both an issue of fact and an issue of law. The issue of fact is the extent to which the actions of the defendant were the factual cause of the plaintiff's loss, referred to as 'cause in fact'. The issue of law is the extent to which the law recognises the loss sustained by the plaintiff and provides compensation for such loss: this is sometimes referred to as 'cause in law'. Essentially, the former question is one to be determined on all the facts of the case, whereas the latter embodies the concept of 'remoteness of damage'.

While it is convenient to categorise the elements of the tort in this way, it is important that one appreciates from the outset that the relationship between these three elements is complex and that in practice they will often overlap and this will cloud conceptual clarity.

Traditionally a consideration of negligence starts with a consideration of duty. It is open to us to question such an approach, since it is perhaps more logical to consider damage first. Why? Quite simply, without damage there can be no tort. There is no recoverable loss unless the plaintiff has sustained some recognised form of damage which was caused by the defendant.

The proper function of duty of care is to mark out the boundaries of what is and what is not recoverable. In some areas, notably economic loss where there has been significant developments in the early 1990s, there has been some confusion: is the issue whether such loss is recoverable one of 'duty' or 'remoteness of damage'? This is illustrated in the judgment of Denning MR in *Spartan Steel & Alloys Ltd* v. *Martin & Co. (Contractors) Ltd* [1972], where he states: 'The more I think about these cases, the more difficult I find it to put each into its proper pigeon-hole. Sometimes I say: "There was not duty". In others I say: "The damage was too remote". So much so that I think that the time has come to discard those tests which have proved so elusive. It seems to me better to consider the particular relationship in hand, and see whether or not, as a matter of policy, economic loss should be recoverable'.

Previously, in *SCM* v. *Whittal* [1971], Buckley and Wynn LJJ held that economic loss caused by the negligent acts of the defendant was not recoverable, there being no legal duty owed in respect of it. Lord Denning had taken the view in that case that whilst such a duty existed, pure economic loss was too remote a consequence of the defendant's breach to be recoverable. Lord Denning's statement is noteworthy for a further reason: it outlines the significance of the relationship between the parties and the role of judicial policy in assessing whether or not such a relationship gives rise to a duty of care.

THE NEIGHBOUR PRINCIPLE

1. The origin of the neighbour principle: *Donoghue* v. *Stevenson* [1932]

The 'neighbour principle', as enunciated by Lord Atkin in the case of *Donoghue* v. *Stevenson* [1932], is the foundation of the tort of negligence. Prior to that case there was no generalised concept of the duty of care in negligence, the law being fragmented. However, the early 1990s have witnessed a shift away from any general principle and a retreat to a more individual and compartmentalised approach, e.g. *Caparo Industries plc* v. *Dickman* [1990] and *Murphy* v. *Brentwood D.C.* [1991] (HL). The neighbour principle was an attempt by Lord Atkin to rationalise and develop the earlier case law into a coherent principle. In *Donoghue* v. *Stevenson* the House of Lords held, by a simple majority, that the manufacturer of a product could be liable in negligence for injury suffered by the ultimate consumer of the product where such injury was caused by the defective condition of the product.

The facts of the case are well known. The plaintiff drank a bottle of ginger-beer manufactured by the defendant which had been purchased by a friend for the plaintiff's consumption. The bottle containing the ginger-beer was opaque, it was opened by the shopkeeper who supplied it and an amount of the drink was poured into a glass. The plaintiff's friend thereafter poured the remainder of the ginger-beer into the glass, when a decomposing snail which had been in the bottle emerged. As a result, the plaintiff claimed that she had contracted a serious illness and sued the manufacturer in negligence.

The basis of the plaintiff's claim in *Donoghue* v. *Stevenson* was that the defendant had been negligent in that, as the manufacturer of a product intended for consumption, contained in a receptacle which prevented intermediate inspection, he owed a duty to her as the ultimate consumer of the product that there was no injurious element in it.

The decision of the House of Lords upheld the plaintiff's claim. It was held that the manufacturer of products which he sells in such a form as to show that he intends them to reach the ultimate consumer in the form in which they left him, with no reasonable possibility of intermediate examination, and with the knowledge that the absence of reasonable care in the preparation or putting up of the products will result in injury to the consumer's life or property, owes a duty to the consumer to take reasonable care. The House of Lords held that the defendant had failed to take reasonable care and was therefore liable to the plaintiff for the injury which she sustained.

The neighbour principle forms part of the broader *ratio decidendi* of the case. Some writers argue that the *ratio decidendi* is in fact limited to the principle stated above with respect to a manufacturer's liability to the ultimate consumer of his product, the neighbour principle forming merely part of the dicta in the case. However, such a view is untenable in the light of the reliance placed upon the principle in subsequent cases. It is unusual to think of negligence as the breach of an antecedent duty, but in real terms the duty always arises after the event; *Donoghue* v. *Stevenson* is the classic example of this.

Lord Atkin seeks to encapsulate in a single principle the previous situations in which the courts had upheld liability for negligence when he states: 'The rule that you are to love your neighbour, becomes in law that you must not injure your neighbour; and the lawyer's question, 'Who is my neighbour?, receives a restricted reply. You must take reasonable care to avoid acts or omissions which you can reasonably foresee would be likely to injure your neighbour. Who, then, in law is my neighbour? The answer seems to be – persons who are so directly affected by my act that I ought reasonably to have them in contemplation as being so affected when I am directing my mind to the acts or omissions which are called in question.' The test of liability expressed by Lord Atkin is reasonable foresight of harm to persons whom it is foreseeable are likely to be harmed by an act or omission. One must be careful not to assume that the infliction of foreseeable injury is always actionable in negligence.

The function of duty of care is to determine when foreseeable damage is actionable. Indeed, in cases subsequent to *Donoghue* v. *Stevenson*, and in particular in *Weller & Co. Ltd* v. *Foot & Mouth Disease Research Institute* [1965] and *Dutton* v. *Bognor Regis UDC* [1972], this function was tested to the limit.

In the House of Lords in the case of *Home Office* v. *Dorset Yacht Co. Ltd* [1970], Lord Reid opined: '*Donoghue* v. *Stevenson* may be regarded as a milestone, and the well known passage in Lord Atkin's speech should, I think, be regarded as a statement of principle. It is not to be treated as if it were a statutory definition. It will require qualification in new circumstances. But I think that the time has come when we should say that it ought to apply unless there is some justification or valid explanation for its exclusion.' The clearest indication of judicial opinion with regard to the neighbour principle is found in the speech of Lord Wilberforce in *Anns* v. *London Borough of Merton* [1977].

2. The development of the neighbour principle: *Anns* v. *London Borough of Merton* [1977]

This case marked a substantial change in judicial attitude towards the concept of duty of care. The issue of substance with which the House of Lords was concerned in *Anns* was whether a local authority is under any duty of care towards owners or occupiers of a building constructed by builders within their area, with respect to the inspection of the property during the building process. In this instance the plaintiffs were lessees of flats, which had been built by the first defendant. The issue of liability was whether the second defendant (the local authority) owed to the plaintiffs a duty of care arising from an inspection by it of the foundations of the building during the construction process. The plaintiffs argued that by failing to inspect properly the foundations of the flats the local authority, through its employees, had been negligent, since upon a proper inspection it would have been clear that the foundations were not of a sufficient depth.

What became known as the 'Wilberforce test' of duty of care was enunciated in *Anns* v. *London Borough of Merton*: 'Through the trilogy of cases in this House, *Donoghue* v. *Stevenson*, *Hedley Byrne & Co. Ltd* v. *Heller & Partners Ltd* and *Home Office* v. *Dorset Yacht Co. Ltd*, the position has now been reached that in order to establish that a duty of care arises in a particular situation, it is not necessary to bring the facts of that situation within those of previous situations in which a duty of care has been held to exist. Rather the question has to be approached in two stages. First one has to ask whether, as between the alleged wrongdoer and the person who has suffered damage, there is a *sufficient relationship of proximity or neighbourhood* such that, in the reasonable contemplation of the former, carelessness on his part may be likely to cause damage to the latter, in which case a *prima facie* duty of care arises. Secondly, if the first question is answered affirmatively, it is necessary to consider whether there are any considerations which ought to negative, or to reduce or limit the scope of the duty or the class of person to whom it is owed or the damages to which a breach of it . . . may give rise.'

The two-stage test laid down by Lord Wilberforce in the *Anns* case may be analysed in the following way:

(a) *The first stage.* A *prima facie* duty of care arises when there is a sufficient relationship of proximity or neighbourhood, such that in the reasonable contemplation of the defendant carelessness on his part may be likely to cause damage to the plaintiff.

Some writers argued that the threshold of liability in *Anns* was set at too low a level, therefore few plaintiffs were unable to succeed in establishing that they were covered by this first stage of the test. That being so, considerable emphasis was placed upon the second stage of limitations and exclusions.

The significance of the Wilberforce test lay in the shift from the neighbour principle, being an argument to support the extension of new areas of liability, where there were policy considerations in favour of such an extension, to a principle which would apply unless there was a policy of justification for it not doing so. This was an important change of emphasis, indeed a fundamental shift in the role of 'policy' in setting the boundaries of duty of care.

Peabody Donation Fund Governors v. *Sir Lindsay Parkinson and Co. Ltd* [1985] marked a turning point, and the decline in importance of the *Anns* two-stage test was begun. This decline accelerated with considerable pace in *Yuen Kun Yeu* v. *Attorney-General of Hong Kong* [1987] and *Caparo Industries plc* v. *Dickman* [1990].

There were three issues which arose from the application of the first stage of the *Anns* test: foresight, reliance and proximity.

(*i*) *Foresight.* Reasonable foreseeability is not itself sufficient to ground liability. There are cases where the defendant will escape liability although it is clear that he must have foreseen the likelihood of harm to the plaintiff. In *Smith* v. *Littlewoods Organisation* [1987], Lord Goff took the view: 'It is very tempting to try to solve all problems of negligence by reference to an all-embracing criterion of foreseeability, thereby effectively reducing all decisions in this field to questions of fact. But this comfortable solution is, alas, not open to us. The law has to accommodate all the untidy complexity of life; and there are circumstances where considerations of practical justice impel us to reject a general imposition of liability for foreseeable damage.'

(*ii*) *Reliance.* This aspect has been most prominent in economic loss cases (*Hedley Byrne and Co. Ltd* v. *Heller and Partners Ltd* [1964], *see* below).

(*iii*) *Proximity.* The nature of the relationship between the parties must be sufficiently proximate (i.e. close) such that in the reasonable contemplation of the defendant a lack of care on his part may be likely to cause damage to the plaintiff.

(b) *The second stage*. The second stage of the Wilberforce test in *Anns* v. *London Borough of Merton* required the court to consider those considerations which ought to negative, reduce or limit the scope of the duty of care, or the class of person to whom such a duty is owed or the damages to which such a breach may give rise.

In the earlier case of *Hedley Byrne and Co. Ltd* v. *Heller and Partners Ltd* [1964] Lord Pearce observed: 'How wide the sphere of duty of care in negligence is to be laid depends ultimately on the court's assessment of the demands of society for protection from the carelessness of others.' The extent to which policy is a justiciable issue was at the centre of their Lordship's decision in *McLoughlin* v. *O'Brian* [1982]. In that case, the appellant's husband and three of their children were in a car driven by the husband. The car was in collision with a lorry, negligently driven by the respondents. At the time of the accident, in which the husband and children suffered serious injury, the appellant was at home. An hour or so later a Mr Pilgrim reported the accident to the appellant, saying that he thought one of the children was dying and that he did not know of the husband's whereabouts or the condition of the other children. The appellant was told by one of her children that another was dead; she saw one child cut and bleeding, heard another's agonised screams, and saw her husband, who was in a battered condition. In all, the circumstances of the appellant's reunion with her family and what she witnessed of their conditions were distressing in the extreme and capable of producing an effect well beyond that of sorrow and grief. The appellant brought proceedings against the respondents for the nervous shock which she sustained.

In the House of Lords much was made of the role of policy in the law, and the need to avoid an over-reliance upon the concept of reasonable foreseeability as not being a universal touchstone to determine the extent of liability for the consequences of wrong doing, thereby approving the dictum of Giffiths LJ in the Court of Appeal. Lord Scarman considered the limitations upon the role of policy: 'Policy considerations will have to be weighed: but the objective of the judges is the formulation of principle. And, if principle inexorably requires a decision which entails a degree of policy risk, the court's function is to adjudicate according to principle, leaving policy curtailment to the judgment of Parliament. . . . If principle leads to results which are thought to be socially unacceptable, Parliament can legislate to draw a line or map out a new path.' The Court of Appeal in *McLoughlin* v. *O'Brian* had placed considerable emphasis upon the role of public policy. Lord Scarman states quite categorically in the House of Lords that 'the policy issue where to draw the line is not justiciable '.

Lord Edmund Davies takes an entirely opposite view, considering that the view that policy is not a justiciable issue is 'as novel as it is startling'. Referring to *Rondel* v. *Worsley* [1969], *Home Office* v. *Dorset Yacht Co. Ltd* [1970] and *BRB* v. *Herrington* [1972] he continues: 'My Lords, in accordance with such a line of authorities, I hold that public policy issues are "justiciable ".' Lord Edmund Davies raises the problem of how the judiciary may get a grasp of public policy, when in some cases it may be rather nebulous. He also considers the argument that the laying down of policy is a Parliamentary function, and cites with approval the view expressed by Professor Winfield: '. . . the better view seems to be that the difficulty of discovering what public policy is at any given moment certainly does not absolve the bench from the duty of doing so. The judges are bound to take notice of it and of changes which it undergoes, and it is immaterial that the question may be one of ethics rather than of law . . . '.

3. The post-*Anns* v. *London Borough of Merton* epoch

In one respect the neighbour principle set out by Lord Atkin in *Donoghue* v. *Stevenson* and the Wilberforce test in *Anns* v. *London Borough of Merton* are similar, in that each extended the boundaries of tortious liability in negligence.

The initial approach taken in cases after the House of Lords' decision in *Donoghue* v. *Stevenson* is substantially different from the judicial response to the decision in *Anns* v. *London Borough of Merton*. The neighbour principle did not attain ready acceptance for some years after 1932, whereas the Wilberforce test in *Anns* was broadly accepted at once. While the courts were initially slow to adopt the neighbour principle there was, in due course, a tendency to apply it to new areas, thereby extending the boundaries of negligence liability (e.g. *Hedley Byrne & Co. Ltd* v. *Heller and Partners Ltd*). In the 1980s there was a reluctance to apply the Wilberforce test culminating in its rejection in the House of Lords' decision in *Murphy* v. *Brentwood District Council* [1991].

Early acceptance of the Wilberforce test was to be found in their Lordships' decisions in *McLoughlin* v. *O'Brian* [1982] and in *Junior Books* v. *Veitchi* [1982]. In *Peabody Donation Fund Governors* v. *Sir Lindsay Parkinson* [1985], whilst the House of Lords approved the Wilberforce test in *Anns*, Lord Keith observed: 'There has been a tendency in some recent cases to treat these passages (in *Anns*) as being themselves of a definitive character. This is a temptation which should be resisted.' This marked the beginning of a change in judicial attitude towards the Wilberforce test in *Anns*.

In *Leigh & Sullivan Ltd* v. *Aliakmon Shipping Co. Ltd* [1986], the above view of Lord Keith was approved, where Lord Brandon stated: 'That passage (in *Anns*) does not provide and cannot in my view have been intended by Lord Wilberforce to provide a universally applicable test of the existence and scope of a duty of care in the law of negligence.'

In *Yuen Kun Yeu* v. *A-G of Hong Kong* [1987] the Privy Council went a stage further, stating the Wilberforce test should only be used in 'rare cases'. Lord Keith, citing the *Peabody Donation Fund Governors* v. *Sir Lindsay Parkinson, Leigh & Sullivan Ltd* v. *Aliakmon Shipping Co. Ltd*, and *Curran* v. *Northern Ireland Housing Assoc.*, endorsed the views expressed in those decisions, stating that the Wilberforce test had been 'elevated to a degree of importance greater than it merited, and greater perhaps than its author intended'.

In *Jones* v. *Department of Employment* [1988] the Court of Appeal was invited to consider whether a social security adjudication officer owed a duty of care to a claimant of benefit. It was held that having regard to the non-judicial nature of the adjudication officer's responsibilities, and the right of the claimant to appeal, a common law duty of care was not owed to a claimant. The Court of Appeal reviewed the Wilberforce test in the light of the subsequent authorities.

In *Hill* v. *Chief Constable of West Yorkshire* [1988], a case arising from the murders carried out by the 'Yorkshire Ripper', Peter Sutcliffe, it was held that as a matter of law, and also of public policy, an action could not be brought against the police in respect of their failure to identify and apprehend a criminal (Sutcliffe) where that failure had resulted in his committing further offences. Lord Keith took the view that injury to potential victims of Sutcliffe was reasonably foreseeable (thus satisfying the first stage of the Wilberforce test in *Anns*); however, there was absent from the case any such ingredient or characteristic capable of establishing a duty of care owed towards the plaintiff (a subsequent victim of Sutcliffe's criminal activities) by the West Yorkshire Police.

In *D. & F. Estates Ltd and Others* v. *Church Commissioners for England and Others* [1988], the House of Lords refused to follow its previous decision in *Anns* v. *London Borough of Merton*. The facts of the case were that Wates were employed as main contractors in the construction of a block of flats in London. The block was owned by the Church Commissioners who granted a lease of one flat to D. & F. Estates Ltd. The flat was occupied by Mr & Mrs T. who, as licensees, had a controlling interest in D. & F. Estates Ltd. The plaster in the flat needed replacing because it had been negligently mixed by the plasterers who were subcontractors of Wates. The plasterers had since gone into liquidation. Proceedings were commenced by D. & F. Estates Ltd and Mr & Mrs T. against Wates for damages, including the cost of replacing the defective plaster. At the trial the judge held that Wates were liable to the plaintiffs on the basis that they had been in breach of their duty to provide adequate and proper supervision of the plastering work and were liable in negligence for that breach. In the Court of Appeal it was held, allowing the defendant's appeal, that the action against Wates must fail for two reasons:

(a) There was no duty owed to D. & F. Estates because, although they were owners, they were not occupiers of the flat.

(b) In any event, Wates owed no duty to third parties (whether occupiers or non-occupiers) to supervise the work of their independent contractor (the plasterers).

In the House of Lords, the Court of Appeal's finding that Wates owed no duty to supervise the work of their sub-contractor was upheld. It was also held that even if the plastering had been undertaken by Wates themselves, the action would still have failed because the defective plaster had not caused damage to other property or injury to persons. *Anns* was not followed.

Murphy v. *Brentwood District Council* [1991] sounded the death knell to the *Anns* principle. In that case the plaintiff purchased from a construction company one of a pair of semi-detached houses newly constructed on an in-filled site on a concrete raft foundation to prevent damage from settlement. The plans and calculations for the raft foundation were submitted to the local council for building regulation approval prior to the construction of the houses. The council referred the plans and calculations to consulting engineers for checking and on their recommendation approved the design under the building regulations and byelaws. In 1981 the plaintiff noticed serious cracks in his house and discovered that the raft foundation was defective and the differential settlement beneath it had caused it to distort. The plaintiff was unable to carry out the necessary repairs to the foundation, which would have cost £45,000, and in 1986 the plaintiff sold the house subject to the defects for £35,000 less than its market value in sound condition. He brought an action against the council claiming that it was liable for the consulting engineers' negligence in recommending approval of the plans and alleging that he and his family had suffered an imminent risk to health and safety because gas and soil pipes had broken and there was a risk of further breaks. The judge, who found as a fact that the plaintiff had been exposed to an imminent risk to health and safety, held the council liable for the consulting engineers' negligence and awarded the plaintiff damages of £38,777, being the loss on the sale of the house and expenses. The council appealed to the Court of Appeal, which held, following existing House of Lords authority, that the council owed a duty of care to the plaintiff to see that the house was properly built so that injury to the safety or health of those who lived in it was avoided and that it was in breach of that duty when it approved plans for a defective raft foundation. The court accordingly dismissed the appeal. The council appealed to the House of Lords.

The House of Lords held that, when carrying out its statutory functions of exercising control over building operations, a local authority was not liable in negligence to a building owner or occupier for the cost of remedying a dangerous defect in the building which resulted from the negligent failure of the authority to ensure that the building was designed or erected in conformity with the applicable standards (prescribed by the building regulations or byelaws) but which became apparent before the defect caused physical injury. The reasoning was that the damage suffered by the building owner or occupier in such circumstances was not material or physical damage but the purely economic loss of the expenditure incurred (in remedying the structural defect to avert the danger or of abandoning the property as unfit for habitation). Since a dangerous defect once known became merely a defect in quality, to permit the building owner or occupier to recover his economic loss would logically lead to an unacceptably wide category of claims in respect of buildings or chattels which were defective in quality, and would in effect introduce product liability and transmissible warranties of quality into the law of tort by means of judicial legislation. The council accordingly had owed no duty of care to the plaintiff when it approved the plans for a defective raft foundation for the plaintiff's house. The appeal was therefore allowed.

Lord Keith in his opinion considered the validity of the *Anns* two-stage test as a principle for determining the scope of duty of care. Referring to *Anns* and the nature of the damage sustained by the plaintiff in that case and in the case before him, Lord Keith took the view that the loss was pure economic loss and it should not be characterised as physical damage.

Lord Keith opined: 'In my opinion it is clear that *Anns* did not proceed on any

basis of established principle but introduced a new species of liability governed by a principle indeterminate in character but having the potentiality of covering a wide range of situations, involving chattels as well as real property, in which it had never hitherto been thought that the law of negligence had any proper place.'
He continued:

'In my opinion there can be no doubt that *Anns* has for long been widely regarded as an unsatisfactory decision. In relation to the scope of the duty owed by a local authority it proceeded on what must, with due respect to its source, be regarded as a somewhat superficial examination of principle and there has been extreme difficulty, highlighted most recently by the speeches in the *D. & F. Estates* case, in ascertaining on exactly what basis of principle it did proceed. I think it must now be recognised that it did not proceed on any basis of principle at all, but constituted a remarkable example of judicial legislation. It has engendered a vast spate of litigation, and each of the cases in the field which have reached this House have been distinguished. Others have been distinguished in the Court of Appeal. The result has been to keep the effect of the decision within reasonable bounds, but that has been achieved only by applying strictly the words of Lord Wilberforce and by refusing to accept the logical implications of the decision itself. These logical implications show that the case properly considered has potentiality for collision with long-established principles regarding liability in the tort of negligence for economic loss. There can be no doubt that to depart from the decision would re-establish a degree of certainty in this field of law which it has done a remarkable amount to upset.

So far as policy considerations are concerned, it is no doubt the case that extending the scope of the tort of negligence may tend to inhibit carelessness and improve standards of manufacture and construction. On the other hand, overkill may present its own disadvantages, as was remarked in *Rowling* v. *Takaro Properties Ltd* [1988]. (See more recently *Lonrho plc* v. *Tebbit* [1992] where the Court of Appeal cited *Takaro* as authority for the difficulties in distinguishing "policy decisions" from "operational activities". The Court held that a government minister's decision to extract an undertaking from a company that it would not proceed with a planned takeover bid whilst the bid was being investigated by the Monopolies and Mergers Commission was a matter of public law but that it remained arguable that the minister owed a private law duty to the bidder to take reasonable care to release the undertaking as soon as it was no longer needed.) There may be room for the view that *Anns*-type liability will tend to encourage owners of buildings found to be dangerous to repair rather than run the risk of injury. The owner may, however, and perhaps quite often does, prefer to sell the building at its diminished value, as happened in the present case.

It must, of course, be kept in mind that the decision has stood for some 13 years. On the other hand, it is not a decision of the type that is to a significant extent taken into account by citizens or indeed local authorities in ordering their affairs. No doubt its existence results in local authorities having to pay increased insurance premiums, but to be relieved of that necessity would be to their advantage, not to their detriment. To overrule it is unlikely to result in significantly increased insurance premiums for householders. It is perhaps of some significance that most litigation involving the decision consists in contests between insurance companies, as is largely the position in the present case. The decision is capable of being regarded as affording a measure of justice, but as against that the impossibility of finding any coherent and logically based doctrine behind it is calculated to put the law of negligence into a state of confusion defying rational analysis. It is also material that *Anns* has the effect of imposing on builders generally a liability going far beyond that which Parliament thought fit to impose on house builders alone by the Defective Premises Act 1972, a statute very material to the policy of the decision but not adverted to in it. There is much to be said for the view that in what is essentially a consumer protection field, as was observed by Lord Bridge in *D. & F. Estates Ltd* v. *Church Comrs. for England* [1988], the precise extent and limits of the liabilities which in the public interest should be imposed on builders and local authorities are best left to the legislature.

My Lords, I would hold that *Anns* was wrongly decided as regards the scope of any private law duty of care resting on local authorities in relating to their function of taking steps to secure compliance with building byelaws or regulations and should be departed from. It follows that *Dutton* v. *Bognor Regis UDC* [1972] should be overruled, as should all cases subsequent to *Anns* which were decided in reliance on it.'

Summary

(a) The *Anns* two-stage test, much criticised in the 1980s, was overruled by the House of Lords in *Murphy* v. *Brentwood District Council* [1991].

(b) A number of factors should be considered on the question of the existence of a duty of care; these include:

(*i*) *Foresight.*

(*ii*) *Proximity*: this has been stated to be an artificial concept depending 'more on the court's perception of what is the reasonable area for the imposition of liability than upon any logical process of analogical deduction' *per* Lord Oliver in *Alcock* v. *Chief Constable of South Yorkshire Police* [1992] (HL).

(*iii*) *Whether the imposition of a duty would be just and reasonable, see* e.g. *Hemmens* v. *Wilson Browne* [1993].

(*iv*) Policy.

(c) These factors will not necessarily all be referred to in any particular case.

4. Duty of care – the current approach

The difficulty of formulating a common approach in establishing the situations in which a duty of care will arise has been amply illustrated by recent case law.

In the House of Lords decision in *The Nicholas H.* [1996] – an action brought against a classification society, which through its employee (a ship surveyor) had certified a ship seaworthy, by owners of a cargo lost when the ship sank – Lord Steyn took the view: '. . . the question is whether in law that carelessness amounted to actionable negligence. In short the question is simply whether in law the classification society owed a duty of care to the owners of the cargo'.

Lord Steyn went on to enumerate the factors which point in favour or against the recognition of a duty of care in the circumstances of this case:

(a) Did the surveyor's carelessness cause direct physical loss?

(b) Did the cargo owners rely on the surveyor's recommendations?

(c) The impact of the contract between the ship owners and the owners of the cargo.

(d) The impact of the contract between the classification society and the ship owners.

(e) The position and role of the ship surveyor.

(f) Policy factors.

It was under policy factors that their Lordships considered:
    (*i*) Is the imposition of a duty fair, just and reasonable?
    and
    (*ii*) Assumption of responsibility.

In *The Nicholas H.* Lord Steyn took the view that: 'Since the decision in *Home Office* v. *Dorset Yacht Co.* [1970] it has been settled law that the elements of foreseeability and proximity as well as considerations of fairness, justice and reasonableness are relevant to all cases whatever the nature of the harm sustained by the plaintiffs'.

At first instance in the Commercial Court, Hirst J. held on the preliminary issue 'Whether on the facts pleaded . . . [the Defendant] owed a duty of care to [the Plaintiff] capable of giving rise to a liability in damages', that such a duty existed, the Court of Appeal unanimously reversed that decision and the House of Lords upheld the judgment of the Court of Appeal.

In *Holt and Another* v. *Payne, Skillington and Another* (1995) the Court of Appeal had to consider the impact of a contract between the parties as a factor in determining the existence of a duty of care. It held that the individual facts and circumstances of a case determined whether any duty of care in tort, which the general law might impose on the parties, was of wider scope than any contract to which the same parties might agree at some stage in the same course of dealing.

NEGLIGENCE AND ECONOMIC INTEREST

5. Nature of economic loss

There are a number of limitations upon the scope of duty of care, one being the type of damage which has been caused by the defendant's breach. In the early stages of the development of duty of care in negligence, economic loss was not recognised as a sufficient form of damage; a duty not to cause economic loss was not recognised by the law. On closer inspection there appear to be four areas where economic loss arises:

(a) *Consequential economic loss* – where the loss arises as a consequence of physical damage caused to the plaintiff's property. A classic example is *Spartan Steel & Alloys Ltd* v. *Martin & Co. Ltd* [1971]. In that case the plaintiffs (Spartan Steel) owned a factory at which they manufactured stainless steel. The defendant contractors, when carrying out repair work to a nearby road, through their negligence damaged the cable supplying electricity to the plaintiff's factory and power was lost to the factory for 14 hours. At the time the power was turned off a melt was lost and subsequent melts proved impossible due to the loss of the power supply. The plaintiffs claimed damages not only for the physical damage caused to the first melt, but also for loss of profit due to their not being able to carry out the second melt through lack of an electricity supply.

The Court of Appeal, by a majority (Edmund Davies LJ dissenting), allowed the plaintiffs to recover damages for the economic loss (loss of profit) occasioned by physical damage to the first melt, but not for the loss of profit from the plaintiff's inability to carry out a second melt due to loss of power. Lord Denning MR stated that: 'at bottom I think the question of recovering economic loss is one of policy. Wherever the courts draw a line to mark out the bounds of duty, they do it as a matter of policy so as to limit the responsibility of the defendant. Wherever the courts set bounds to the damages recoverable – saying that they are, or are not, too remote – they do it as a matter of policy so as to limit the liability of the defendants. . . . In many of the cases where economic loss has been held not to be recoverable it has been put on the ground that the defendant was under no duty to the plaintiff. . . . In other cases, however, the defendant seems clearly to have been under a duty to the plaintiff, but the economic loss has not been recovered because it was too remote. . . . On the other hand, in the cases where economic loss by itself has been held to be recoverable, it is plain that there was a duty to the plaintiff and the loss was not too remote. . . .'

(b) *Pure economic loss* – where the loss which is sustained by the plaintiff consists solely of loss of profit. An example of pure economic loss is *Weller & Co. Ltd* v. *Foot & Mouth Disease Research Institute* [1966]. It is in this area of economic loss that there has been the greatest scope for divergence of opinion.

(c) *Liability for negligent statements* – where the loss sustained by the plaintiff arises from statements made by the defendant to the plaintiff in circumstances where a special relationship exists between the parties, a duty of care arises (*see Hedley Byrne & Co. Ltd* v. *Heller & Partners Ltd* [1964]).

(d) *The tort of deceit* – this forms the final instance where a plaintiff may obtain recovery for economic loss inflicted by the defendant (*see Derry* v. *Peek* (1889)).

6. Financial loss caused by negligent acts

The general rule is that if, as a consequence of the defendant's negligent act, the plaintiff suffers pure financial loss which is not accompanied by any physical loss to his person or property, such loss cannot be recovered.

This rule has been applied in *Cattle* v. *Stockton Waterworks* (1875), where the plaintiff who had contracted with a landowner to build a tunnel under his land could not recover extra expenses incurred in finishing the work after the defendant's waterworks had negligently flooded the land. This rule was confirmed in a number of cases, e.g. *Weller* v. *Foot & Mouth Disease Institute* (above), where auctioneers failed to recover profits from cattle auctions cancelled because of an outbreak of disease.

In other cases where a plaintiff suffered economic loss flowing from physical loss, both types of damage were recoverable. In *British Celanese Ltd* v. *A.H. Hunt*

Capacitors Ltd [1969] the defendant negligently allowed metal strips stored on his land to blow onto a power line, thereby cutting the power supply to the plaintiff's factory. The plaintiff's machines were damaged and economic loss suffered. The plaintiff obtained full recovery for both categories of loss, i.e. physical damage to property and economic loss (*see also SCM* v. *Whittal* [1971], and *Spartan Steel & Alloys Ltd* v. *Martin & Co.* [1971]).

There would *appear* to be a number of qualifications to the general rule that while consequential economic loss based upon the defendant doing some physical act is recoverable, pure economic loss is not. These qualifications are:

(a) Economic loss arising from a negligent mis-statement made by the defendant, rather than from the defendant's negligent action, may be recoverable.

(b) Claims for economic loss made by dependants lie under the Fatal Accidents Act 1976.

(c) Economic loss caused by the plaintiff's attempt to avoid physical damage is recoverable: *see Rivtow Marine Ltd* v. *Washington Ironworks* [1973].

It is clear that the simple distinction drawn in *Spartan Steel & Alloys Ltd* v. *Martin & Co. Ltd* between consequential economic loss (arising from the defendant's actions causing physical damage to the plaintiff or his property) and pure economic loss (where the only interest damaged is the economic interest of the plaintiff) has been eroded in recent decisions. The distinction between acts and statements has been swept away to a large extent by cases such as *Midland Bank Trust Co. Ltd* v. *Hett, Stubbs & Kemp* [1979] and *Ross* v. *Caunters* [1980].

7. *Hedley Byrne* v. *Heller* [1964]: negligent statements

In *Hedley Byrne & Co. Ltd* v. *Heller & Partners Ltd* [1964], Heller & Partners were bankers to Easipower Ltd, which was a client of the plaintiffs, who were advertising agents. Through their own bank the plaintiffs made an enquiry to the defendants as to the financial standing of Easipower, mentioning an advertising contract for £1,000,000. The reply was headed 'Confidential. For your private use and without responsibility on the part of the bank or its officials.' The letter said that Easipower was a 'respectably constituted company, considered good for its ordinary business engagements. Your figures are larger than we are accustomed to see.' Relying on this the plaintiffs incurred expenditure on behalf of Easipower and lost £17,000 when the company went into liquidation. The plaintiffs alleged that the reference had been made carelessly and that the defendants owed them a duty to take reasonable care in giving this information. The House of Lords agreed that in the appropriate circumstances there could be such a duty. The defendants were not liable on the facts, however, because the disclaimer of responsibility made it unreasonable for the plaintiffs to place reliance on the statement.

When does such a duty of care arise? The House referred to a '*special relationship*'. A 'special relationship' is, in the view of Lord Reid, 'where it is plain that the party seeking information or advice was trusting the other to exercise such a degree of care as the circumstances required, where it was reasonable for him to do that, and where the other gave the information or advice when he knew or ought to have known that the enquirer was relying on him'. Lord Morris said that where a person 'is so placed that others could reasonably rely upon his judgment or his skill or upon his ability to make careful inquiry, [and] a person takes it upon himself to give information or advice to, or allows his information or advice to be passed on to, another person who, as he knows or should know, will place reliance upon it, then a duty of care will arise.'

The crucial issue is what constitutes a 'special relationship'? It is apparent that three requirements have to be satisfied:

(a) The plaintiff relied on the defendant's skill and judgment or his ability to make careful enquiry.

(b) The defendant knew, or ought reasonably to have known, that the plaintiff was relying on him; and

(c) It was reasonable in the circumstances for the plaintiff to rely on the defendant.

As to the third requirement of 'reasonable reliance', the question remains, however, in what circumstances will reliance be reasonable? It would not be reasonable to rely on opinions expressed on social or informal occasions, or even in a professional or business context, unless it was clear that the plaintiff was seeking considered advice: *see Mutual Life & Citizen's Assurance Co. Ltd* v. *Evatt* [1971] (*per* Lords Morris and Reid, dissenting).

An opinion given 'off the cuff' over the telephone does not create a duty (*Howard Marine & Dredging Co. Ltd* v. *Ogden & Sons (Excavations) Ltd* [1978], *per* Denning MR). A contrary view is to be found in *Chaudhry* v. *Prabhakar & Another* [1988] (CA) where the defendant, at the request of a friend, found a second-hand car for sale and advised the friend to buy it, knowing that she was relying on his skill and judgment. The Court of Appeal held that the defendant owed to the friend a duty of care and would be liable to her for any negligent mis-statement concerning the car if she relied on it and thereby suffered loss.

It was once thought, following *Mutual Life & Citizens' Assurance Co. Ltd* v. *Evatt* [1971], where a majority of the Privy Council held that the duty applied only to defendants who were in the business of giving advice or information or who claimed that they had the requisite expertise, that the imposition of the duty would unfairly require others to achieve the same standard of competence as those in the business of giving advice. Lords Reid and Morris dissented; in their Lordships' opinions the duty could arise when an enquirer consulted a business-man in the course of his business and made it plain that he was seeking considered advice and intended to act on that advice. If the businessman chooses to give advice without any warning or qualification he would be under a duty to take such care as is reasonable in the circumstances. This minority view has been followed by the Court of Appeal in *Esso Petroleum Co. Ltd* v. *Mardon* and *Howard Marine & Dredging Co. Ltd* v. *Ogden & Sons (Excavations) Ltd*. In *Esso Petroleum Co. Ltd* v. *Mardon*, although the defendants were not in the business of giving advice, it was significant that they were experienced and had special knowledge and skill in estimating the petrol throughput at a filling station, whereas the plaintiff did not. *See also James McNaughton Paper Group Ltd.* v. *Hicks Anderson & Co.* [1991].

The courts use the concept of '*reasonable reliance*' as a way of placing limits on the range of liability for negligent statements.

In *JEB Fasteners Ltd* v. *Marks Bloom & Co.* [1983] it was held that auditors who prepared a company's accounts, knowing that the company was in difficulty and needed finance, ought to have foreseen that a takeover was a possible source of finance and that someone contemplating a takeover might rely on the accounts. Accordingly, the auditors owed a duty of care to that person in preparing the accounts. The accountants' duty would not extend, however, to 'strangers of whom they have heard nothing and to whom their employer without their knowledge may choose to show their accounts'. The defendants in *JEB Fasteners Ltd* v. *Marks Bloom & Co.* were held not liable because even though the plaintiffs had 'relied' on the accounts this was not the cause of the loss, because they would have taken over the company in any event. The plaintiff's reliance will only constitute a cause of his loss 'as long as a misrepresentation plays a real and substantial part, though not be itself a decisive part, in inducing the plaintiff to act', *per* Stephenson LJ.

The use of a disclaimer in *Hedley Byrne & Co. Ltd* v. *Heller & Partners Ltd* was most effective. It is apparent, however, that 'disclaimers' will not always succeed in avoiding liability. In *Yianni* v. *Edwin Evans & Sons* [1981], Park J appears to have accepted that the fact that most purchasers of property do place reliance on building society valuation reports makes it reasonable that they should rely on such reports despite warnings in the building society literature that they should have an independent survey. In this particular situation the report is not truly gratuitous because the purchaser pays a fee to the building society for the valuation, and that must go some way to making the purchaser's reliance reasonable.

In *Harris and Another* v. *Wyre Forest District Council* [1989] the plaintiffs, a young couple contemplating marriage, applied to the authority for a mortgage loan to purchase a small Victorian terraced house in Kidderminster. They completed and signed one of the Council's standard mortgage application forms which stated, immediately above their signatures: 'To be read carefully and signed by all applicants . . . I / We understand that . . . the valuation is confidential and is intended solely for the information of Wyre Forest District Council in determining what advance, if any, may be made on the security and that no responsibility whatsoever is implied or accepted by the Council for the value or condition of the property by reason of such inspection and report. (You are advised for your own protection to instruct your own surveyor/architect to inspect the property.) I / We understand that the valuation report is the property of the Council and that I/we cannot require its production.' The judge found that neither of the plaintiffs read these words. Nobody suggested to them that they should have their own survey done, nor did they think of it themselves, although they knew such a thing could be arranged for a certain price.

In due course Mr Lee, who was employed by the Council as a valuation surveyor, was sent to inspect and value the property. His report valued the house at the asking price of £9,450 and recommended a loan of 90 per cent of the valuation for a maximum period of 25 years. Under the heading 'essential repairs' he wrote: 'Obtain report for district council from MEB regarding electrics and carry out any recommendations. Make good mortar fillets to extension.' The judge held that it was implicit in Mr Lee's report that structural repairs were not, in his view, essential.

The Council wrote to the plaintiffs and told them it was prepared to make the advance necessary subject to a number of conditions, one of which was that they should undertake to carry out the 'essential repairs' detailed by the surveyor. The plaintiffs bought the house. When, three years later, they attempted to sell it, they were advised that it needed considerable underpinning and other works and was unsaleable. The plaintiffs' submission was that, being under a duty to others to make a valuation which they knew would necessarily come to the knowledge of the plaintiffs, the defendants owed a duty to them to make it with care. The question was whether a duty was owed. That question had to be answered by an application of established principles relating to negligent mis-statements which depended on there being the necessary proximity between the maker and the recipient of the statement.

In the Court of Appeal Nourse LJ opined: 'The essential question was: were the circumstances such that the defendants ought reasonably to have recognised both the importance which would be attached to Mr Lee's valuation by the plaintiffs and the Council's own answerability to them in making it?'

The Court of Appeal allowed the appeal by the defendant District Council. The plaintiffs appealed to the House of Lords, where allowing the plaintiff's appeal it was held that a valuer instructed by a prospective mortgagee to carry out a valuation of a modest house for the purpose of deciding whether or not to grant a mortgage on it to the prospective mortgagor owed a duty of care to the mortgagor to exercise reasonable skill and care in carrying out the valuation, if he was aware that the mortgagor would probably purchase the house in reliance on the valuation without an independent survey, unless the valuer had made a disclaimer of liability to the mortgagor; that a disclaimer of liability by or on behalf of a valuer was a notice which purported to exclude liability for negli-gence within the meaning of the Unfair Contract Terms Act 1977 and would be ineffective by virtue of s. 2(2) unless it satisfied the requirement of reasonable-ness provided by s. 11(3) of the Act; and that, since the valuer was a professional man, whether he was acting as an independent contractor or as an employee of the mortgagee, whose services were paid for by the mortgagor, who might or might not be supplied with a copy of the valuation report, it would not be fair and reasonable to allow the valuer to rely on such a disclaimer to exclude his liability to the mortgagor for the accuracy of the valuation. This case was heard as a consolidated appeal together with a claim raising very similar issues, namely *Smith* v. *Eric S. Bush* [1990].

The true significance of *Hedley Byrne* v. *Heller* does not lie in establishing liability for negligent words. *Hedley Byrne* opened up the possibility of claims in negligence for pure economic loss in circumstances where the conceptual tools were available to place a limit on the extent of liability. This is exemplified by the way in which actions nominally based on *Hedley Byrne* have been extended to include what are essentially negligent acts: *see Midland Bank Trust Co. Ltd* v.

Hett, Stubbs & Kemp [1979], where the defendants were held liable in tort for failing to register an option to purchase land as a land charge. In *Ross* v. *Caunters* [1980], Megarry V-C regarded *Hedley Byrne* as important for 'opening the door' to the recovery of pure financial loss in negligence. The plaintiff was the named beneficiary under a will who lost her bequest because her solicitors had failed to warn the testator not to allow the spouse of a beneficiary to witness the will. The solicitors were held liable, although the plaintiff had not 'relied' on the defendants at all. Megarry V-C considered that in these circumstances liability could be based on *Donoghue* v. *Stevenson* [1932].

In *Spring* v. *Guardian Assurance plc* [1994] the House of Lords closely examined the decision in *Hedley Byrne* in deciding that an employer who gives a reference in respect of an employee, whether past or present, to a prospective future employer ordinarily owes a duty of care to the employee in respect of the preparation of that reference and will be liable in damages to the employee in respect of economic loss suffered by him by reason of the reference being prepared negligently.

8. *Caparo Industries plc* v. *Dickman* [1990]: corporate and professional conduct

The House of Lords decision in *Caparo* and the cases which have followed from it potentially have considerable impact upon the conduct of many corporate transactions and the role and responsibilities of professional advisers.

Caparo, after considering the audited accounts of a target company (in which it already had a minority stake), purchased more shares in the target before making a successful takeover bid. Caparo then brought an action against the target's auditors alleging negligence in that the target's accounts were inaccurate and misleading since they showed a pre-tax profit of £1,200,000 when in fact there had been a loss of over £400,000.

The case was decided on a preliminary issue when the House of Lords held that an auditor owed no duty of care to an individual shareholder in the company who wished to buy more shares. The auditor's statutory duty to prepare accounts was owed to the body of shareholders as a whole, and the purpose for which accounts were prepared and audited was limited to enabling the shareholders as a body to exercise informed control of the company (and not to enable individual shareholders to buy shares with a view to profit). *See also Berg Sons and Co. Ltd* v. *Adams* (1992) in which the *Caparo* approach to the purpose of an auditor's duty prevented a duty of care being owed to a company in a case where it was alleged that an unqualified audit certificate had permitted the company to continue trading and thus to increase the losses suffered.

The House of Lords considered that, in making a statement, a duty of care is owed only where there is a relationship of sufficient proximity between the maker of the statement and the person relying on it. This will arise in particular situations where the maker of the statement knows that his statement will be communicated to the person relying on it specifically in connection with a particular transaction, and that the person will rely on it for the purpose of deciding whether or not to enter into that particular transaction.

The problem highlighted in *Caparo* is that, as Lord Bridge puts it, ideas of fair, just and reasonable, neighbourhood and proximity are 'not susceptible of any precise definition as would be necessary to give them utility as practical tests'.

Lord Roskill goes further: 'Subsequent attempts to define both the duty and its scope have created more problems than the decisions have solved.'

In relation to economic loss, Lord Oliver takes the view that: 'Although the cases in which the courts have imposed or withheld liability are capable of an approximate categorisation, one looks in vain for some common denominator by which the existence of the essential relationship can be tested. . . . I think that it has to be recognised that to search for any single formula which will serve as a general test of liability is to pursue a "will-o-the-wisp".'

Lord Oliver goes on, however, to set out the principles which can be deduced from *Hedley Byrne* v. *Heller & Partners*:

> 'What can be deduced from the *Hedley Byrne* case, therefore, is that the necessary relationship between the maker of a statement or giver of advice ("the adviser") and the recipient who acts in reliance upon it ("the advisee") may typically be held to exist where (1) the advice is required for a purpose, whether particularly specified or generally described, which is made known, either actually or inferentially, to the adviser at the time when the advice is given; (2) the adviser knows, either actually or inferentially, that his advice will be communicated to the advisee, either specifically or as a member of an ascertainable class, in order that it should be used by the advisee for that purpose; (3) it is known, either actually or inferentially, that the advice so communicated is likely to be acted upon by the advisee for that purpose without independent enquiry; and (4) it is so acted upon by the advisee to his detriment. That is not, of course, to suggest that these conditions are either conclusive or exclusive, but merely that the actual decision in the case does not warrant any broader propositions.'

Following *Caparo*, it appeared that the Lords had decided that it is impossible to use a single general principle of liability – an approach which was once encouraged by Lord Reid in *Home Office* v. *Dorset Yacht Co*. This in part arises from the House of Lords adopting the views expressed by Brennan J in the High Court of Australia where he stated: 'It is preferable, in my view, that the law should develop novel categories of negligence incrementally and by analogy with established categories, rather than by a massive extension of a prima facie duty of care restrained only by indefinable "considerations which ought to negative, or to reduce or limit the scope of the duty or the class of person to whom it is owed." '

In *Morgan Crucible Co. plc* v. *Hill Samuel Bank Ltd and Others* [1991] it was held by the Court of Appeal that if during the course of a contested takeover bid the directors and financial advisers of the target company make express representations after an identified bidder has emerged, intending that the bidder will rely on those representations, they owe the bidder a duty of care not to be negligent in making representations which might mislead him.

In 1985, Morgan Crucible announced a takeover bid for First Castle Electronics plc which recommended its shareholders not to accept the bid. First Castle sent a defence circular to shareholders forecasting a 38 per cent increase in pre-tax profits for the then current financial year and containing letters from both its accountants stating that the forecast had been properly compiled and from

Hill Samuel that the forecast had been made after due and careful enquiry. Shortly afterwards, Morgan Crucible increased its bid and succeeded in acquiring its target.

Subsequently, however, it sued Hill Samuel, the accountants, and the directors, claiming the accountancy policies adopted on the profit forecast were negligently misleading and grossly overstated the profits.

Following the House of Lords decision in *Caparo*, which was a blow to the way Morgan Crucible had pleaded its case, an application was made to amend its statement of claim to raise an arguable case for the existence of proximity. On hearing the *Morgan Crucible* summons for leave to amend the statement of claims, Hoffmann J considered the substantive issues raised by the case and noted that despite the proposed amendments the entire case based on negligence was bound to fail. He concluded that the case fell squarely within the House of Lords' decision in *Caparo*. It was clear from the City Code on Takeovers and Mergers that the purpose of the defence document was to advise shareholders whether to accept the bid. There was nothing to suggest it was meant for the bidder. Therefore, the defendants owed no duty to the bidder to take reasonable care in making financial statements on which it could reasonably rely.

The Court of Appeal reversed Hoffmann J's decision; however, before the case came to court for a full hearing of the substantive issues it was settled.

It can be argued that *Morgan Crucible* should be distinguished from *Caparo*, both because the information was produced for a specific transaction and also because the identity of the bidder was known at the time the information was published.

In *James McNaughton Paper Group Ltd* v. *Hicks Anderson & Co.* [1991] the Court of Appeal held that in deciding whether a duty of care is owed by the maker of a statement to a person other than the person directly intended by the maker to act on the statement the factors to be considered include the purpose for which the statement was made, the purpose for which the statement was communicated, the relationship between the adviser, the advisee and any relevant third party, the size of any class to which the advisee belongs, the state of knowledge of the adviser, and any reliance by the advisee. Having regard to those factors, an accountant who is asked by a company which is the subject of an agreed takeover bid to produce draft accounts as soon as possible owes no duty of care to the bidder to produce accurate accounts.

The facts of the case were that the plaintiff company (McNaughton) entered into negotiations with a rival company, MK Paper Group, for an agreed takeover of MK at a time when MK was in financial trouble and making substantial losses. The chairman of MK, Mr Topsom, asked the company's accountants, Hicks Anderson & Co., to prepare draft accounts as quickly as possible for use in the negotiations. The accounts were prepared by Mr Pritchard of Hicks Anderson and were shown to McNaughton. At a meeting between the negotiating parties on 7 September 1982 Mr Pritchard stated in response to a question by the chairman of McNaughton that as a result of rationalisation MK was breaking even or doing marginally worse. After the takeover was completed McNaughton discovered certain discrepancies in the accounts and brought an action against

Hicks Anderson alleging that the draft accounts had been negligently prepared and that McNaughton had relied on them and Mr Pritchard's statement on 7 September 1982 as to the current state of MK in going through with the takeover. The judge held that Hicks Anderson owed a duty of care to McNaughton and awarded McNaughton £75,000 damages for breach of duty. The accountants appealed to the Court of Appeal.

Lord Justice Neill in his judgment considered the state of the authorities and the applicability or otherwise of a general principle of liability:

'It therefore becomes necessary, in the absence of some general principle, to examine each individual case in the light of the concepts of foreseeability, proximity and fairness. The last of these concepts, however, is elusive and may indeed be no more than one of the criteria by which proximity is to be judged. It is perhaps sufficient to underline that in every case the court must not only consider the foreseeability of the damage and whether the relationship between the parties is sufficiently proximate but must also pose and answer the question: in this situation is it fair, just and reasonable that the law should impose on the defendant a duty of the scope suggested for the benefit of the plaintiff?'

Lord Justice Neill in the final part of his judgment considers the applicability of the speeches in the House of Lords decision *Murphy* v. *Brentwood District Council*; he concludes:

'There is nothing in any of these speeches which alters what was said earlier this year in *Caparo*. Indeed it may be noted **(a)** that Lord Keith referred again to the judgment of Brennan J in *Sutherland Shire Council* v. *Heyman* where Brennan J emphasised that the question is always whether the defendant was under a duty to avoid or prevent the kind of damage which the plaintiff in fact suffered, **(b)** that Lord Oliver underlined the same point.'

In *Al-Nakib Investments (Jersey) Ltd and Another* v. *Longcroft and Others* [1990] it was held that although directors of a company owed a duty of care to persons who subscribed for shares in reliance on a prospectus they did not owe a duty of care to a shareholder or anyone else who relied on the prospectus for the purpose of deciding whether to purchase shares in the company through the stock market, because the prospectus was addressed to shareholders for the particular purpose of inviting a subscription for shares and if it was used by a shareholder for the different purpose of buying shares in the stock market there was not a sufficiently proximate relationship between the directors and the shareholder for a duty of care to arise on the part of the directors. *See also Barings plc and Another* v. *Coopers and Lybrand (a firm) and Others* [1996] where the Court of Appeal considered the duty owed by auditors, to a parent holding company, where it audited the accounts of an overseas subsidiary.

Reference should also be made to the decision of the House of Lords in *Spring* v. *Guardian Assurance plc* [1994]. It was held that an employer providing a reference owed a duty of care to the employee in preparing that reference.

Accordingly, the defendants were held liable in damages to the employee in respect of the economic loss suffered by him by reason of the reference being prepared negligently.

9. *Hedley Byrne* revisited

The *Hedley Byrne* decision has recently been subject to considerable scrutiny and analysis in *Henderson* v. *Merrett Syndicates Ltd* [1994]. The facts of that case were that 'names' at Lloyds (individuals who were rich enough to provide a certificate of wealth and become 'names') agreed to being placed, either by their own agents or by a person selected by those agents, on syndicates which issued insurance policies rendering the 'names' personally liable to the full extent of their means, should an insured event occur. Such events did occur, and 'names' sued both their own agents and the sub-agents, whom their own agents had retained. The court accepted that those placing the insurance had been negligent in overexposing the 'names'.

In a long speech in which Lord Goff held the sub-agents liable in tort, and the agents liable (i) in tort as well as contract for their own negligence, and (ii) in contract for the negligence of the sub-agents, Lord Goff opined:

> 'In subsequent cases concerned with liability under the *Hedley Byrne* principle in respect of negligent mis-statements, the question has frequently arisen whether plaintiff falls within the category of persons to whom the maker of the statement owes a duty of care. In seeking to contain that category of persons within reasonable bounds, there has been some tendency on the part of the courts to criticise the concept of "assumption of responsibility" as being "unlikely to be a helpful or realistic test in most cases" (*see Harris* v. *Wyre Forest D.C.* [1989] per Lord Griffiths, and *Caparo Industries plc* v. *Dickman* [1990] per Lord Roskill). However, at least in cases such as the present, in which the same problem does not arise, there seems to be no reason why recourse should not be had to the concept, which appears after all to have been adopted, in one form or another, by all of their Lordships in *Hedley Byrne* v. *Heller*'.

Lord Goff goes on to say:

> 'It follows that, once the case is identified as falling within the *Hedley Byrne* principle, there should be no need to embark upon any further inquiry whether it is "fair, just and reasonable" to impose liability for economic loss – a point which is, I consider, of some importance in the present case'.

The House of Lords later returned to the issue of duty of care in negligence in the case of *White* v. *Jones* [1995]. In that case a solicitor had failed to prepare a Will and was sued by the disappointed beneficiaries who would have inherited part of the testator's estate had the Will been drawn up. At first instance the claims of the disappointed beneficiaries were rejected on the grounds that whilst the solicitor had failed to act, his omission was not itself negligent. The Court of Appeal unanimously reversed the first instance decision, and the House of Lords by a majority dismissed the defendant solicitor's appeal.

Lord Browne-Wilkinson stated in his opinion:

> 'I agree that your Lordships should hold that the defendant solicitors were under a duty of care to the plaintiffs arising from an extension of the principle of assumption of responsibility explored in *Hedley Byrne* v. *Heller*. In my view although the present case is not directly covered by the decided cases, it is legitimate to extend the law to the limited extent proposed using the incremental approach by way of analogy advocated in *Caparo Industries plc* v. *Dickman*'.

Lord Browne-Wilkinson goes on to comment on the House of Lords decision in *Henderson* v. *Merrett Syndicates Ltd* [1994]:

'In *Henderson* v. *Merrett Syndicates Ltd*, your Lordships recently applied the concept of assumption of liability to cases where the defendants (the managing agents) had pursuant to a contract with a third party (the members' agents) undertaken the management of the underwriting affairs of the plaintiffs. For the present purposes the case is important for two reasons. First, it shows (if it was previously in doubt) that the principle of a special relationship arising from the assumption of responsibility is as applicable to a case of negligent acts giving rise to pure economic loss as it is to negligent statement. Second, it demonstrates that the fact that the defendant assumed to act in the plaintiffs' affairs pursuant to a contract with a third party is not necessarily incompatible with the finding that, by so acting, the defendant also entered into a special relationship with the plaintiff with whom he had no contract'.

Lord Browne-Wilkinson continues:

'The law of England does not impose any general duty of care to avoid negligent mis-statements or to avoid causing pure economic loss even if economic damage to the plaintiff was foreseeable. However, such a duty of care will arise if there is a special relationship between the parties. Although the categories of cases in which such a special relationship can be held to exist are not closed, as yet only two categories have been identified, *viz.* (1) where there is a fiduciary relationship and (2) where the defendant has voluntarily answered a question or tenders skilled advice or services in circumstances where he knows or ought to know that an identified plaintiff will rely on his answers or advice. In both these categories the special relationship is created by the defendant voluntarily assuming to act in the matter by involving himself in the plaintiff's affairs or by choosing to speak. If he does so assume to act or speak he is said to have assumed responsibility for carrying through the matter he has entered upon'.

Lord Browne-Wilkinson concludes:

'The solicitor who accepts instructions to draw a Will knows that the future economic welfare of the intended beneficiary is dependant upon his careful execution of the task. It is true that the intended beneficiary (being ignorant of the instructions) may not rely on the particular solicitor's actions. But, as I have sought to demonstrate, in the case of a duty of care flowing from a fiduciary relationship liability is not dependant upon actual reliance by the plaintiff on the defendant's actions but on the fact that, as the fiduciary is well aware, the plaintiff's economic well-being is dependant upon the proper discharge by the fiduciary of his duty. Second, the solicitor by accepting the instructions has entered upon, and therefore assumed responsibility for, the task of procuring the execution of a skillfully drawn Will knowing that the beneficiary is wholly dependant upon his carefully carrying out his function. That assumption of responsibility for the task is a feature of both the two categories of special relationship so far identified in the authorities'.

10.   *Banque Bruxelles S.A.* v. *Eagle Star Insurance* [1996]

The House of Lords has recently considered the scope of duty of care in the *BBL* appeals [1996], including *South Australia Asset Management Corporation* v. *York Montague Ltd* [1996].

In the three cases the subject of the appeals the defendants, as valuers, were required by the plaintiffs to value properties on the security of which they were considering advancing money on mortgage. In each case, the defendants considerably overvalued the property. Following the valuations, the loans were made, which they would not have been if the plaintiffs had known the true values of the properties. The borrowers subsequently defaulted, and in the meantime the property market had fallen substantially, greatly increasing the losses eventually suffered by the plaintiffs. The plaintiffs brought actions against the defendants for damages for negligence and breach of contract.

In *South Australia Asset Management Corporation* v. *York Montague Ltd* (*S.A.A.M. Co.*) the defendants had valued the property at £15 million and the plaintiffs had advanced £11 million to the borrower. The judge found that the actual value of the property at the time of valuation had been £5 million. Following the borrower's default, the plaintiffs had sold it for £2,477,000. The plaintiffs claimed as damages the outstanding amount of the loan less net recovery from realisation of the security plus unpaid interest. The judge gave judgment for the sum claimed less 25% in respect of the plaintiff's contributory negligence. Leave was given by the judge for appeal direct to the House of Lords.

The House of Lords dismissed the appeal, and held:

(a) The duty of the defendants was the same in tort as in contract: to provide the plaintiffs with a correct valuation of the property, namely the figure that a reasonable valuer would have considered it most likely to fetch if sold on the open market.

(b) Where a person was under a duty to take reasonable care to provide information on which someone else would decide on a course of action he was, if negligent, responsible not for all the consequences of the course of action decided on but only for the foreseeable consequences of the information being wrong.

(c) The measure of damages was the loss attributable to the inaccuracy of the information suffered by the plaintiff through embarking on the course of action on the assumption that the information was correct.

In *S.A.A.M. Co.* the consequence of the valuation being wrong had been that the plaintiffs had had £10 million less than they had thought; that if they had had that margin they would have suffered no loss and the whole loss had been within the scope of the defendant's duty.

Lord Hoffmann, with whom Lords Goff, Jauncey, Slynn and Nicholls concurred, opined:

> 'A duty of care such as the valuer owes does not however exist in the abstract. A plaintiff who sues for breach of duty imposed by the law (whether in contract or tort or under statute) must do more than prove that the defendant has failed to comply. He must show that the duty was owed to him and that it was a duty in respect of the kind of loss which he has suffered. Both of these requirements are illustrated by *Caparo Industries plc* v. *Dickman* [1990].'

Lord Hoffmann then cites the speech of Lord Bridge in *Caparo* where he states:

'It is never sufficient to ask simply whether A owes B a duty of care. It is always necessary to determine the scope of the duty by reference to the kind of damage from which A must take care to save B harmless'.

Lord Hoffmann later in his opinion observes:

'. . . a person under a duty to take reasonable care to provide information on which someone else will decide upon a course of action is, if negligent, not generally regarded as responsible for all the consequences of that course of action. He is responsible only for the consequences of the information being wrong. A duty of care which imposes upon the informant responsibility for losses which would have occurred even if the information which he gave had been correct is not in my view fair and reasonable as between the parties. It is therefore inappropriate either as an implied term of a contract or as a tortious duty arising from the relationship between them'.

A further case of interest in this area is *Verity* v. *Lloyds Bank* [1995]. This case attracted wide publicity and relates to advice given in a written pamphlet to potential borrowers by a bank. The impact of the decision is considered in an interesting article in the *Solicitors Journal* (1996, vol. 140, p. 128).

PUBLIC POLICY ISSUES

11. As a limiting factor upon duty of care

There have been many cases which intentionally or otherwise have extended the scope of duty of care in the tort of negligence, however a smaller number of equal importance have sought to restrain such expansions and to limit its scope. Quite where the boundaries of duty of care lie is to a considerable extent an issue of public policy. Lord Scarman in *McLoughlin* v. *O'Brian* clearly took the view that public policy was a non-justiciable issue and one which should properly be left by judges for Parliament to determine. This is a view which was echoed in subsequent cases: *see Curran* v. *N. Ireland Housing Assoc.* [1987], *per* Lord Bridge and *Yuen Kun Yeu* v. *Attorney-General of Hong Kong* [1987], *per* Lord Keith. In *Jones* v. *Department of Employment* [1988], the Court of Appeal took the view that by reason of the statutory framework within which an adjudication officer operates, he did not owe a duty of care to claimants. Moreover, as a matter of public policy in view of the above, the officer's decision was not susceptible to challenge by common law unless it could be shown that his decision amounted to misfeasance. The House of Lords in *Hill* v. *Chief Constable of West Yorkshire* [1988] (*see* 3 above) took the view that as a matter of law and also of public policy an action could not be brought against the police in respect of their failure to identify and apprehend a criminal, where that failure had resulted in his committing further offences, thereby causing the death of the plaintiff's daughter.

The scope of duty of care and the issue of public policy as a limiting factor upon it has in recent cases been discussed in relation to public authorities, e.g. the Department of Employment, a police authority or a local authority. Whereas the courts have not been slow to limit the scope of duty of care in negligence for reasons of public policy, in areas where negligence can be linked with another tort, i.e. trespass to the person, they have stepped in to ensure a remedy. The extent of local authorities' liability in tort continues to cause difficulty for the courts. *Stovin* v. *Wise (Norfolk C.C. third party)* [1996] in the House of Lords was inconclusive; it was held by majority that no duty was to be imposed on Norfolk C.C. as highway authority for failing to ensure a landowner removed an obstacle which would improve visibility at a junction where the plaintiff was injured in a road accident by the defendant.

In *Calveley and Others* v. *Chief Constable of Merseyside* [1988] (CA) police officers against whom disciplinary proceedings had been taken under the Police (Discipline) Regulations 1977 had, during the investigations, all been suspended on basic pay, and had been in receipt of some of their allowances, in accordance with the Regulations. All had been reinstated save one, who was medically discharged before the investigation relating to him had been completed. On reinstatement they received backdated payment of other allowances to which they were entitled. The police officers brought actions in negligence against the defendants who by virtue of s. 48(1) of the Police Act 1964 were vicariously liable for the officers responsible for the investigations, alleging that the latter had failed to conduct the proceedings properly or expeditiously and claiming damages, *inter alia*, in respect of the loss of overtime earnings they would have received during the periods of suspension, and for injury to reputation. The defendants applied to strike out the proceedings as disclosing no cause of action on the grounds that no duty of care was owed by an investigating officer to an officer under investigation, and no private law claim arose in negligence in respect of any alleged breach of statutory duty under the Regulations. The judge struck out the actions, holding, *inter alia*, that other remedies were available to the plaintiffs, in particular by way of judicial review, in which they might also claim damages.

In dismissing the plaintiffs' appeal, the Court of Appeal held that in the context of the relationship between an investigating officer and an officer under investigation, and having regard to the statutory origin and control of the investigating officer's duties and to the officer's statutory appellate rights, together with the supervisory judicial review jurisdiction of the High Court, it was neither just and reasonable, nor in the public interest in the free and fearless investigation of complaints, that a common law duty of care should exist. Since the purpose of the Regulations was to ensure that breaches of discipline were, and were seen to be, properly investigated and punished, and since there was express provision for an officer's reimbursement on reinstatement, the statutory framework was not such as to confer on individual officers private law rights founding in damages in respect of breaches of statutory duty Accordingly, there being no cause of action, the proceedings had properly been struck out.

The Court of Appeal applied their own decision in *Jones* v. *Department of Employment* and distinguished that of the House of Lords in *Hill* v. *Chief Constable of West Yorkshire*. Lord Donaldson MR in *Calveley* took the view that *Jones* v. *Department of Employment* applied generally to all cases where an officer is exercising a statutory power to investigate and adjudicate.

The danger of public policy intervening in the area of duty of care is highlighted by Lord Keith in *Murphy* v. *Brentwood District Council* [1991].

PROFESSIONAL NEGLIGENCE

'Professional negligence' is the epithet often applied to the liability of professional advisers to provide advice of a certain standard. In many instances this may be a label for liability which arises under a more general heading, e.g. liability for negligent mis-statements or for economic loss. There have, however, been a number of cases which specifically address the relationship between a professional adviser and his client, the earliest and most notable of which was *Rondel* v. *Worsley* [1969].

12. Lawyers

Rondel v. *Worsley* [1969] lays down that as between barrister and client there is a special relationship giving rise to a duty of care, when the barrister can bring himself within the immunity which applies to an advocate. There are clear policy reasons why the barrister in the role of an advocate, i.e. conducting proceedings before a court, should not be within the scope of any duty of care to the person whom he is representing. These policy considerations arise from the need to ensure a free and independent Bar, the 'cab-rank principle' that a barrister cannot refuse to act for a client and the fact that a barrister owes a primary duty as an officer of the court to ensure the proper administration of justice. A barrister is not immune, however, where he is not acting as an advocate, so liability may ensue from an opinion given in chambers on a point of law or from paperwork drawn up by a barrister, where it is not immediately connected with prospective litigation: *see Saif Ali* v. *Mitchell & Co.* [1980].

The position of the solicitor is more clear-cut. A solicitor, unlike a barrister, is in a direct contractual relationship with his client; he may also be liable to a client in tort as well as liable for breach of contract: *see Midland Bank* v. *Hett, Stubbs & Kemp* [1979]. When acting as an advocate, it is assumed that a solicitor may take advantage of the same immunity afforded to barristers. A solicitor not only owes a duty of care to his client, but also to those persons whom he knows will rely on his professional skill, or who may suffer as a result of his carelessness: *see Ross* v. *Caunters* [1980]. The scope of the duty of care owed by solicitors was the subject of judicial comment in *Somasundaram* v. *M. Julius Melchior & Co.* [1988]; the Court of Appeal took the view that it was an abuse of the process of the court to bring an action for negligence against solicitors where the action necessarily involved a collateral attack on the judgment of another court in a criminal or a civil matter. Solicitors were not, however, immune from suit in negligence in respect of their advice as to plea in criminal proceedings.

In *Al-Kandari* v. *J.R. Brown* [1988] solicitors had, in the course of custody proceedings between their client and the plaintiff, his former wife, given an undertaking to the court to retain their client's passport in circumstances where there was a real risk that if their client (a Kuwaiti citizen) obtained the passport he would abduct the children. The Court of Appeal held that the solicitors owed a duty of care to the plaintiff to inform her if the passport ceased, for any reason, to be in their possession. Lord Donaldson MR opined:

'In the context of hostile litigation public policy would usually require that a solicitor be protected from a claim in negligence by his client's opponent, since such claims could be used as a basis for endless re-litigation of disputes: *Rondel* v. *Worsley* [1969].

The present case was different because the passport was not only that of the husband but also of the two children who were in custody, care and control of the plaintiff. In voluntarily agreeing to hold that passport to the order of the court the solicitors had stepped outside their role as solicitors for their client and had accepted responsibilities towards both their client and the plaintiff and the children.

One such responsibility was clearly a duty not to hand over the passport to the husband upon his request, and there had been no breach of that duty. The question was whether there was a wider responsibility.

The plaintiff fell squarely within Lord Atkin's concept of the defendants' "neighbour" (*see Donoghue* v. *Stevenson* [1932]) and, accordingly, in the absence of contra-indications, of which there were none, the law required the defendants to take reasonable care to avoid acts or omissions likely to injure her.

The defendants owed the plaintiff a duty in tort.'

A solicitor may not always be held to be negligent simply because a duty is held to exist; many of the cases of professional negligence hinge more on breach rather than the scope of the duty owed. In *Booth & Andler* v. *Davey* [1988], a solicitor was held to be not liable in negligence in a transaction for the sale of land where, prior to exchange of contracts, he read aloud to his clients the terms of the draft contract and gave them a copy to consider before signing it.

The Court of Appeal in *Clarke* v. *Bruce Lance & Co. and Others* [1987], held that a testator's solicitors owed no duty of care to a potential beneficiary under the Will to advise the testator that a particular transaction which the testator had entered into was likely to harm the potential beneficiary's interest. In *Hemmens* v. *Wilson Browne* [1993] it was accepted that there could be instances where a solicitor will owe a duty of care to third parties in *inter vivos*, i.e. lifetime transactions, although in that case the Court rejected the plaintiff's claim against the solicitor where the solicitor had negligently drawn up a document for the client allowing payment to the plaintiff and the client has refused to pay the plaintiff.

In *White* v. *Jones* [1995] the Court of Appeal expressly affirmed *Ross* and applied that decision to a case where a solicitor had failed to prepare a Will as opposed to providing incorrect advice. The remedy in negligence was required in this situation to aid the disappointed beneficiary who would otherwise have no protection. The House of Lords held by a bare majority (Lords Mustill and Keith dissenting) that the defendant's appeal should be dismissed. Lord Mustill in his opinion observed:

'The solicitor does of course undertake the task of preparing the Will, in the sense of agreeing to take it on. But this is between himself and his client. By virtue of his response to the testator's instructions the solicitor does assume or undertake a legal liability for doing it properly.'

Lord Mustill took the view that this situation is outside the scope of the *Hedley Byrne* principle. There could in his view be no rationale for an incremental extension of the *Hedley Byrne* principle to encompass this situation.

For solicitors, from a practical point of view, the existence of a client's spouse and his/her proprietary interests in the matrimonial home have raised the issue: Does the solicitor owe a duty of care to his client's wife to ascertain her consent to a proposed disposal of the property jointly owned by them? In *Penn* v. *Bristol & West Building Society* (1995) such a duty was imposed.

A further situation which has given rise to a number of claims for professional negligence is where a solicitor has acted for both the borrower and lender on a mortgage. Where a lender sues a solicitor for negligently having given incorrect information, the lender does not have to prove that it would not have made the mortgage if it had known the true facts. The lender is required to establish what it has lost as a consequence of a second charge over the property, which had been negligently overlooked by the defendant solicitor, so held the Court of Appeal in *Bristol & West Building Society* v. *Mothew (trading as Stapley & Co.)* [1996].

13. Medical practitioners

Medical practitioners have not been immune from negligence liability. Cases involving doctors have been concerned primarily with the standard of care owed rather than the actual existence or nature of any duty of care owed by a doctor to his/her patients: *see Sidaway* v. *Bethlem Royal Hospital Governors* [1985].

The courts were confronted with the issue of whether a doctor owes a duty of care to the unborn child of his/her patient in *B.* v. *Islington Health Authority* [1992]. In that case medical staff at a hospital managed by the defendant health authority carried out a gynaecological operation on the plaintiff's mother when she was pregnant with the plaintiff. The plaintiff was born with numerous abnormalities, including deformed limbs and an inability to conceive, and was greatly embarrassed by her appearance, which she considered would impair her relationships with men and her earning capacity. She brought an action against the health authority alleging that her condition had been caused by the carrying out of the operation on her mother while the plaintiff was in utero, that the operation should not have been performed on a pregnant woman and that the medical staff had been negligent in carrying out the operation without first ascertaining whether the plaintiff's mother was pregnant. The health authority applied to strike out the plaintiff's statement of claim on the ground that it disclosed no reasonable cause of action because at the time the alleged negligence occurred and the injury was caused to the plaintiff she had no legal status, being no more than an embryo, and therefore was not a legal person to whom a duty of care could be owed and had no right to sue.

At first instance it was held that it was not an essential requirement of the tort of negligence for the negligent act which caused the injury to be contemporaneous with the injury itself or for the person committing the negligent act and the person injured to have correlative rights and duties at the time of the wrongful act. Breach of a duty of care would be established if at the time the wrongful act was committed there was merely a potential or contingent duty of care which crystallised into an actual duty when the person injured suffered the injury, and it was irrelevant that at the time the wrongful act was committed there was no specific person towards whom the duty could be said to exist. Accordingly, since the medical staff ought reasonably to have foreseen that the operation carried out on the plaintiff's mother was liable to damage any embryo being carried in her womb and since on birth the plaintiff not only suffered damage by being born with physical deformities but also acquired legal status and legal rights to sue in respect of that damage, she had a cause of action in respect of the injury caused to her by the medical staff's negligence before she was born. The application to strike out would therefore be dismissed. This traditional *Donoghue* v. *Stevenson* foreseeability approach was affirmed by the Court of Appeal, and is somewhat of an exception to the more favoured incremental approach now being adopted by the House of Lords in determining the issue of duty of care.

14. Surveyors

The concept of duty of care has recently been re-examined in the context of the duty owed by a surveyor to those who may suffer loss as a consequence of his valuation of property: see the House of Lords' decision in *Banque Bruxelles Lambert S.A.* v. *Eagle Star* [1996] – *South Australia Asset Management Corporation* v. *York Montague Ltd* [1996] (**10** above).

The key issue in the House of Lords' decision is the issue whether or not the plaintiff's loss is of a kind against which the defendant has assumed responsibility to safeguard the plaintiff. In the ordinary type of valuation cases, the loss which the valuer assumes responsibility to safeguard the lender is loss due to the inadequacy of the security. The loss which the lender sustains is that which is attributable to having made an advance on a security which is worth less than the lender intended to have for that advance.

Lord Hoffmann narrows the scope of the duty of care owed by surveyors to include only: the kinds of damage against which the valuer has assumed responsibility to safeguard the lender; and which the lender was entitled to rely upon the valuer to prevent – namely the loss due to the inadequacy of the security at the time of the advance. On this analysis, the proportion of the valuation that the lender chooses to advance, and the reasons why, in the event, he suffers the loss that he actually suffers (e.g. a fall in the property market, destruction of the property), are entirely irrelevant.

Lord Hoffmann explains:

> 'A duty of care such as the valuer owes does not however exist in the abstract. A plaintiff who sues for breach of a duty imposed by the law (whether in contract or tort or under statute) must do more than prove that the defendant has failed to comply. He must show that the duty was owed to him and that it was a duty in respect of the kind of loss which he has suffered.'

The significance of the House of Lords' decision is that it effectively narrows the scope of the duty of care owed by a surveyor. The basis for such duty appears to be 'assumption of risk' only.

An interesting article on the *BBL* appeals, 'Property finance negligence damages after BBL' by H. Tomlinson and T. Grant, is to be found at page 654 of vol. 40, no. 26 of the *Solicitors Journal*.

It is important to consider the scope of the duty owed by surveyors in the light of that which is owed by solicitors. In circumstances where a lender has sustained financial loss as a consequence of a surveyor's valuation and the advice of the lender's solicitor, the duty owed by each professional adviser is different. Following the House of Lords' decision in *S.A.A.M. Co.* the surveyor's duty is narrower than that of the solicitor (see below).

15. Persons responsible for building control

The position of consultant engineers and others who are responsible for the supervision/control of the construction of buildings or their inspection has been much litigated in tort. Reference should be made to the House of Lords' decision in *Murphy* v. *Brentwood District Council* [1991], and *D. & F. Estates Ltd and Others* v. *Church Commissioners for England and Others* [1988].

In relation to builders, the House of Lords considered their liability for economic loss arising from defective construction work in *Department of Environment* v. *Thomas Bates and Son Ltd* [1990]. In that case their Lordships applied their decision in *Murphy* v. *Brentwood District Council,* holding that the plaintiff's claim for economic loss was not recoverable in tort.

The facts of the case were: The owners of a building site granted a lease of it to lessees, who contracted with the defendants for the construction on it of a complex including a two-storey building with a flat roof and an 11-storey tower block, the upper nine floors of which were to be used as offices. The building operations took place during 1970 and 1971. In September 1971, the lessees granted an underlease of parts of the complex, including parts of the two-storey building and the upper nine storeys of the tower block, to the plaintiffs. During subsequent remedial work to the flat roof of the two-storey building it was discovered that some of the concrete used was soft, and it was subsequently discovered that the concrete in pillars supporting the floors of the tower block was also soft, due to its having contained an excess of concrete and a deficiency of cement. The plaintiffs' expert expressed the opinion that nine of the pillars were insufficiently strong to support the design load of the building, and they were accordingly strengthened. The plaintiffs commenced proceedings against the defendants by writ issued in October 1982, claiming payment of the amount that they had paid in respect of remedial works to the flat roof of the two-storey building, the amount that they had paid in respect of alternative accommodation while those works were being carried out and £71,016.61 in respect of the cost of strengthening the pillars. They pleaded their cause of action in negligence, alleging that the defendants had owed them a duty to use reasonable skill and care in the construction of the complex. The judge found in the plaintiffs' favour in respect of part of their claim relating to the flat roof but dismissed their claim in respect of the pillars. He found that at no time had the weakness of the concrete in the pillars given rise to imminent danger to the health or safety of either the plaintiffs' employees or the public: the purpose of the strengthening of the pillars had been not to avert such imminent danger but to cure a defect that had otherwise prevented the plaintiffs from making full use of the building to the extent for which it had been designed. The Court of Appeal dismissed an appeal by the plaintiffs in respect of their claim relating to the pillars.

On appeal by the plaintiffs, the House of Lords, dismissing the appeal, held that, since the tower block had not been unsafe by reason of the defective construction of the pillars but had merely suffered from a defect of quality making the plaintiffs' lease less valuable since the building could not be used to its full design capacity unless it was repaired, the loss suffered by the plaintiffs was pure economic loss, which was not recoverable in tort by them against the defendants.

For the position of environmental health officers, *see Welton* v. *North Cornwall D.C.* (1996).

For building inspectors, *see Invercargill City Council* v. *Hamlin* (1996) (PC).

16. Police and prison staff

In *Kirkham* v. *Chief Constable of the Greater Manchester Police* [1990], the scope of the duty of care owed by the police to persons in their custody was considered. The facts of the case were that the plaintiff's husband (the deceased) was an alcoholic with suicidal tendencies who had a long criminal record. After a suicide attempt he was admitted to hospital but was allowed to discharge himself the next day. The day after, following a domestic argument, he was arrested and charged with criminal damage. The plaintiff told the police that the deceased had recently tried to commit suicide and that he needed to be watched. The hospital also informed the police of the deceased's history of mental illness. At the police station the station sergeant noted the deceased's suicidal tendencies and ordered that he be placed in a detention room and visited every half hour in accordance with the procedure adopted in cases of potential suicide. However, the procedure for informing the prison authorities of a prisoner's suicidal tendencies, by completing the form for exceptional risk prisoners, stating that the prisoner had suicidal tendencies, giving the relevant details and handing that form to the magistrate's court gaoler for transmission to the prison authorities if the prisoner was remanded in custody, was not carried out in the case of the deceased. At his appearance before the magistrates the next day the prosecution asked that he be kept in custody for his own protection in view of his attempted suicide. The magistrates remanded him to a remand centre, where he was treated like a normal prisoner and placed in a cell alone, where he committed suicide by hanging. The plaintiff brought an action against the chief constable claiming damages for negligence by the police in failing to pass on to the remand centre information relating to the deceased's suicidal tendencies. The defendant contended (*i*) that the police did not owe a duty of care to prevent the deceased inflicting harm on himself because they were in the position of mere bystanders and (*ii*) that the plaintiff's cause of action was barred by the maxim *ex turpi causa non oritur actio* or some general ground of public policy because the claim arose out of an act of suicide.

Mr Justice Tudor Evans held that the defendant owed a duty of care to prevent the deceased committing suicide because the police had been expressly put on notice of the deceased's mental state and the risk of suicide, and by taking him into custody and detaining him at the police station the police assumed a duty to take reasonable care of his safety. Moreover, that duty did not end when the deceased was taken to court and was passed over to the prison authorities, since the procedure of completing a form for exceptional risk prisoners for the purpose of informing the prison authorities of a prisoner's suicidal tendencies showed that it was reasonably foreseeable by the police that their actions would affect the deceased after he passed out of their charge. The discharge of the duty of care required the police to pass on to the remand centre all information available to them relevant to the risk of suicide by the deceased and by failing to pass on that information they were in breach of their duty of care. That omission was an effective cause of the deceased's death, since if the remand centre had known of the risk of the deceased's suicide he would probably have been placed in the hospital wing rather than a cell by himself and would probably have been prevented from committing suicide. Furthermore, the deceased's act of suicide was not too remote from the defendant's negligence, there was no contributory negligence and the defendant was not entitled to avoid liability by relying on the maxim *ex turpi causa non oritur actio* or some general ground of public policy because there was no causally related criminal act and, having regard to the circumstances of the deceased's high suicide risk and the defendant's failure to carry out the duty of care owed to him, there was no moral turpitude attaching to the deceased's suicide which prevented the plaintiff from recovering damages. Accordingly, the defendant was liable to the plaintiff for damages, which, on the basis of the deceased's future earnings, would be assessed at £5,000. This approach was affirmed by the Court of Appeal. *See* by way of former case examples: *Hill* v. *Chief Constable of West Yorkshire* [1988]; *Alexandrov* v. *Oxford* [1990]; and *Clough* v. *Bussan* [1990]. With regard to the liability of prison staff *see Knight and Others* v. *Home Office* [1990].

17. Teachers

The scope of the duty owed by teachers towards the pupils whom they supervise was considered in *Van Oppen* v. *Clerk of Bedford Charity Trustees* [1989]. In that case the plaintiff was seriously injured in 1980 when he tackled another pupil in a game of rugby at school. In the previous year the school had received a report from the school medical officers' association recommending that schools take out accident insurance for pupils playing rugby, but at the time of the plaintiff's accident the school had not decided on what sort of insurance was required and how it was to be obtained. The plaintiff brought an action against the school's trustees alleging that the school had been negligent in failing (*i*) to take reasonable care for the plaintiff's safety on the rugby field, in that the school had failed to coach or instruct the plaintiff in proper tackling techniques, (*ii*) to insure the plaintiff against accidental injury and (*iii*) to advise the plaintiff's father of the risk of serious injury in rugby, of the need for personal accident insurance for the plaintiff and of the fact that the school had not arranged such insurance. The plaintiff claimed damages for pain, suffering and loss of amenity, loss of earnings and the cost of future assistance.

The plaintiff's claim was dismissed:

(a) On the facts, the school was not negligent in its coaching or teaching of rugby and it was not liable for the plaintiff's injuries, since they were the result of an accident rather than negligence on anyone's part.

(b) There was no general duty arising simply from the relationship between a school and its pupils requiring the school to insure its pupils against accidental injury or to protect the pupils' economic welfare by insuring them, because such a duty would be in excess of the school's obligations to educate and care for the pupils and would be wider than the duty imposed on a school in its position *in loco parentis*. Similarly, a school was under no duty to advise a parent of the dangers of rugby football or of the need for personal accident insurance, just as a parent was under no duty to insure if he was advised to do so. Furthermore, the plaintiff's school had never assumed legal responsibility for advising on the need for insurance or for insuring its pupils, since it did not hold itself out as having the expertise to advise parents on insurance or to deal with insurance itself, and there was no evidence that the plaintiff's father had relied on the school for such advice. *See also Nwabudike* v. *Southwark L.B.C.* The courts have very recently had to struggle with actions based on the bullying of pupils, where their schools have failed to intervene to protect them from the actions of their fellow pupils.

18. Auditors

The accountancy profession is exposed to significant claims for damages for negligence arising from auditing activities. So much so that accountancy practices are considering the extent to which they can protect themselves effectively, e.g. by incorporation. At the root of the problem is the rule on joint and several liability of partners.

In *Galoo Ltd* v. *Bright Grahame Murray* [1995] the Court of Appeal considered the issue of 'voluntary assumption of responsibility' in circumstances where the defendant can be shown not merely to have known that the individual plaintiff would or might rely upon the representation, but to have intended that it should be relied upon by him for a particular purpose.

In assessing the position of auditors, reference must be made to the House of Lords' decision in *Caparo Industries plc* v. *Dickman* [1990] (see **8** above).

An auditor in his report provides information on which someone else may decide upon a course of action. If the auditor is negligent in the preparation of his report he is not generally regarded as responsible for all the consequences of that course of action. The auditor is responsible only for the consequences of the information contained in the report being wrong. No duty arises which imposes upon the auditor responsibility for losses which would have occurred even if the information contained in his report was correct.

In *South Australia Asset Management Corporation* v. *York Montague Ltd* [1996], Lord Hoffmann provides the following analysis:

'The principle thus stated distinguishes between a duty to *provide information* for the purpose of enabling someone else to decide upon a course of action and a duty to *advise* someone as to what course of action he should take. If the duty is to advise whether or not a course of action should be taken, the adviser must take reasonable care to consider all the potential consequences of that course of action. If he is negligent he will therefore be responsible for all the foreseeable loss which is a consequence of that course of action having been taken. If his duty is only to supply information, he must take reasonable care to ensure that the information is correct and, if he is negligent, will be responsible for all the foreseeable consequences of the information being wrong'.

19. Rescue services

There have been three recent first instance cases of note on the liability in negligence of fire authorities. In *Church of Jesus Christ of Latter-Day Saints (Great Britain)* v. *Yorkshire Fire and Civil Defence Authority* [1996], where the plaintiff alleged a failure to inspect and maintain water hydrants, resulting in the fire brigade's inability to put out a fire effectively, the court held that although the risk of harm was foreseeable and there was sufficient proximity, public policy demanded that an emergency service should be immune.

Conversely, in *Capital and Counties plc* v. *Hampshire C.C.* [1996] the trial judge considered that public policy did not justify immunity.

In *John Munroe (Acrylics) Ltd* v. *London Fire and Civil Defence Authority* [1996], the trial judge held on the particular facts (the plaintiff was the owner of an adjacent property damaged by a fire attended by the defendant's employees) that there was insufficient proximity and furthermore that public policy prevented the imposition of any duty of care.

As to the coastguard, in *Skinner* v. *Secretary of State for Transport* [1995], it was held in the High Court that the coastguard does not owe any duty of care when exercising its functions of watching, listening and its emergency rescue co-ordination activities.

EXCLUSIONS AND LIMITATIONS UPON DUTY OF CARE

20. Omissions

A clear distinction must be drawn between the infliction of harm through the conduct of the defendant and, on the other hand, where the defendant merely allows the harm to occur through his omitting to take positive steps to prevent it. It is rare to find a 'simple omission' – usually the failure to take action forms part of a course of conduct and therefore forms part of the negligent conduct.

There is no general duty to act to prevent harm occurring to others, even where such harm is reasonably foreseeable. Foreseeability of damage cannot itself impose an obligation to act. This is clearly to be seen in *Perl (Exporters) Ltd* v. *Camden London Borough Council* [1984]. Thieves entered the plaintiffs' premises by breaching the wall of an adjoining flat owned by the defendants. The defendants were not liable for the theft. The flaw in the plaintiffs' case was the use of mere foreseeability of damage as the sole foundation of the duty of care. But a further point must be emphasised: the defendants' liability, if established, would have been for a simple failure to act, since the basis of the plaintiffs' case was that the defendants had done nothing to exclude vagrants and others from their own property, thereby facilitating the theft.

The House of Lords in *Smith and Others* v. *Littlewoods Organisation & the Chief Constable of Fife Constabulary* [1987] had the opportunity to review the law on omissions. The facts of the case were that the respondents purchased a cinema with a view to demolishing it and replacing it with a supermarket. They took possession on 31 May 1976, closed the cinema and employed contractors to make site investigations and do some preliminary work on foundations, but from about the end of the third week in June the cinema remained empty and unattended by the respondents or any of their employees. By the beginning of July the main building of the cinema was no longer lockfast and was being regularly entered by unauthorised persons. Debris began to accumulate outside the cinema and on two occasions attempts to start fires inside and adjacent to the cinema had been observed by a passer-by but neither the respondents nor the police were informed. On 5 July a fire was started in the cinema which seriously damaged two adjoining properties, one of which had to be demolished. The appellants, the owners of the affected properties, claimed damages against the respondents on the ground that the damage to their properties had been caused by the respondent's negligence. The judge found the claims established and awarded the appellants damages. An appeal by the respondents was allowed by the Court of Session. The appellants appealed to the House of Lords, contending that it was reasonably foreseeable that if the cinema was left unsecured children would be attracted to the building, would gain entry and would cause damage which, it was reasonably foreseeable, would include damage by fire which, it was reasonably foreseeable, would in turn spread to and damage adjoining properties.

The House of Lords held, dismissing the appeal, that the respondents were under a general duty to exercise reasonable care to ensure that the condition of the premises they occupied was not a source of danger to neighbouring property. Whether that general duty encompassed a specific duty to prevent damage from fire resulting from vandalism in the respondents' premises depended on whether a reasonable person in the position of the respondents would foresee that if he took no action to keep the premises lockfast in the comparatively short time before the premises were demolished, they would be set on fire with consequent risk to the neighbouring properties. On the facts and given, particularly, that the respondents had not known of the vandalism in the area or of the previous attempts to start fires, the events which occurred were not reasonably foreseeable by the respondents and they accordingly owed no such specific duty to the appellants. Furthermore (*per* Lord Mackay), where the injury or damage was caused by an independent human agency the requirement that the injury or damage had to be the probable consequence of the tortfeasor's own act or omission before there could be liability referred not to a consequence determined according to the balance of probabilities but to a real risk of injury or damage, in the sense of the injury or damage being a highly likely consequence of the act or omission rather than a mere possibility. The more unpredictable the conduct in question, the less easy it was to affirm that any particular result from it was probable and, unless the court could be satisfied that the result of the human action was highly probable or very likely, it might have to conclude that all the reasonable man could say was that it was no more than a mere possibility. Furthermore, Lord Goff and Lord Keith took the view that there was no general duty at common law to prevent persons from harming others by their deliberate wrongdoing, however foreseeable such harm might be, if a defendant did not take steps to prevent it. Accordingly, liability in negligence for such harm caused by third parties could only be made out in special circumstances, namely

(a) where a special relationship existed between the plaintiff and the defendant

(b) where a source of danger was negligently created by the defendant and it was reasonably foreseeable that third parties might interfere and cause damage by sparking off the danger

(c) where the defendant had knowledge or means of knowledge that a third party had created or was creating a risk of danger on his property and he failed to take reasonable steps to abate it.

On the facts, no such special circumstances were present, and accordingly the respondents owed no duty of care to the appellants.

A case in which the duty to protect the plaintiff from the wrongs of a third party was considered in *Topp* v. *London County Bus Ltd* [1993]. The defendants had left their minibus unattended with the keys in the ignition. The minibus was stolen by X who crashed it into the plaintiff's wife, killing her. The Court of Appeal held there was no duty of care.

In *Minories Finance Ltd* v. *Arthur Young* [1988] and *Johnson Matthey plc* v. *Arthur Young* [1988], the issue of liability for omission again arose. The case developed from the conduct of the commercial loan banking business of Johnson Matthey Bankers Ltd between 1980 and 1984. It had been alleged that the business had been conducted in such an imprudent and careless way that it became insolvent and had to be rescued by the Bank of England.

It had been claimed that in the course of audits between 1981 and 1983 Arthur Young should have discovered and reported on what was happening and that, had they done so, much of the loss sustained would have been avoided. The damages being claimed by the plaintiffs exceeded £100 million in each case. Arthur Young had denied any breach of duty on their part and had asserted in the present proceedings that if they were under any liability, they were entitled to an indemnity or contribution from the Bank of England. The basis of that claim was that the Bank of England, as the body responsible for the supervision of banks in the UK, had owed a duty of care to the plaintiffs to carry out its supervisory functions with reasonable care and skill and had failed to do so.

Mr Justice Saulle held that:

> 'No duty of care arose out of the relationship between the Bank of England and commercial banks in the UK. Principles of common sense and reason did not indicate that such an obligation should exist. On the contrary, it seemed to offend those principles to suggest that a commercial concern such as Johnson Matthey Bankers Ltd could look to the Bank of England to make good its losses arising from its own imprudence or carelessness on the basis that the Bank of England should have discovered and dealt with those shortcomings.'

He opined:

> 'In the present case it was important to bear in mind that the negligence alleged against the Bank of England was not that wrong or misleading advice or instruc-

tions had been given in the course of supervision. What was alleged was that the Bank of England negligently failed to discover or comment upon or take any appropriate action in relation to the imprudent and careless manner in which Johnson Matthey Bankers Ltd were conducting their commercial loan portfolio.'

His Lordship took the view that there was nothing just or fair or reasonable in making the Bank of England assume or share any part of the commercial responsibilities which private banks owed to themselves to conduct their commercial dealings prudently and carefully so as to make profits and avoid losses.

The position of professional bodies and regulatory authorities should also be considered. The Court of Appeal in *Wood* v. *The Law Society* (1995) held that The Law Society was not under any general duty to clients of solicitors practices. In that case a client complained to The Law Society regarding the conduct of her solicitor as The Law Society regulates the professional conduct of the solicitors' profession. The plaintiff's case was that The Law Society omitted to investigate her complaint effectively and was thus in breach of its duty to her. The Court of Appeal held that no such duty existed.

As a final point on omissions it should be noted that a problem arises with regard to omissions where, for instance, the defendant has voluntarily embarked upon an undertaking where there was not a duty to do so, e.g. the rescue of an injured person, or the giving of first aid, then omits to complete the undertaking or does so negligently.

In such a situation, the person who embarks on the endeavour is not liable unless his intention, or the discontinuance of it, has put the other person in a worse position than he was in before the intervention of that person: *see East Suffolk Rivers Catchment Board* v. *Kent* [1941]. Insofar as this case considers the liability of a public authority for its failure to act, it must be reviewed in the light of the decision in *Anns*. In that case the defendant Borough Council were held liable since they failed to confer a benefit, namely to prevent damage caused by the builder's negligent construction of the flats. Here one sees the imposition of a duty to act, and a simple omission to do so resulted in liability on the part of the local authority. Arguably, the point is capable of extension outside the statutory context of the *Anns* case.

Certain relationships between plaintiff and defendant can give rise to a positive duty to prevent harm:

(a) *Employer and employee*: the employer owes a duty not to put the employee at risk of attack: Charlton v. *Forrest Printing Ink Co. Ltd* [1980]. In *Spring* v. *Guardian Assurance* [1994] the House of Lords held that an employer owes a former employee a duty of care when writing a reference to a prospective employer. In *Walker* v. *Northumberland C.C.* [1995] it was held that an employer owes a duty of care not to cause psychiatric injury to an employee whom the employer knows to be susceptible to such harm (*see* 3:**3** and 6:**11**).

(b) *Parent and child*: *Carmarthenshire County Council* v. *Lewis* [1955].

(c) *School and pupil*: *Barnes* v. *Hampshire County Council* [1969], where a child of five was let out of school early and ran out into the road and was badly injured in a road accident. The Council were held liable for releasing the child from school early since at the due time her mother would have met her and been able to prevent the girl running into the road.

(d) *Licensee of bar and customer*: Munro v. *Porthkerry Park Holiday Estates Ltd* [1984].

(e) *Occupier and lawful visitor, see* Chapter 5.

(f) *Occupier and trespasser, see* Chapter 5.

21. Nervous shock

Nervous shock is the way in which lawyers describe psychiatric illness. No action lies for mere mental suffering: *see Heinz* v. *Berry* [1970]. Mental distress, anguish or grief will not be actionable unless it leads to a positive psychiatric or physical illness, such as a heart attack: *see McLoughlin* v. *O'Brian* [1982]. Where, however, mental distress or grief exacerbates other injuries received in the same accident, preventing the plaintiff from making a recovery as quickly as he would otherwise have done, this can be reflected in the quantum of damages in respect of the other injuries: *see Kralj* v. *McGrath* [1986].

The courts have been extremely cautious about admitting claims for nervous shock which were not the result of physical injury to the plaintiff (although shock or distress consequent upon physical injury to the plaintiff has always been recoverable). The initial fear of a flood of fraudulent claims was gradually replaced with the fear of a multiplicity of genuine claims if the neighbour principle was applied in an unqualified way to this type of harm.

The initial response was to deny any action for nervous shock which was not the product of some form of physical impact with the plaintiff. In *Dulieu* v. *White* [1901] the plaintiff succeeded for shock sustained as a result of being put in fear for her own safety by the defendant's negligence. In *Hambrook* v. *Stokes Bros* [1925] a mother suffered nervous shock when she saw a runaway lorry which she feared might have injured her children, but she did not see the accident itself. A majority of the Court of Appeal held the negligent driver liable. It would be absurd, it was said, not to compensate a mother who feared for her children's safety, when on similar facts another mother would succeed if, not thinking about her children, she was frightened only for herself.

Four things emerged from the case law:

(a) That the test of liability for shock is foreseeability of injury by shock: *see King* v. *Phillips* [1953], *per* Denning LJ.

(b) In determining what is foreseeable the shock must be the product of what the plaintiff perceived with his own unaided senses. There would be no action in respect of shock sustained as a result of what the plaintiff was told by others: *see Hambrook* v. *Stokes Bros* [1925]. Situations may therefore arise where a claim for nervous shock resulting from a television broadcast would be accepted by the Courts: *see Alcock* v. *Chief Constable of South Yorkshire* [1992].

(c) Claims were admitted of plaintiffs who were in fairly close physical proximity to the accident, although it was necessary that they saw the accident itself:

see Boardman v. *Sanderson* [1964], where the plaintiff heard the accident and saw the aftermath, and *Chadwick* v. *British Railways Board* [1967], where the plaintiff saw the consequences of a major train crash. In *King* v. *Phillips* the test was said to be reasonable foreseeability of shock. The fact that the plaintiff was 70 yards from the scene rendered her shock 'unforeseeable', despite the fact that she saw her child's tricycle under a taxi. The result would be different today: *see McLoughlin* v. *O'Brian* [1982]. Note in this context the decision of the Court of Appeal in *Mcfarlane* v. *E.E. Caledonia Ltd* [1994].

(d) The nature of the relationship between the accident victim and the person who suffered the shock was important. Thus a parent or spouse of a victim would more readily be regarded as foreseeably affected, although a workman has succeeded for anticipated injury to fellow workers: *Dooley* v. *Cammell Laird & Co. Ltd* [1951]. A total stranger such as a bystander is likely to be treated as an unforeseeable plaintiff: *see Bourhill* v. *Young* [1943]. In *Chadwick* v. *British Railways Board*, however, the plaintiff was not related to the victims of the train disaster. The fact that he was assisting the victims at the scene and therefore could be regarded as a 'rescuer' undoubtedly influenced the Court of Appeal's decision to admit his claim. Note in this context the decision of the Court of Appeal in *Mcfarlane* v. *E.E. Caledonia Ltd* [1994].

The purpose of these restrictions was to narrow the potential number of claimants, firstly by excluding those who did not witness the event and secondly by excluding bystanders not related to the victim.

These cases have to be considered in the light of the decision of the House of Lords in *McLoughlin* v. *O'Brian* [1982] and *Page* v. *Smith* [1996]. In *McLoughlin* v. *O'Brian*, the Court of Appeal decided that the shock was foreseeable, but as a matter of policy the defendant did not owe a duty of care to someone who was not at or near the scene of the accident. The plaintiff's appeal was unanimously allowed by the House of Lords. The central problem was the fact that the plaintiff had not been at the scene of the accident. All members of the appellate tribunal agreed that the shock was readily foreseeable, but the question was whether as a matter of policy there should be some other limit on the duty of care. Lord Wilberforce, with whom Lord Edmund-Davies agreed, adopted an 'aftermath test'. Foreseeability alone was not sufficient; there had to be some additional limits, based on:

(a) The class of persons who can sue – the closer the emotional tie the greater the claim for consideration.

(b) Physical proximity to the accident, which must be close in both time and space, although this would be extended to persons who did not witness the accident but came upon the 'aftermath' of the events. By analogy with the 'rescue' cases, persons who would normally come to the scene, such as a parent or spouse, would be within the scope of duty. On the facts of *McLoughlin* v. *O'Brian* the 'aftermath' would be given a fairly wide interpretation.

(c) The shock must come through the plaintiffs own sight or hearing of the event or its immediate aftermath. Communication by a third party would not be sufficient.

Lord Bridge of Harwich, with whom Lord Scarman agreed, preferred a test based upon foreseeability alone, 'untrammelled by spatial, physical or temporal limits' (per Lord Scarman). Lord Bridge observed that: 'A policy which is to be relied on to narrow the scope of the negligent tortfeasor's duty must be justified by cogent and readily intelligible consideration, and must be capable of defining the appropriate limits of liability by reference to factors which are not purely arbitrary.'

The drawing of a line by reference to the criteria suggested by Lord Wilberforce 'must impose a largely arbitrary limit of liability'. Those factors would have a bearing on the degree to which shock was foreseeable, but they would not necessarily preclude a claim. Thus a bystander of normal fortitude would not usually be foreseeably affected, but if the accident was particularly gruesome, as in *Chadwick* v. *British Railways Board*, then a spectator, such as an uninjured passenger on the train, might have an action even though he was not acting as a rescuer. Nor was there any logic in denying an action to a mother who reads a newspaper report of a fire at a hotel where her children were staying and subsequently learns of their death, simply because an 'important link in the chain of causation of her psychiatric illness was supplied by her imagination of the agonies of mind and body in which her family died, rather than direct perception of the event', *per* Lord Bridge in *McLoughlin* v. *O'Brian* [1982]. Indeed, this may be a more likely cause of shock than witnessing the events.

In *McLoughlin* v. *O'Brian* [1982], Lord Russell, without expressly agreeing with Lord Bridge, concluded that if the shock to Mrs McLoughlin was foreseeable there was no justification for not finding the defendant liable. Policy might be relevant in an appropriate case but his Lordship declined to lay down guidelines in advance for hypothetical cases. Although not entirely free from doubt, this suggests that Lord Russell agreed that foreseeability of injury by shock should not be arbitrarily limited by the physical circumstances of the manner in which it arose. Policy considerations were 'rooted in a fear of floodgates opening', an argument with which his Lordship was not impressed. The 'floodgates' argument was also rejected by Lords Wilberforce, Edmund-Davies and Bridge. 'Both the number of successful claims in this field and the quantum of damages they will attract are likely to be moderate', said Lord Bridge. On this basis it is arguable that, following *McLoughlin* v. *O'Brian*, liability for nervous shock has been brought within the mainstream of the neighbour principle, and depends on foreseeability of injury by shock *simpliciter*. See *Page* v. *Smith* [1996] (**23** below).

Nervous shock has until recently been associated with mental illness caused through witnessing physical harm to others or in anticipation of physical injury to oneself. In *Attia* v. *British Gas plc* [1987] the Court of Appeal awarded damages for psychiatric damage resulting from the plaintiff witnessing the consequences of the defendants' negligence, namely the destruction of the plaintiff's home and possessions by a fire caused by the defendants' negligence. The defendants were engaged by the plaintiff to install central heating in her house. While they were doing so the plaintiff returned home one afternoon to see smoke pouring from the loft of the house. She telephoned the fire brigade but by the time they arrived the whole house was on fire. It took over four hours to get the fire under control and the house and its contents were extensively damaged.

22. The Hillsborough disaster

The Hillsborough disaster has provided the House of Lords with an opportunity to re-examine the rules of liability for nervous shock. *Alcock* v. *Chief Constable of South Yorkshire Police (sub nom. Jones and Others* v. *Wright)* enabled the House of Lords to review its earlier decisions in *Bourhill* v. *Young* [1943] and *McLoughlin* v. *O'Brian* [1982] and consider all the key issues concerning recovery of damages for nervous shock: category of relationship to the primary victim, definition of immediate aftermath, perception of the incident, e.g. by television pictures, etc.

The facts of the case were that shortly before the commencement of a major football match at a football stadium the police responsible for crowd control at the match allowed an excessively large number of spectators into a section of the ground which was already full, with the result that 95 spectators were crushed to death and over 400 injured. Scenes from the stadium were broadcast live on television during the course of the disaster. In accordance with broadcasting guidelines none of the TV reports depicted suffering by or the deaths of recognisable individuals.

Sixteen persons, none of whom was present in the area where the disaster occurred but who were either relatives or the fiancé of persons who were in that area, brought actions against the Chief Constable of the force responsible for policing the match, claiming damages for nervous shock resulting in psychiatric illness alleged to have been caused by seeing or hearing news of the disaster. The Chief Constable admitted liability in negligence in respect of those who were killed and injured in the disaster but denied that he owed any duty of care to the plaintiffs. The question whether, assuming that each plaintiff had suffered nervous shock causing psychiatric illness as a result of the experiences inflicted on them by the disaster, they were entitled in law to recover damages for nervous shock against the defendant was tried as a preliminary issue.

Mr Justice Hidden in *Alcock and Others* v. *Chief Constable of South Yorkshire Police* [1991] held that nervous shock in the nature of a psychiatric illness, suffered by a plaintiff as a result of witnessing, discovering or apprehending serious physical injury caused to another by the defendant's negligence, was a reasonably foreseeable consequence of that negligence only if the plaintiff and the physically injured person were closely related, or the plaintiff was a rescuer or was otherwise within the defendant's contemplation by reason of carrying on a particular activity, and there was a high degree of proximity of time and place between the incident in which the physical injury had been sustained or apprehended and the plaintiff's discovery of it.

Furthermore, that a parent, spouse or sibling of a victim who had died, been injured or been feared injured was sufficiently closely related for such psychiatric illness to have been reasonably foreseeable, but other relatives and friends were not; that the plaintiffs present in or immediately outside the stadium at the time of the disaster had been sufficiently close in time and place for it to be reasonably foreseeable that what they witnessed would cause them to suffer psychiatric illness; that, since the defendant had known that television crews were in the stadium and it was therefore reasonably foreseeable that if such a disaster took place live pictures would be seen by relatives of the victims, the plaintiffs who had watched the events as they were happening on live television broadcasts had likewise been sufficiently close; but that plaintiffs who had been told of the disaster or had heard of it on the radio but had not seen recorded television pictures until some hours later had not been sufficiently close in time and place for it to be reasonably foreseeable that psychiatric illness would ensue; and that, accordingly, on the assumption that the psychiatric illness alleged had been proved, there would be judgment for ten of the plaintiffs, for damages to be assessed, and judgment for the defendant against the remaining six plaintiffs. The defendant appealed and the six unsuccessful plaintiffs cross-appealed.

In *Alcock* v. *Chief Constable of South Yorkshire Police* (*sub nom. Jones* v. *Wright*) [1991] the Court of Appeal held, allowing the appeal and dismissing the cross-appeals, that the category of those entitled to recover damages for nervous shock is limited to those who fall within the spouse/parent relationship with the victim or in exceptional cases relatives who were in the same position vis-a-vis the victim as a parent/spouse would have been, and relationships outside that category are excluded on the presumption that the love and affection normally to be expected in the former category is so powerful that psychiatric injury through shock is foreseeable, whereas those whose relationship is more remote can be expected to withstand the shock without injury.

Since it is unlikely that any television broadcast would do no more than communicate the fact of the accident or disaster, it is not to be equated with the plaintiff being within 'sight or hearing of the event or its immediate aftermath' and therefore shock sustained by reason of the broadcast will not suffice to found a claim for damages for nervous shock.

Ten of the plaintiffs appealed to the House of Lords, where their appeals were dismissed. In the opinions of their Lordships, a person who sustains nervous shock which causes psychiatric illness as a result of apprehending the infliction of physical injury or the risk thereof on another person may recover damages from the person whose negligent act caused the physical injury or the risk to the primary victim if, but only if, the relationship of the plaintiff to the primary victim is sufficiently close that it is reasonably foreseeable that the plaintiff might sustain nervous shock if he or she apprehends that the primary victim has been or might be injured, if the plaintiff's proximity to the accident in which the primary victim was involved or its immediate aftermath is sufficiently close both in time and space, and if the plaintiff suffers nervous shock through seeing or hearing the accident or its immediate aftermath.

The plaintiff's appeal relied substantially upon the speech of Lord Bridge in *McLoughlin* v. *O'Brian* for the proposition that the test for establishing liability is the unfettered application of the test of reasonable foreseeability. The defendants based their arguments upon Lord Wilberforce's opinion in *McLoughlin* v. *O'Brian*, namely that foreseeability does not of itself automatically lead to a finding that a duty of care existed. Lord Wilberforce considered there to be three elements inherent in any claim: (i) the class of persons whose claims should be recognised, (ii) the proximity of such persons to the accident in both time and space, (iii) the means by which the shock was caused.

To have succeeded in their appeals the plaintiffs needed to extend the boundaries of liability beyond those recognised in *McLoughlin* v. *O'Brian* by (a) removing any restrictions on the categories of persons who may sue, (b) extending the means by which shock is caused, so that it includes the viewing of a simultaneous television broadcast of the incident which caused the shock and (c) modifying the requirement that the aftermath must be 'immediate'. In the result, none of the plaintiffs succeeded in their claims. The majority failed because they had not perceived the incident or its immediate aftermath with their own unaided senses. Perception via a live television broadcast could not be equated with presence at the ground. Attendance at the temporary mortuary no earlier that nine hours after the incident was not the same as participation in the immediate aftermath. The two remaining plaintiffs who were actually present at the stadium failed because they offered no direct evidence to establish a sufficiently close relationship with their relatives (brothers and brother-in-law). It would appear that a sufficiently close relationship is only presumed in the case of a parent or spouse. In November 1996 an agreement was reached with the families of the child victims who were murdered by nurse Beverley Allitt. This settlement breaks new ground in that it disregards the restrictions which deprived the Hillsborough families of compensation.

In *Frost* v. *C.C. of South Yorkshire* [1996] the Court of Appeal held that the Chief Constable owed a duty to police officers exposed to the aftermath of the Hillsborough disaster either as employees acting in the course of their duty or as rescuers not to expose them to unnecessary risk of physical or psychiatric injury. Where such injuries had been suffered as a result of his negligence the officers who suffered such injury can claim damages.

The Courts have again had an opportunity to consider the area of nervous shock in the case of *Mcfarlane* v. *E.E. Caledonia Ltd* [1994]. This claim arose out of the Piper Alpha disaster in 1988. The plaintiff, employed as a painter on the Piper Alpha oil rig, witnessed the explosions on the rig from a support vessel some 550 metres away. The fire ultimately caused the deaths of 164 men. The plaintiff claimed for psychiatric illness suffered as a result of the events he had witnessed. The Court of Appeal held that a person who was a mere bystander or witness of horrific events could not recover damages for psychiatric illness resulting from that experience unless there was a sufficient degree of proximity. This required both nearness in time and place and a close relationship of love and affection between the plaintiff and victim. Neither of these elements were proven in that given case and the plaintiff's claim consequently failed. It should also be borne in mind that the decision of the Court was based in large part upon public policy.

The scope of damages for nervous shock were recently considered by the Court of Appeal in *Vernon* v. *Bosley* [1996], where it was held that damages can be recovered for nervous shock even if it is partly attributable to the pathological consequences of grief and bereavement.

23. *Page* v. *Smith* [1996]

In applying the test of foreseeability of injury by shock it has been assumed that the plaintiff is a person of reasonable fortitude and is not unduly susceptible to that type of reaction. This is intended to exclude from compensation those persons who are abnormally sensitive to shock: *see Bourhill* v. *Young* [1943] and *McLoughlin* v. *O'Brian* [1982].

In the House of Lords decision of *Page* v. *Smith* [1996] the plaintiff (aged 46) was driving his Volvo car at 30 mph when the defendant's oncoming car suddenly turned across in front of him; although the plaintiff braked hard, the two cars collided. Nobody in either car was physically hurt and the plaintiff drove himself home. Some three hours after the accident the plaintiff went to bed, he sensed a relapse of 'chronic fatigue syndrome' (ME) from which he had suffered on and off for some 20 years. At the time of the court hearing the plaintiff's ME had become chronic and the prognosis was poor.

The trial judge awarded the plaintiff £162,153 in damages. The Court of Appeal unanimously reversed the first instance decision, holding that no person of reasonable fortitude would have suffered any psychiatric harm from such an accident. The House of Lords by a majority reinstated the judgment of the trial judge.

Lord Lloyd considered the earlier House of Lords authorities – *Bourhill* v. *Young* [1943], *McLoughlin* v. *O'Brian* [1982], *Alcock* v. *Chief Constable of South Yorkshire Police* [1992]:

> 'In all these cases the plaintiff was the secondary victim of the defendant's negligence. He or she was in the position of a spectator or bystander. In the present case, by contrast, the plaintiff was a participant. He was himself directly involved in the accident, and well within the range of foreseeable physical injury. He was the primary victim. This is thus the first occasion on which your Lordships have had to decide whether in such a case the foreseeability of physical injury is enough to enable the plaintiff to recover damages for nervous shock'.

The factual distinction between primary and secondary victims of an accident is long established. In *Alcock* v. *Chief Constable of South Yorkshire Police* [1992] Lord Oliver noted:

> 'Broadly they divide into two categories, that is to say those cases in which the injured plaintiff was involved, either mediately or immediately, as a participant, and those in which the plaintiff was no more than the passive unwilling witness of injury caused to others'.

Lord Lloyd in *Page* v. *Smith* observes:

> 'Though the distinction between primary and secondary victims is a factual one, it has, as will be seen, important legal consequences. So the classification of all nervous shock cases under the same heading is misleading. It is of cardinal importance in the present case to bear that warning in mind. Foreseeability of psychiatric injury remains a crucial ingredient when the plaintiff is a secondary victim, for the very reason that the secondary victim is almost always outside the area of physical impact, and therefore outside the range of foreseeable physical injury. But, where the plaintiff is the primary victim of the defendant's negligence,

the nervous shock cases, by which I mean the cases following *Bourhill* v. *Young*, are not in point'.

Lord Lloyd further observes:

'Since the defendant was admittedly under a duty of care not to cause the plaintiff foreseeable physical injury, it was unnecessary to ask whether he was under a separate duty of care not to cause foreseeable psychiatric injury.'

Referring to policy arguments regarding 'opening the door' for numerous claims, Lord Lloyd comments:

'As for opening the door, this is a very important consideration in claims by secondary victims. It is for this reason that the courts have, as a matter of policy, rightly insisted on a number of control mechanisms. Otherwise, a negligent defendant might find himself being made liable to all the world. Thus in the case of secondary victims, foreseeability of injury by shock is not enough. The law also requires proximity – *see Alcock* v. *Chief Constable of South Yorkshire Police* [1992] and *Mcfarlane* v. *E.E. Caledonia Ltd* [1994]'.

The *proximity* referred to by Lord Lloyd means not only proximity to the event in time and space, but also proximity of relationship between the primary victim and the secondary victim.

Lord Lloyd notes that with regard to secondary victims:

'A further control mechanism is that the secondary victim will only recover damages for nervous shock if the defendant should have foreseen injury by shock to a person of normal fortitude or "ordinary phlegm".'

With regard to primary victims Lord Lloyd explains:

'In the case of a primary victim the question will almost always turn on whether the foreseeable injury is physical. But it is the same test in both cases, with different applications. There is no justification for regarding physical and psychiatric injury as different "kinds" of injury. Once it is established that the defendant is under a duty of care to avoid causing personal injury to the plaintiff, it matters not whether the injury in fact sustained is physical, psychiatric or both.'

Summary

Page v. *Smith* is authority for the following propositions:

(1) It is essential to distinguish in cases involving nervous shock between primary and secondary victims.

(2) In claims by secondary victims certain control mechanisms are used as a matter of policy to limit the number of potential claims. A defendant will not be liable unless the psychiatric damage is foreseeable in a person of normal fortitude. These control mechanisms have no place where the plaintiff is the primary victim.

(3) The approach in all cases should be uniform, namely whether the defendant can reasonably foresee that his conduct will expose the plaintiff to the risk of personal injury, whether physical or psychiatric. Where the answer to the above is 'yes' then the duty of care is established, even though physical injury does not, in fact, occur. There is no justification therefore in treating physical and psychiatric injury as different kinds of damage.

(4) A defendant who is under a duty of care to the plaintiff, whether as primary or secondary victim, is not liable for damages for nervous shock unless the shock results in some recognised psychiatric illness. Nor is it relevant that the illness takes a rare form or is of unusual severity. The defendant must take his victim as he finds him.

Progress test 2

1. What remains of the House of Lords decision in *Anns* v. *London Borough of Merton* [1977]?

2. Of what significance is the case of *White* v. *Jones* [1995]?

3. To what extent, if any, is there a duty not to cause economic loss? Is this duty limited to consequential economic loss?

4. What is the significance of the House of Lords decision in *Henderson* v. *Merrett Syndicates Ltd* [1994]?

5. To what extent, if at all, can there be liability for omission?

6. Outline the scope of the duty not to cause psychological injury after the House of Lords decision in *Page* v. *Smith* [1996].

3

NEGLIGENCE 2: STANDARD OF CARE

INTRODUCTION

In this chapter we will review the rules as to breach of duty, that is the extent to which the law requires a person to exercise reasonable care and skill to prevent harm to others. It has been stated that: 'Negligence is the omission to do something which a *reasonable man*, guided upon those considerations which ordinarily regulate the conduct of human affairs, would do, or doing something which a prudent and reasonable man would not do' (*see* Alderson B., *Blyth* v. *Birmingham Waterworks Co. Ltd* (1856).

The reasonable man, and the objective standard of care derived from this notional moral exemplar, are the key to understanding breach of duty.

The concept of negligence in the law of tort is an unhappy compromise between a principle of 'no liability without fault' and the desire to ensure that those who have suffered injury are compensated for their loss. The former has held back the development of 'no fault' compensation based upon principles of strict liability, the latter has retarded the use of the 'subjective' concept of blameworthiness, since it would lead to a considerable reduction in the number of plaintiffs who would succeed in being able to recover damages. The law makes use of the concept of the 'reasonable man', thereby ignoring the realities of the defendant's situation in so far as they differ from the objective standard.

THE REASONABLE MAN

Who is the 'reasonable man'? He is the ordinary man, the average man, the 'man on the Clapham omnibus' (*see Hall* v. *Brooklands Auto Racing Club* [1933]). The ordinary 'reasonable man' is a notional person, who is neither unduly apprehensive nor over-confident. The purpose of utilising this notional exemplar is to ensure objectivity and uniformity in that it 'eliminates the personal equation and is independent of the idiosyncrasies of the particular person whose conduct is in question' *per* Lord Macmillan in *Glasgow Corporation* v. *Muir* [1943]. The concept of the reasonable man is not without criticism, and has been particularly criticised due to the differing judicial interpretations of who is a reasonable man, and what he may properly be said to be able to foresee.

THE OBJECTIVE STANDARD

1. Interpretation

The standard of care expected of the reasonable man is objective; we have seen that it does not take account of the particular idiosyncrasies or weaknesses of the defendant. It is, in each case, left to the trial judge to determine what is reasonable and what could have been foreseen. This permits a limited amount of subjectivity, for what to one judge may seem far-fetched may seem to another both natural and probable.

The objective standard applies to skills which can be acquired by training (e.g. driving), as well as attributes which most ordinary people can be expected to possess. The standards of professional people fall into a specific category and are discussed at 5, below. The point is well illustrated by *Nettleship* v. *Weston* [1971], where the defendant was a learner-driver who crashed into a lamppost injuring the front seat passenger. The defendant was convicted of driving without due care and attention, but at first instance the plaintiff's claim was dismissed because the defendant had been doing her best to control the car. The Court of Appeal held that the standard of care required for a learner-driver is the same as that required of any other driver, namely that of a reasonably competent and experienced driver. The driver's 'incompetent best is not good enough'. The defendant's driving had fallen below this standard and it was irrelevant that this was because of her inexperience. A variable standard for different levels of experience, or competence, or temperament would create much uncertainty and, indeed, unfairness for plaintiffs, and result in the court having the impossible task of specifying a subjective level of competence for each defendant.

The objective standard also applies to a driver who becomes physically incapable of controlling the vehicle properly because of some impairment, e.g. as a result of a stroke, even though he was unaware of his condition: *see Roberts* v. *Ramsbottom* [1980].

2. Unforeseen harm

If a particular danger could not reasonably have been anticipated, the defendant has not acted in breach of his duty of care, because a reasonable man would not take precautions against an unforeseeable consequence.

The concept of reasonable foreseeability does not mean that liability will be imposed whenever it might conceivably have crossed the mind of a normal person that the occurrence of damage was a possibility. Lord Dunedin in *Fardon* v. *Harcourt-Rivington* (1932) took the view that '. . . people must guard against reasonable probabilities, but they are not bound to guard against fantastic possibilities'. The law takes account also of the degree of *probability* of the consequence occurring. Foresight of consequence is measured by reference to knowledge at the time of the event. In *Roe* v. *Minister of Health* [1954], during the course of an operation, the plaintiff was paralysed by anaesthetic which had become contaminated by disinfectant. The anaesthetic had been kept in glass ampoules which were stored in the disinfectant and became contaminated by seepage through invisible cracks in the glass. At the time of the accident in 1947 this risk was not known. The Court of Appeal held that the hospital authorities were not liable because the danger was not reasonably foreseeable. The court 'must not look at the 1947 accident with 1954 spectacles' opined Denning LJ but it would have been negligent to adopt the same practice in 1954. In *Glasgow Corporation* v. *Muir* [1943], the defendants were not liable for a spillage of scalding water because there was no reason to anticipate the accident and therefore no precautions were reasonably necessary. It is not necessary, however, for the particular damage that occurred to be foreseeable in a general way.

The House of Lords has had to consider foreseeability of harm in *Owgo* v. *Taylor* [1987] (*see* **5** below) and in *Wilsher* v. *Essex Area Health Authority* [1988] (*see* **4:2**).

3. The risk of harm

A defendant is not negligent if the damage was not a foreseeable consequence of his conduct. It does not follow, however, that a defendant is negligent if the damage was foreseeable. In *Bolton* v. *Stone* [1951], the defendant cricket club was exonerated from liability when a cricket ball was hit out of the cricket ground onto the highway, striking and injuring the plaintiff. The possibility of such an event occurring was clearly foreseeable as balls had been hit from the ground before. But the fact that this had happened only on very rare occasions (six times in 30 years) meant that the risk in the circumstances was one which a reasonable man could appropriately choose not to guard against. Lord Oaksey in *Bolton* v. *Stone* opined:

> 'The standard of care in the law of negligence is the standard of an ordinarily careful man, but in my opinion, an ordinarily careful man does not take precautions against every foreseeable risk. He can, of course, foresee the possibility of many risks, but life would be almost impossible if he were to attempt to take precautions against every risk which he can foresee. He takes precautions against risks which are reasonably likely to happen. Many foreseeable risks are extremely unlikely to happen and cannot be guarded against except by almost complete isolation.'

However, it may be the case that a risk is both obvious and the likelihood of harm resulting is high, e.g. the risk to an employee's mental health, where the impact on him of the stress of job is known to cause psychological illness: *see Walker* v. *Northumberland C.C.* [1995]. The same proposition can apply to physical harm to an employee whose work involves some element of danger and risk of personal injury: *see King* v. *Smith* [1995] where a window cleaner fell some 75 feet and sustained serious injuries.

STANDARD OF CARE

Apart from the risk of the harm occurring, other factors are of vital importance when evaluating the scope of standard of care.

4(i). The magnitude of the risk

In *Read* v. *J. Lyons & Co. Ltd* [1947], Lord Macmillan took the view that 'The law in all cases exacts a degree of care commensurate with the risk created.' Simply put, the greater the risk of the harm the more stringent the precautions which must be taken.

The magnitude of the risk is the product of two factors: (*i*) the likelihood of the risk materialising and (*ii*) the potential severity of the damage should it occur. As to the likelihood of harm, this is referred to above when considering the case of *Bolton* v. *Stone*. However two further points should be noted, firstly that *Bolton* v. *Stone is a case which 'is not far from the borderline'* (*per* Lord Reid at [1951] AC 867–8), and should be contrasted with the subsequent decisions in *Miller* v. *Jackson* [1977] and *Hilder* v. *Associated Portland Cement Manufacturers* [1961]. Secondly, *Bolton* v. *Stone* is not authority for the view that it is always reasonable to ignore a small risk of harm occurring. The risk must always be measured against the defendant's purpose and the practicalities of taking effective precautions.

4(ii). The defendant's knowledge

Where the defendant has knowledge of some fact which makes harm to the plaintiff more likely than would otherwise be the case, then as a reasonable man he must take account of that. In *Haley* v. *London Electricity Board* [1965], the plaintiff, who was blind, fell into a hole in the pavement that had been dug by the defendants' employees. The precautions taken by the defendants' workmen to warn the public of the danger were adequate for sighted persons but not for the blind. The defendants were held liable, it being common knowledge that blind persons walk along city pavements and the defendants would have had no difficulty in providing appropriate and adequate warning for such persons. It could not be said that the risk of causing injury to this *special group* was so small that it could be ignored. Lord Reid in that case approved a dictum of Lord Sumner in *Glasgow Corporation* v. *Taylor* [1922], where he stated: 'A measure of care appropriate to the inability or disability of those who are immature or feeble in mind or body is due from others who know, or ought to anticipate, the presence of such persons within the scope and hazard of their own operations' – *see also Knight and Others* v. *Home Office and Another* [1990].

Where the injured party is or should have been known to the defendant and the defendant has some responsibility for his welfare the defendant should have in mind the particular needs of that person.

In *Johnstone* v. *Bloomsbury Area Health Authority* [1992] (CA) discussing the duty owed by the employer authority to junior doctors required to work excessive hours Stuart Smith LJ stated:

> 'It must be remembered that the duty of care is owed to an individual employee and different employees may have different stamina. If the authority in this case knew or ought to have known that by requiring him to work the hours they did, they exposed him to risk of injury to his health, then they should not have required him to work in excess of the hours that he safely could have done.'

Human frailty must also be taken into account: *Pape* v. *Cumbria County Council* [1992]. *See also Walker* v. *Northumberland C.C.* [1995]: foreseeable risk that overwork would cause employee to suffer psychological breakdown.

4(iii). Severity of the damage

The more serious the potential consequences, the greater the precautions that should be taken. 'Those who engage in operations inherently dangerous must take precautions which are not required of persons engaged in the ordinary routine of daily life': *see Glasgow Corporation* v. *Muir* [1943], *per* Lord Macmillan. In *Paris* v. *Stepney Borough Council* [1951], the defendants knew that the plaintiff employee was blind in one eye. In the course of the plaintiff's work a chip of metal entered his good eye blinding him completely. He alleged that the defendants were negligent in failing to provide goggles, although it was not usual to do so for that type of work. In the House of Lords the defendants were held liable. The duty of an employer was owed to each individual employee and in determining the requisite degree of care an employer must have regard to the gravity of the consequences of the potential injury to each person rather than the consequences of a similar injury to a fully sighted man.

4(iv). Defendant's purpose

The social utility of the defendant's activity may justify taking greater risks than would otherwise be the case. So in *Daborn* v. *Bath Tramways Motor Co. Ltd* [1946], it was held that it was not negligent to use a left-hand-drive vehicle as an ambulance in wartime when there was a shortage of vehicles for the task, even though it was difficult to give hand signals and this had caused an accident. Asquith LJ said that in assessing what is reasonable care the risk must be balanced against the consequences of not assuming the risk. 'The purpose to be served, if sufficiently important, justifies the assumption of abnormal risk', and so the need for ambulances justified the risks involved in using the vehicle. Similarly, in *Watt* v. *Hertfordshire County Council* [1954], the plaintiff was a fireman called out to an emergency where a woman was trapped under a lorry. A vehicle designed to carry a heavy lifting jack was not available so the jack was taken on an ordinary lorry with three firemen steadying it. The jack slipped, injuring the plaintiff. His employers were not liable. The risk had to be balanced against the end to be achieved. This does not mean that the purpose of saving life or limb justifies taking any risk. There is little point racing to save one person if in the process others are killed and injured. Thus it can be negligent for the driver of a fire engine to ignore a red traffic light: *see Ward* v. *London County Council* [1938].

4(v). Practicability of precautions

Some risks are unavoidable. Others can be eliminated or reduced only at great expense. The question that arises is at what point the cost or precautions would justify a reasonable man in not taking them. In *Latimer* v. *AEC Ltd* [1953] the defendant's factory was flooded after a heavy rainfall, and water became mixed with oil leaving the floor very slippery when the flooding subsided. Sawdust was spread over the surface but there was not enough to cover the entire area. A workman slipped on the uncovered part and was injured. The trial judge held the defendants liable for failing to close down that part of the factory. The House of Lords agreed that this might be necessary if the risk to employees was sufficiently grave, but that had not been the position in this case.

The approach taken was to ask, if steps to remedy fully the situation were not possible, would a reasonably prudent employer have closed down the factory rather than allow his employees to run the risk of injury involved in continuing to work? Reasonable is a matter of achieving a balance, thus where a large reduction of risk can be obtained by minimal expenditure, the defendant has acted unreasonably if he does not take precautions. Where considerable expense would produce only a minimal reduction in risk, it is reasonable for the person to do nothing. In sum, it is a question of degree in each situation.

In *Overseas Tankship (UK) Ltd* v. *Miller Steamship Co. Pty Ltd* (*The Wagon Mound II*) [1967], a large quantity of bunkering oil was spilled in Sydney harbour as a result of the carelessness of the defendants' engineer. This is a high flash-point oil and very difficult to ignite in the open; however, it did catch fire (probably as a consequence of hot metal falling to the water from welding operations carried out on a wharf) and caused extensive damage. The Privy Council concluded that a reasonable engineer would have foreseen the *possibility* of the oil catching fire though the *likelihood* of it doing so was extremely small. It did not follow, however, that, no matter what the circumstances, it is justifiable to neglect a small risk. 'A reasonable man would only neglect such a risk if he had some valid reason for doing so, e.g. that it would involve considerable expense to eliminate the risks. He would weigh the risk against the difficulty of eliminating it.' It would have been simple to stop the discharge of oil – it was a matter of closing a valve. A reasonable man would not ignore even a small risk 'if action to eliminate it presented no difficulty, involved no disadvantage and required no expense'.

When precautions are not practicable then the risks of continuing the activity have to be weighed against the disadvantages of stopping the activity altogether. Where it was not possible to give an employee, who was susceptible to dermatitis, work which did not involve a risk of contracting the disease it was held that the employers were not liable: *see Withers* v. *Perry Chain Co. Ltd* [1961]. There were no further precautions that the employers could have taken short of dismissing the plaintiff, and there was no obligation to do this in order to avoid an action in negligence.

5. Professional standards

A person who possesses a special skill is not judged simply by the standard of the man on the Clapham omnibus, but by the standards of other persons with those special skills. A doctor must therefore conform to the standards of a reasonably competent man exercising and professing to have that skill – the 'ordinary man'. In *Bolam* v. *Friern Hospital Management Committee* [1957] McNair J took the view that 'a doctor is not guilty of negligence if he has acted in accordance with a practice accepted as proper by a responsible body of medical men, skilled in that particular art. . . .' It can be said, therefore, that a doctor is not negligent when acting in accordance with recognised medical practice and that this is so even if there is a body of opinion that takes a contrary view. The Bolam test enunciated by McNair J has been approved by the House of Lords in *Maynard* v. *West Midlands Regional Health Authority* [1984] and *Whitehouse* v. *Jordan* [1981] and applies not only to diagnosis and treatment but also to the disclosure of information by doctors to patients: *see Sidaway* v. *Bethlem Royal Hospital Governors* [1985].

The net effect of the law taking such an approach is to make proof of professional negligence virtually impossible where the doctor, solicitor, architect or other professional has followed the accepted practice in his/her profession. Professional practice may change over time so that what was once accepted as the correct procedure is no longer considered to be appropriate or responsible. A professional person cannot obstinately and pig-headedly carry on with some old technique if it has been proved to be contrary to what is substantially informed professional opinion. This imposes an obligation to keep up to date in the exercise of a particular skill.

Where a person holds himself out as having specialist skill he will be judged by the objective standards of a reasonably competent man exercising the skill, even though he does not in fact possess the requisite skill. Therefore, as with learner-drivers: *(see Nettleship* v. *Weston* [1971] (above)), the inexperienced professional is negligent if he does not achieve the standards of a reasonably competent and experienced person exercising the particular skill of his/her profession. This is illustrated by the case of *Wilsher* v. *Essex Area Health Authority* [1988], and the decision is fully discussed at 4:**2**.

In the context of property valuations, and the standard of care to be exercised by a surveyor, the *Bolam* test can be effectively applied. The scope of the duty of care owed by a surveyor and the extent of the damages for which a surveyor may be liable have recently been considered by the House of Lords in *Banque Bruxelles S.A.* v. *Eagle Star* [1996], also cited as *South Australia Asset Management Corporation* v. *York Montague Ltd.* (*see* 2:**10**). In that case there is little stated regarding breach of duty; however, causation is dealt with in some detail by Lord Hoffmann (*see* 4:**1** below). The *Bolam* test regarding the appropriate standard of care to be exercised by a professional person is as applicable to the surveying professional as it is elsewhere. In the area of valuation, the Statement of Asset Valuation Practice promulgated by the Royal Institution of Chartered Surveyors is appropriate guidance as to the standard of care which is applied.

In an entirely different context, namely that of the prison service, the issue of standard of care has recently been considered in *Knight and Others* v. *Home Office and Another* [1990].

The facts of that case were that the deceased attacked a man and subsequently pleaded guilty to wounding with intent to cause grievous bodily harm and assault occasioning actual bodily harm. The court ordered that he be detained in hospital pursuant to s. 60 of the Mental Health Act 1959 and further ordered that he be detained in a remand prison pending his admission to hospital. Because he was known to have suicidal tendencies he was subject to the prison's 'special watch' procedure but because he was also known to be violent it was not possible to put him in a ward in the prison hospital wing, where a continuous watch could be kept on him. Instead he was put in a cell where prison officers observed him at not less that 15-minute intervals. In between two 15-minute inspections the deceased committed suicide by hanging. His personal representatives brought an action against the Home Office claiming that the standard of care provided for the deceased in the prison hospital was inadequate.

Mr Justice Pill held that the standard of care provided for a mentally ill prisoner detained in a prison hospital was not required to be as high as the standard of care provided in a psychiatric hospital outside prison, since psychiatric and prison hospitals performed different functions and the duty of care in respect of each type of hospital had to be tailored to the act and function to be performed. Accordingly, the facilities and numbers of staff for the provision of medical care for persons detained in prison did not have to be the same as for the specialist function of psychiatric hospitals of treating and if possible curing mental illness. It followed that there had been no negligence on the part of the prison service in failing to provide in the hospital wing of the prison in which the deceased had been detained the patient/staff ratio which existed in psychiatric hospitals. Furthermore, applying the accepted test for medical negligence, the prison medical staff had not been negligent in failing to keep the deceased under continuous observation since their decision to observe him at 15-minute intervals was a decision which ordinary skilled medical staff in their position could have made. The action would therefore be dismissed.

A question to which no clear answer has yet emerged is whether a defendant who is particularly experienced or eminent and who practises in a highly specialised field within his profession must exercise *greater* care than the ordinarily competent professional. In *Maynard* v. *West Midlands Regional Health Authority* [1984] Lord Scarman said that 'a doctor who professes to exercise a special skill must exercise the ordinary skill of his speciality'.

So far in this chapter we have considered the standard of care expected to be exercised by a professional person towards persons in his care or who seek his advice. It is appropriate at this juncture to consider the standard of care expected of a lay person with regard to a professional who is assisting him; in particular whether a lay person owes a lower standard of care since he might reasonably expect a professional to guard against injury inherent in the exercise of his calling. The House of Lords has had to consider this point in the case of *Owgo* v. *Taylor* [1987]. The defendant negligently started a fire by using a blowlamp to burn off the paint on the fascia board under the guttering of the roof of his house thereby causing the timbers to catch on fire. The plaintiff, a fireman, went into the roof space to tackle the fire and sustained serious injuries caused by steam generated by water poured onto the fire, notwithstanding that he was wearing standard protective clothing. There was no suggestion that the contents of the roofspace were unusually combustible or that there was any special danger from such hidden cause. The plaintiff brought an action in negligence against the defendant, contending that because the fire had been started negligently and because he had been injured as a result, he was entitled to recover damages from the defendant. The judge held that the defendant had been negligent but that he could not reasonably have foreseen the injury suffered by the plaintiff and rejected the claim. The plaintiff appealed. The Court of Appeal held that a person who negligently started a fire was liable for any injury sustained by a fireman or another person fighting the fire which was a foreseeable consequence of the negligent starting of that fire, and accordingly gave judgment for the plaintiff. The defendant appealed to the House of Lords, where it was decided that a person who negligently starts a fire is liable for injuries suffered by a fireman while attempting to put out the fire, regardless of whether the particular injuries suffered by the fireman were reasonably foreseeable or whether the injuries were suffered as the result of exceptional or merely ordinary risks undertaken by the fireman.

6. Sport

In *Wooldridge* v. *Sumner* [1963] the plaintiff was a photographer at a horse show who was knocked down by a horse being ridden in a competition when it got out of control. The Court of Appeal held that a spectator at a game or competition takes the risk of any damage caused by the act of a participant in the course of and for the purposes of the game, unless the participant's conduct shows a 'reckless disregard of the spectators' safety'. This appears to set a lower standard than 'reasonable care in all the circumstances' and for this reason the case has been criticised and was followed with some diffidence in *Wilks* v. *Cheltenham Home Guard Motor Cycle and Light Car Club* [1971]. However, in *Harrison* v. *Vincent* [1982], a case involving a side-car passenger in a motorcycle race, the Court of Appeal extended the 'reckless disregard of safety' test from spectators to fellow competitors in the sport, at least where the injury was caused 'in the flurry and excitement of the sport'.

In *Condon* v. *Basi* [1985] the plaintiff, an amateur footballer whose leg was broken when he was tackled during a local league game, succeeded in his claim at first instance and in the Court of Appeal. Donaldson MR identified that there are two possible views that can be taken, each yielding the same answer:

> 'One is to take a more generalised duty of care and to modify it on the basis that the participants in the sport or pastime impliedly consent to taking risks which otherwise would be a breach of duty of care. . . . The other . . . [is] that there is a general standard of care, namely the Lord Atkin approach in *Donoghue* v. *Stevenson*, that you are under a duty to take all reasonable care taking into account the circumstances in which you are placed, which in a game of football are quite different from those which affect you when you are going for a walk in the countryside'.

It can be argued, following Lord Donaldson's judgment in *Condon* v. *Basi*, that there is a 'sliding scale' of standard of care to be expected of players, a higher standard being expected of professional footballers than those who play in amateur games.

An interesting article, 'Sporting negligence', is to be found in the *Solicitors Journal* (1996, vol. 140, no. 2, p.38).

The duty of care owed by a referee to players in a rugby match is being considered by the Court of Appeal in *Nolan* v. *Smolden* (*Daily Telegraph*, 27 November 1996). In this case the High Court held that a referee owes a duty to the players to control the game in accordance with the rules. Mr Smolden was paralysed when a scrum collapsed on him in the course of a game refereed by Mr Nolan.

7. Children

Due to lack of clarity as to the standard of care expected of children as potential defendants, coupled with the fact that in practical terms children may not be worth suing, this area of the law is muddled.

Infancy is not a defence to an action in tort: *see Gorley* v. *Codd* [1967]. Where a child is a defendant the standard of care expected of him is unclear, but may be said to be that of a 'reasonable child' of the same age as the defendant. Older children may be judged by the standards of an adult.

A parent is generally not liable for the torts of his children, but he may be liable for his own negligence in failing to supervise the child whereby the child causes injury to a third party or himself: *see Barnes* v. *Hampshire County Council* [1969] and *Carmarthenshire County Council* v. *Lewis* [1955]. Persons who have control over children, such as an education authority, are in the same position.

It is usually said that the standard required is that of a 'reasonably prudent parent'.

Progress test 3

1. Who is the reasonable man? What is his significance regarding standard of care?

2. Of what significance is foreseeability of harm to standard of care?

3. What factors do the courts consider when determining whether a particular defendant has failed to comply with the standard of care which can be expected of him?

4. Is the standard of care expected of professional persons in the exercise of their calling different from that expected of a reasonable man?

5. Does the standard of care vary either:
   (a) according to the characteristics of the plaintiff, or
   (b) the nature of the defendant?

4

NEGLIGENCE 3: CAUSATION AND REMOTENESS OF DAMAGE

It is of vital importance to distinguish the concept of remoteness of damage from that of causation. Causation is concerned with the physical connection which links the defendant's negligence with the plaintiff's damage. The law utilises the 'but for' test to determine whether this connection has been established on the facts in issue in any particular case. Remoteness of damage is used to set the limits of legal accountability.

Considering the elements of the tort of negligence, duty, breach and damage, we can say that each is a device for limiting the scope of the law and the range of liability for negligence. Lord Denning took the view in *Lamb* v. *Camden London Borough Council* [1981], that: 'Sometimes it is done by limiting the range of the persons to whom the duty is owed. Sometimes it is done by saying that there is a break in the chain of causation. At other times it is done by saying that the consequence is too remote to be a head of damage. All these devices are useful in their way. But ultimately it is a question of policy for the judges to decide.'

CAUSE IN FACT

1. The 'but for' test

The first issue is whether the defendant's act or omission to act was the cause of the plaintiff's loss. The methodology which lawyers use to determine this issue is called the 'but for' test. If harm to the plaintiff would not have occurred 'but for' the defendant's negligence then that negligence is a cause of the harm. Putting this another way, if the loss would have been incurred in any event, that defendant's conduct is not a cause. In *Barnett* v. *Chelsea & Kensington Hospital Management Committee* [1969], a doctor in a casualty department sent a patient away without treatment, telling him to see his own doctor. The patient died from arsenic poisoning. It was held that the doctor's conduct was negligent, but the expert evidence indicated that the patient was way beyond help and would have died in any event. Therefore the doctor's negligence did not cause the death. Similarly, in *Robinson* v. *Post Office* [1974], a doctor's omission to test for an allergic reaction to an anti-tetanus vaccination was not causally related to the patient's subsequent reaction, because the test would not have revealed the allergy in time.

It may be difficult to draw conclusions using the 'but for' test where, rather than being based upon objective scientific proof, the court has to speculate as to what might have occurred had the defendant behaved in a different way. In *McWilliams* v. *Sir William Arrol & Co. Ltd* [1962] a steel erector who was not wearing a safety belt fell to his death. His employees were in breach of a statutory duty to supply safety belts, but the House of Lords held that they were not liable because it was probable that the deceased would not have worn the belt if it had been available. The deceased had rarely, if ever, used a safety belt in the past and so it was a natural inference that he would not have worn a belt on this occasion. Lord Reid commented that it would not be right to draw such an inference too readily because people do sometimes change their minds unexpectedly, but the evidence in this case was 'overwhelming'.

This type of causation problem also arises in cases where a patient alleges that his doctor has been negligent in failing to disclose information about the risks of a proposed medical procedure. Even if the plaintiff overcomes the problems of establishing negligence (*see Sidaway* v. *Bethlem Royal Hospital Governors* [1985]) he still has to prove that, had the information been disclosed, he would have declined the treatment, thereby avoiding the risk.

The courts do not always make it clear whether or not they are considering the scope of the duty of care in negligence or some direct causal link, i.e. did the defendant's act or omission cause injury to the plaintiff? Recently in *South Australia Asset Management Corporation* v. *York Montague Ltd.* [1996], Lord Hoffmann used to considerable impact the illustration of the mountaineer:

> 'A mountaineer about to undertake a difficult climb is concerned about the fitness of his knee. He goes to a doctor who negligently makes a superficial examination and pronounces the knee fit. The climber goes on the expedition, which he would not have undertaken if the doctor had told him the true state of his knee. He suffers an injury which is an entirely foreseeable consequence but has nothing to do with his knee'.

Lord Hoffmann analyses the situation in terms of the scope of the duty of care owed by the doctor to his patient:

> 'On the Court of Appeal's principle, the doctor is responsible for the injury suffered by the mountaineer because it is damage which would not have occurred if he had been given correct information about his knee. He would not have gone on the expedition and would have suffered no injury. On what I have suggested is the more usual principle, the doctor is not liable. The injury has not been caused by the doctor's bad advice because it would have occurred even if the advice had been correct'.

In *South Australia Asset Management Corporation* v. *York Montague Ltd.* the issue was one of the scope of the duty owed; the illustration of the mountaineer has some utility when considering causation. As Lord Hoffmann points out it is possible to argue that the doctor 'caused' the mountaineer's injury – the mountaineer would not have embarked on the climb if his knee was not passed fit. The doctor in passing the knee fit sets in motion the chain of events which leads to the mountaineer's injury. This may be so, but it is insufficient to determine the extent of the doctor's liability, for in point of fact the mountaineer's injury was caused by something entirely foreseeable and unconnected with the weak knee, e.g. a rope snapping.

The point to be remembered is that causation becomes an issue only where a duty of care exists – Lord Hoffmann's analysis is part of the deliberations as to whether or not in the circumstances of the case a duty does or does not exist. Furthermore, causation is but one step; if causation is established the court will then consider other issues, 'cause in law' (i.e. the cause for the purpose of attributing legal liability) and remoteness of damage.

It is also important to have in mind the distinction between what *would* have happened and what *might* have happened. In *Bolitho* v. *City and Hackney Health Authority* [1993] the defendant doctor, urgently summoned by a nurse to attend a two-year-old with respiratory problems, failed to attend and could not contact her 'standby' as that doctor's pager had flat batteries. If a doctor had attended and intubated the child, the child would have lived. Not all doctors would have taken that medical step; the defendant doctor said if she had attended, she would not have done so. A majority of the Court of Appeal applied the *Bolam* test and upheld the trial judge's dismissal of the case against the defendant. Their decision is based on the proposition that applying the *Bolam* test a body of competent professional opinion would not have intubated the child and therefore it would have been wrong of the defendant not to do so. Brown L.J. dissented, indicating that he would entered judgment for the plaintiff, the proposition being that the *Bolam* test is irrelevant to issues of causation. Furthermore, since intubation alone would have saved the child and any doctor attending would have done that which he/she should have done, intubation was the appropriate step to take and a failure to do so was negligent. For further analysis of this case, *see* 'Causation in Medical Negligence Cases' (*Sol. Jo.*, 1996, vol. 140, p. 1098). *See also Joyce* v. *Wandsworth Health Authority* [1996] which applies the majority view in *Bolitho*.

The cases we have examined are each concerned with the risk of some physical harm occurring. Do the same principles apply where one is dealing with a risk other than physical harm, e.g. the loss of an opportunity to make a profit?

In the case of *Allied Maples Group* v. *Simmons & Simmons* [1995], the lost chance was the opportunity to renegotiate a deal thus avoiding a financial loss. In that case the defendant solicitors negligently failed to alert the plaintiff to a risk, to which it was exposed by the terms proposed for a take-over. If alerted, the plaintiff *would* have sought to renegotiate the terms; however, in the event of it not being able to do so the plaintiff *would* have gone ahead with the deal and suffered the same loss. The Court of Appeal by a majority affirmed judgment for the plaintiff for discounted damages to be assessed. *Allied Maples Group* has been followed in *Stovold* v. *Barlows* [1995] in the Court of Appeal.

There are limits to the 'lost chance' doctrine: *see Nestlé* v. *National Westminster Bank* [1994]. A plaintiff must prove what *would* have happened, the plaintiff cannot base its claim on what *might* have happened.

The 'but for' test operates as a preliminary filter to exclude events which did not affect the outcome. It cannot, however, resolve all problems of factual causation.

2. Proof of causation

It is for the plaintiff to prove, on the balance of probabilities, that the defendant's breach of duty caused the damage. In some cases the precise cause of the damage may be unknown, and this can be a particular problem with some types of medical condition. This can place an impossible burden on the plaintiff. In *McGhee* v. *National Coal Board* [1972], the plaintiff, who worked at the defendants' brick kilns, contracted dermatitis. There were no facilities for washing off the brick dust after work and this materially increased the risk of contracting the disease. At the time the current state of medical knowledge could not say whether it was probable that the plaintiff would not have contracted the disease if he had been able to take a shower after work. The House of Lords held that it was sufficient for a plaintiff to show that the defendants' breach of duty made the risk of injury more probable even though it was uncertain whether it was the actual cause. The case is note-worthy in that the plaintiff succeeded without proving that the defendants caused him any harm. They merely increased the risk of injury to him.

The House of Lords had the opportunity to consider the rule in *McGhee's* case in *Wilsher* v. *Essex Area Health Authority* [1988]. The facts of the case were that the plaintiff was born prematurely and was placed in a special care baby unit at a hospital managed by the defendants. If he was to survive, he needed extra oxygen and to ensure that the correct amount was administered it was necessary to insert a catheter into an umbilical artery so that his arterial blood oxygen levels would be accurately read on an electronic monitor. A junior doctor mistakenly inserted the catheter into the umbilical vein with the result that the monitor would give a low reading. Neither he nor the senior registrar appreciated that the X-rays taken showed the catheter in the vein but both realised that there was something wrong with the readings on the monitor. The senior registrar inserted another catheter but into the same vein and other means of monitoring the arterial blood oxygen were also adopted. The following day, it was realised that the plaintiff had been supersaturated with oxygen for a period of about 8 to 12 hours and within 30 hours of the plaintiff being received into the special unit the second catheter was replaced by one in the artery. Thereafter, the monitoring of the arterial blood oxygen levels continued and at times during the following weeks there were periods when the levels were considered too high. The plaintiff developed retrolental fibroplasia, a condition of the eyes which resulted in blindness. A likely cause of the condition, but not a definite or only possible cause, was that too much oxygen had been administered within the first 30 hours or at a later stage. The plaintiff claimed damages from the defendant health authority for the negligent medical treatment he had received in their special care baby unit. The judge held that the defendants were liable since they had failed to prove that the plaintiff's condition had not been caused by the negligence of their employees. The Court of Appeal, by a majority, dismissed the defendants' appeal.

On the defendants' appeal to the House of Lords it was held that where injury to a plaintiff was attributable to any one of a number of causes but the evidence was insufficient to establish the particular cause, then the mere existence of a duty of care owed by the defendant to the plaintiff and the breach of that duty by conduct which enhanced an existing risk of injury did not raise a presumption, or entitle the court to make an inference, as to causation in favour of a particular cause. The onus remained on the plaintiff to prove on a balance of probabilities that the cause led to the injury.

In *Bryce* v. *Swan Hunter Group plc and Others* [1988], the deceased was employed for most of his working life from 1937 until 1975 in shipyards owned by the three defendant companies. In the course of his employment the deceased was exposed to asbestos dust which caused him to contract mesothelioma from which he died in 1981 at the age of 60. His widow, as administratrix of his estate, brought an action against the defendants claiming damages in respect of his death. She contended, *inter alia,* that the methods of work and the processes employed by the defendants had caused the release of asbestos dust into the deceased's working environment which had resulted in him contracting the disease. The defendants contended that even if they had been in breach of the duties they owed as the employers of the deceased there was no evidence that those breaches had caused the disease and therefore the plaintiff had failed to discharge the burden of proof.

The High Court held, applying the standards of knowledge at the relevant time (i.e. when the deceased was in the defendants' employment), although not under a duty of care to prevent all exposure of the deceased to dangerous quantities of asbestos dust, the defendants were under a duty to take all reasonably practicable steps to reduce the amount of asbestos dust to which the deceased was exposed. On the facts, the defendants were in breach of that duty. Albeit that the plaintiff had established breaches of duty on the part of the defendants, she had not established on a balance of probabilities that such breach had caused the deceased to contract the disease. However, the defendants were liable, under the principle that if they owed the deceased a duty not to use methods of work etc. which created or increased a risk that the deceased would contract that disease (by reason of the employer/employee relationship) and if they were in breach of that duty and the deceased had in fact contracted the disease, they were to be taken to have caused the disease by their breach of duty. This was held notwithstanding that the existence and extent of the contribution made by their breach could not be ascertained.

CAUSE IN LAW

Once the court has eliminated irrelevant factual causes by use of the 'but for' test it is still faced with the task of selecting which factual cause is to be regarded as the cause in law of the plaintiffs damage, namely the cause for the purpose of attributing legal liability.

3. Where there are two causes

Where two independent events, each of which would be sufficient to cause the harm, occur simultaneously the practical solution is to say that both caused the harm. Where the two events are separated in time it might be thought that the simple answer would be that the first event should be treated as the cause. Certainly this is so where it is the tort that comes second. In *Performance Cars Ltd* v. *Abraham* [1961], the defendant collided with the plaintiff's Rolls-Royce and the damage would have necessitated a respray of part of the vehicle. However, the car had previously been damaged in the same position in an earlier accident and would have needed a respray to repair that damage. The defendant was not liable for the cost of the respray because, having damaged an already damaged car, his negligence was not the cause of the loss. The decision in *Performance Cars* v. *Abraham* stems from the basic rule that the object of an award of damages in tort is to restore the plaintiff to the position he would have been in if he had not sustained the tort.

In *Baker* v. *Willoughby* [1970], the plaintiff's left leg was injured in a road accident, caused by the defendant's negligence, which affected his mobility and reduced his earning capacity. Subsequently the plaintiff was shot in the same leg during the course of an armed robbery at his place of work, and the leg had to be amputated. The defendant argued that the amputation obliterated the original injury so that he should only have to compensate for the loss up to the date of the robbery. Thereafter the loss of mobility and earning capacity was the result of the shooting. The House of Lords held that the defendant remained responsible for the initial disability after the amputation.

If the robbers had been sued they would have been liable only for the additional loss that they had inflicted, not the whole disability. The defendant's argument would have left the plaintiff under-compensated because he would not have been compensated at all for the original injury after the robbery had occurred. It was clearly wrong that the plaintiff should fall between two tortfeasors in this way, receiving less in damages than he would have received had there been no interval between the two torts.

In *Jobling* v. *Associated Dairies Ltd* [1982], the facts were similar to *Baker* v. *Willoughby*, except that the second event was non-tortious. In 1973 the plaintiff sustained a back injury as a result of his employers' negligence which reduced his earning capacity by 50 per cent. In 1976 he was found to be suffering from a disease unconnected with the accident, which prevented him from working at all. The House of Lords held that the defendants were liable only for the reduced earning capacity between 1973 and 1976, when the supervening disease terminated their responsibility. *Jobling* v. *Associated Dairies Ltd* is a policy decision based on the idea that compensation for the period after the supervening illness would 'put the plaintiff in a better position that he would be in if he had never suffered the tortious injury'.

4. Intervening acts

Where the defendant's negligence forms part of a sequence of events leading to harm to the plaintiff and the act of another person (without which the damage would not have occurred) intervenes between the defendant's negligence and the damage, the court must decide whether the defendant remains responsible or whether the act can be regarded as breaking the chain of causation between the negligence and the damage, i.e. as a *novus actus interveniens*.

There is some confusion as to the principles to be applied to determine whether a particular action breaks the chain of causation. Firstly, there is the causation test, which asks whether the intervening act was reasonable in all the circumstances of the case. Was it part of the ordinary course of things which flowed from the wrongful act? – see *The Argentino* (1889). This has to be measured against the nature of the risk created by the defendant. Secondly, the fault approach turns on the foreseeability of the intervening act occurring.

It may be that it is the act of the plaintiff which intervenes. In *McKew* v. *Holland & Hannen & Cubitts (Scotland) Ltd* [1969] the defendants negligently injured the plaintiff's leg, which as a result was liable to give way without warning. Without asking for assistance he attempted to descend a steep flight of stairs with no handrail and he fell suffering further injuries. The House of Lords held that the defendants were not liable for his additional injury because the plaintiff's conduct was unreasonable and constituted a *novus actus*. It was not a question of what was foreseeable, because it was not at all unlikely or unforeseeable that in these circumstances someone might take just such an unreasonable risk (*per* Lord Reid). However, it did not follow that a defendant was liable for every foreseeable consequence.

McKew v. *Holland & Hannen & Cubitts (Scotland) Ltd* can be contrasted with *Wieland* v. *Cyril Lord Carpets Ltd* [1969] where the plaintiff had to wear a surgical collar as a result of the initial injury. This restricted the movement of her head which reduced her ability to use her bifocal glasses. Eveleigh J held the defendants liable for further injuries sustained in a fall down some steps on the basis that it was foreseeable that one injury may affect a person's ability to cope with the vicissitudes of life and thereby be a cause of another injury. It would seem that the distinction between these two cases is that in *Wieland* v. *Cyril Lord Carpets Ltd* the plaintiff did not act unreasonably in attempting to descend the steps.

Negligence by an intervening third party will not necessarily break the chain of causation, and in *Sayers* v. *Harlow UDC* [1958] the plaintiff's own negligence did not constitute a *novus actus*. In Sayers the plaintiff was trapped in a public lavatory by a faulty door lock. After calling for assistance without response she decided to climb out, but fell when she placed her weight on a toilet-roll holder which gave way. It was reasonable to attempt the escape but she was careless in the manner of performing the attempt, for which she was held contributorily negligent.

In *Pigney* v. *Pointer's Transport Services Ltd* [1957] the plaintiff's husband sustained a head injury which produced a depressive mental illness leading to his suicide. The defendants were held liable for his death because the act, i.e. suicide, was not sufficiently unreasonable to constitute a *novus actus interveniens*.

In *Wright* v. *Lodge* [1993] the driver of a car which broke down at night on an unlit dual carriageway in foggy conditions was held to have been negligent in failing to move the car off the road. She was therefore held to have broken the duty of care she owed to a passenger in the car and to be liable to that passenger for injuries inflicted when a lorry crashed into the car. The lorry driver's act of driving at excessive speed which itself was reckless and the injuries caused to other motorists when the lorry crossed the central reservation and overturned were held to be attributable to the negligence of the lorry driver.

The logic of the decision can be summarised as follows:

(*i*) D's lorry swerved out of control in D's attempt to avoid P's car.

(*ii*) The presence of the stationary car on the carriageway was due to S's negligence.

(*iii*) The presence of D's lorry on the opposite carriageway was caused by S.

(*iv*) Given S's initial negligence the only question was whether the chain of causation between her initial negligence and the injuries sustained by her passenger had been broken by a *novus actus interveniens* – it had not.

(*v*) The presence of the lorry on the opposite carriageway was entirely due to D's negligence.

REMOTENESS OF DAMAGE

5. The test of foreseeability and its complexities

In order that a defendant may be held to be in breach of duty it must have been reasonably foreseeable that his conduct might cause harm to someone. How does the law view the situation where the defendant has acted carelessly, but the resulting damage is more extensive, or of a different type, or occurred in a different way from that which might reasonably have been expected from such conduct? There are two differing approaches which the law can take. The first states that a defendant is liable for all the direct consequences of his negligence, no matter how unusual or unexpected. This is essentially a test based on *causation*. Some independent intervening cause, either voluntary conduct or coincidence, would render the damage indirect. The second holds that a person is only responsible for consequences that could *reasonably have been anticipated*. Although in theory it is now accepted that foreseeability is the correct test, in reality decisions as to exactly how foreseeable the consequences must be, in combination with the principles that a tortfeasor must 'take his victim as he finds him', means that the limits of actionability set by remoteness of damage lie somewhere between these two approaches.

The first approach, based upon directness of consequence, has its origins in the Court of Appeal decision in *Re Polemis* [1921]. Bankes LJ said that given the damage was a direct result of the negligence 'the anticipations of the person whose negligent act had produced the damage appear to me be to be irrelevant'. Similarly, Scrutton LJ observed that 'once the act is negligent, the fact that its exact operation was not foreseen is immaterial'.

In *The Wagon Mound* [1961], the Privy Council described this proposition as fundamentally false. The trial judge had found that it was not reasonably foreseeable that bunkering oil with such a high flashpoint would catch fire when spread on water. Indeed, the plaintiffs' works manager had made enquiries and then allowed welding to continue on the wharf. Viscount Simonds said that although an action for negligence can be analysed in terms of duty, breach of duty and consequent damage, there can be no liability until the damage has been done.

Despite being only a persuasive authority, as a decision of the Privy Council, the strong disapproval of *Re Polemis* in *The Wagon Mound* has led subsequent courts to adopt foreseeability as the test of remoteness of damage in negligence. The same test was extended to nuisance in *Overseas Tankship (UK) Ltd* v. *Miller Steamship Co. Pty Ltd* (*The Wagon Mound II*) [1967], in which the owners of two ships damaged in the same fire that damaged the wharf sued the owners of the *Wagon Mound*. The plaintiffs in this case were successful on the basis that damage by fire was foreseeable, albeit only as a remote risk, notwithstanding the fact that the Privy Council had concluded in *The Wagon Mound* that the fire was unforeseeable. For the purpose of remoteness, once it is established that the damage sustained by the plaintiff was foreseeable, the likelihood that it would have occurred is irrelevant. In *The Heron II* [1969], for example, Lord Upjohn said that 'the tortfeasor is liable for any damage which he can reasonably foresee may happen as a result of the breach however unlikely it may be, unless it can be brushed aside as far-fetched'. After *The Wagon Mound* the courts quickly came to the conclusion that, provided the type or kind of harm sustained by the plaintiff could have been foreseen, it did not matter that its extent or the precise manner of its occurrence could not have been foreseen.

The fact that damage occurred in an unforeseeable way does not necessarily mean that it was not foreseeable. In *Hughes* v. *Lord Advocate* [1963], employees of the Post Office negligently left a manhole open in the street. This was covered by a canvas tent and surrounded by paraffin warning lamps. Out of curiosity, two young boys entered the tent, taking one of the lamps with them.

The lamp was knocked into the hole and there was a violent explosion in which one of the boys suffered severe burns. The evidence indicated that an explosion was unforeseeable in the circumstances, although burns from a conflagration could have been anticipated. The House of Lords held the defendants liable. Lord Guest said that it was not necessary that the precise details leading up to the accident should have been reasonably foreseeable, 'it is sufficient if the accident which occurred is of a type which should have been foreseeable by a reasonably careful person'. The accident was simply a 'variant of the foreseeable' (*per* Lord Pearce) and, having been caused by a known source of danger, it was no defence that it was caused in a way which was unforeseeable (*per* Lord Reid).

Two cases appear to run contrary to this line of reasoning. In *Doughty* v. *Turner Manufacturing Co. Ltd* [1964] an asbestos cover was knocked into a bath of molten liquid. Shortly after, due to a chemical reaction which was unforeseeable at the time, there was an eruption of the molten liquid that burned the plaintiff who was standing nearby. The Court of Appeal, distinguishing *Hughes* v. *Lord Advocate*, held that burning by an unforeseeable chemical eruption was not a variant of burning by splashing, which was within the foreseeable risk created by knocking the cover into the liquid. The second case is *Crossley* v. *Rawlinson* [1981], in which the plaintiff, whilst running towards a burning vehicle with a fire extinguisher, tripped in a concealed hole and was injured. It was held that because the plaintiff had not approached the scene of the danger the injury was unforeseeable and therefore too remote.

More recently, in *Owgo* v. *Taylor* [1987], the House of Lords has again considered *Hughes* v. *Lord Advocate*. Lord Bridge in *Owgo* v. *Taylor* (*see* 3:5) took the view that the proper question to be asked is not whether the particular injuries sustained by the plaintiff were reasonably foreseeable, still less whether they were actually foreseen. As Lord Reid put it in *Hughes* v. *Lord Advocate* [1963], a negligent defendant 'can only escape liability if the damage can be regarded as differing in kind from what was foreseeable'. Lord Bridge opined:

> 'Of course, the plaintiff entering the loft did not foresee the nature or severity of the injuries he was going to suffer. He could see there was danger, but a man with the courage which a fireman must constantly be called on to show has no time in such a situation to reflect on the precise nature and extent of the risks he is running. Looked at, as it should be, from the point of view of the negligent defendant who started the fire in the loft, he could foresee that the fire brigade would be called, that firemen would use their skills to do whatever was both necessary and reasonably practicable to extinguish the fire, and that if this involved entering the loft and playing a hose on the fire, they would be subject to any risks inherent in that operation, of which the risk of a scalding injury was certainly one. This was a real risk occasioned by setting fire to the rafters of a small terrace house, a risk which the defendant could have avoided by elementary care and without difficulty or expense to himself and certainly not a risk which a reasonable man would brush aside as far fetched.'

Lord Bridge in his judgment also refers to the first instance decision of *Salmon* v. *Seafarer Restaurants Ltd* [1983] where Woolf J specifically examines remoteness of damage in the context of fire fighting. Lord Bridge observes:

> 'I would particularly wish to adopt and endorse a passage in the judgment where Woolf J said, "Where it can be foreseen that the fire which is negligently started is of the type which could, first of all, require firemen to attend to extinguish that fire, and where because of the very nature of the fire, when they attend they will be at risk even though they exercise all the skill of their calling, there seems no reason why a fireman should be at any disadvantage when the question of compensation for his injuries arises." '

The damage will be too remote if it is not of the same type or kind as the harm that could have been foreseen. The difficulty is to know how to categorise the 'type' of damage that must be foreseeable, and this is at the centre of most of the problems concerning remoteness. It is possible to take a broad view of the classification of harm, dividing it into personal injury, property damage and financial loss.

How the court draws the distinction between various forms of damage to property is less clear. *The Wagon Mound* [1961] indicates that there is a distinction between damage by impact and damage by fire, because of the disapproval of *Re Polemis* [1921], and damage by fouling and damage by fire. Beyond that it gives no guidance about how to categorise harm. *Hughes* v. *Lord Advocate* [1963] makes it clear that burning by explosion is the same type of harm as burning by conflagration, and this would presumably be equally applicable to property damage. In *Vacwell Engineering Co. Ltd* v. *BDH Chemicals Ltd* [1971], Rees J said: 'It would also be foreseeable that some damage to property would or might result. In my judgment the explosion and the type of damage being foreseeable, it matters not in the law that the magnitude of the former and the extent of the latter were not.' This suggests a wide classification of *damage to property*, at least where the manner of the occurrence is foreseeable.

As to physical injury, if the injury is of a foreseeable type and this leads to injury of a different, unforeseeable type the defendant is responsible. The defendant will not be liable, however, if there is no injury of a foreseeable type. In *Bradford* v. *Robinson Rentals Ltd* [1967], the plaintiff suffered frostbite when he was sent on a journey by his employers in a vehicle without a heater, at a time of very severe winter weather. Rees J held that frostbite was damage of the same kind as that which was a foreseeable consequence of exposure to extreme cold. In *Tremain* v. *Pike* [1969], on the other hand, a farm employee contracted a rare disease transmitted by contact with rats' urine. Payne J said that although injury by rat bites or from contaminated food was foreseeable, this particular disease was unforeseeable, and by implication harm of a different type.

Where the plaintiff suffers physical injury, nervous shock is a foreseeable consequence, albeit that it is damage of a different kind, it is reasonable and not too remote. If the type of harm and the manner of its occurrence were foreseeable it is irrelevant that the physical extent of the damage was unforeseeable. In *Hughes* v. *Lord Advocate* [1963], Lord Reid took the view that: 'No doubt it was not to be expected that the injuries would be as serious as those which the appellant in fact sustained. But a defender is liable, although the damage may be a good deal greater in extent than was foreseeable. He can only escape liability if the damage can be regarded as differing in kind from what was foreseeable.' In this context *see also Alcock* v. *Chief Constable of South Yorkshire Police* [1992].

The same principle applies to property damage. In *Vacwell Engineering Co. Ltd* v. *BDH Chemicals Ltd* [1971] it was known that a chemical distributed by the defendants reacted with water to produce toxic vapour. Some of the chemical came into contact with water and the reaction led to an explosion of unforeseeable violence causing extensive damage. Rees J held that it was irrelevant that the magnitude of the explosion and resulting damage was unforeseeable.

6. Eggshell skull

Where the plaintiff is suffering from a latent physical or psychological predisposition to a particular form of illness, which the harm inflicted by the defendant triggers off, the defendant is responsible for the additional, unforeseeable damage that his negligence has produced. This is known as the eggshell-skull rule.

The eggshell-skull rule applies to almost any form of weakness or predisposition: *see Owens* v. *Liverpool Corporation* [1939]. The latent physical defect in *Love* v. *Port of London* [1959] was a weak heart; in the Canadian case of *Bishop* v. *Arts and Letters Club of Toronto* [1978], it was haemophilia. This rule applies provided that some harm was foreseeable to establish the breach of duty: *see Bourhill* v. *Young* [1943].

In *Smith* v. *Leech Brain & Co. Ltd* [1962], the plaintiff's husband was burned on the lip by a piece of metal. The burn was treated and healed, but due to a premalignant condition the burn promoted a cancerous growth which ultimately led to his death. Lord Parker CJ held the defendants liable for the death, taking the view that: 'The test is not whether these (defendants) could reasonably have foreseen that a burn would cause cancer and that (Mr Smith) would die. The question is whether these (defendants) could reasonably foresee the type of injury he suffered, namely the burn. What, in the particular case, is the amount of damage which he suffers as a result of that burn, depends upon the characteristics and constitution of the victim.' In *Robinson* v. *Post Office* [1974], the plaintiff was injured as a result of the defendant's negligence. He suffered a serious allergic reaction to an anti-tetanus injection given to him at the hospital. The Court of Appeal held the defendants liable for this injury, stating that a person who could reasonably foresee that the victim of his negligence may require medical treatment is liable for the consequences of the treatment 'although he could not reasonably foresee those consequences or that they could be serious.'

The eggshell-skull rule has been applied to an *eggshell personality*, where the injury to the plaintiff merely aggravated a pre-existing nervous condition: *see Malcolm* v. *Broadhurst* [1970]. The net result of the eggshell-skull rule is that the defendant must take his victim as he finds him, it would appear both in body and in mind. The decision in *Walker* v. *Northumberland County Council* [1995] offers a pertinent example of taking your victim's mind as you find it. The case is essentially about the scope of an employer's duty to provide a safe system of work, i.e. one that does not cause stress-related illness to its employee. Mr. Walker's employer knew because of Mr. Walker's previous nervous breakdown due to stress at work that he was vulnerable to psychological injury. The employer took steps to encourage Mr. Walker to return to work by reassuring him that he would get the support which he needed to do his job effectively without the risk of further psychological harm to him. In fact that support was not forthcoming, Mr. Walker suffered further psychological injury. The significant point is that the employer knew Mr. Walker was vulnerable to such harm and failed to take specific additional steps to safeguard him from it. There is however one final aspect which should be considered in relation to the eggshell-skull rule and this arises from *Liesbosch* v. *SS Edison* [1933], when the plaintiffs' dredger was sunk due to the defendants' fault. The plaintiffs could not afford to purchase a new vessel and so hired a substitute at an exorbitant rate and this made the performance of their contractual obligations much more expensive. The House of Lords held that they were not entitled to claim this additional expense because it was not an immediate physical consequence of the negligence, but was the result of their own want of means which was an 'extraneous matter'. The defendant did not have to take the plaintiff as he found him with respect to his impecuniosity.

Progress test 4

1. Distinguish between cause in fact and cause in law. How does the law draw a distinction?

2. Of what significance is the House of Lords decision in *Wilsher* v. *Essex Area Health Authority* [1988]?

3. What is a *novus actus interveniens*? Of what significance is this concept?

4. What is meant by the phrase 'remoteness of damage'?

5. Of what significance are the House of Lords decisions in *Hughes* v. *Lord Advocate* [1963] and *Owgo* v. *Taylor* [1987]?

6. Explain what is meant by the 'eggshell-skull rule'. How does this rule operate?

7. Of what significance is the case of *Walker* v. *Northumberland County Council* [1995]?

5

OCCUPIERS' LIABILITY

INTRODUCTION

The liability of an occupier for loss sustained by persons at the occupier's premises falls into four categories:

(a) Liability to *lawful visitors* under the Occupiers' Liability Act 1957 (OLA 1957).

(b) Liability to *non-visitors* and trespassers under the Occupiers' Liability Act 1984 (OLA 1984).

(c) Liability under the common law tort of negligence.

(d) Contractual liability towards those who enter the premises under a contract to occupy, e.g. hotel guests.

The Occupiers' Liability Acts of 1957 and 1984 embody statutory duties; under the 1957 Act the duty is to lawful visitors, under the 1984 Act the duty is to non-visitors. Liability under the common law still exists outside of these statutes; this liability may take any of three forms.

Contractual liability may arise by virtue of an implied term of contract, namely, that the occupier will take reasonable care regarding the safety of the person entering the premises under the contract: *see Maclenan* v. *Segar* [1917].

1. Common law tort of negligence

It is arguable that the *activity duty* (the duty owed by persons carrying out an activity on their premises to take reasonable care for the safety of persons who may be injured by their activity) has survived the OLA 1957. For example there may be a common law duty to ensure that a hotel is reasonably safe apart from the duty owed by the hotelier, as an occupier under the OLA 1957, to visitors to the hotel. It is important also to note the case of *Murphy* v. *Brentwood District Council* [1991] in this context.

2. The duty to ensure that premises are reasonably safe

An outline knowledge of the common law rules which were replaced (although not abolished) by the Occupiers' Liability Act 1957 is essential to a proper understanding of the present law. At common law, there were three categories of persons entering premises. A person who, before the passing of the Occupiers' Liability Act 1957, entered premises in the occupation or control of another was one of a *licensee*, an *invitee* or a *trespasser*. The standard of care owed to him by the occupier depended upon the category which covered him.

(a) *Licensees.* At common law, a licensee is one who has the gratuitous permission (express or implied) of the occupier to be on the premises for a purpose in which the occupier has no interest. A licensee must take the premises as he finds them, subject only to the occupier's duty to warn of concealed dangers, not to set traps and not to injure the licensee by a positive act of misfeasance.

(b) *Invitees.* At common law an invitee is a person who comes into the occupier's premises with the latter's consent, in pursuit of a common interest with the occupier. Thus, a customer in a shop is an invitee at common law, as shopkeeper and customer have a common interest in the customer's being there. An occupier owes his invitee (provided he remains within the terms of his invitation) a duty to take reasonable care for his safety. This is a more stringent duty than that owed to a licensee.

(c) *Trespassers.* A trespasser is a person without any kind of permission to be on the premises, and whose 'presence is either unknown to the proprietor or, if known, is practically objected to': *R. Addie & Sons Ltd* v. *Dumbreck* [1929], *per* Lord Dunedin. A trespasser entered the premises entirely at his own risk, the only duty of the occupier being not to inflict damage intentionally or recklessly on a trespasser he knew to be there.

An illustration of the common law duty to ensure that premises are reasonably safe is *Maclenan* v. *Segar* [1917]. A guest upon arrival at the hotel was taken directly to the room by lift. During her night's stay a fire broke out in the hotel and the guest in a panic attempted to leave her second floor room through the window by means of a 'rope' made from bed linen. She fell through a glass roof and sustained injuries. It was held that the fire was caused by the negligence of the hotel management and furthermore the premises were not reasonably safe. The trial judge in finding for the plaintiff enunciated two grounds for the decision:

> (*i*) 'Where the occupier of premises agrees for reward that a person shall have the right to enter and use them for a mutually contemplated purpose, the contract between the parties (unless it provides to the contrary) contains an implied warranty that the premises are as safe for that purpose as a reasonable care and skill on the part of anyone can make them.
> (*ii*) '. . .The defendant had been personally negligent in that he had failed to take such steps and to make such inquiries as would have revealed to him the defects in his structure and the risks of fire thereby occasioned.'

The first ground for the decision appears to be derived from the contract of booking. In other words there is an implied term of the contract that the premises are reasonably safe. What if the plaintiff in this case had been a tradesman (e.g. a lawful visitor to the premises, but one who was not in a contractual relationship with the hotel) who was injured whilst trying to escape from the fire? It would, of course, not be possible to argue along the lines of an 'implied term' of contract since no contract exists. However, the tradesman would surely be a 'neighbour' under the 'neighbour principle' in *Donoghue* v. *Stevenson* and be owed a duty of care in accordance with that principle. It may, however, be argued that such a duty is identical with the statutory duty set out in s. 2 OLA 1957.

The second ground for the decision appears to be straightforward negligence liability. The case of course predates the 'neighbour principle' in *Donoghue* v. *Stevenson*, but there is no reason to doubt that if the facts of the case were to occur once more, it could be dealt with as an application of the 'neighbour principle'. The case of *Salmon* v. *Seafarer Restaurants Ltd* [1983] is an illustration of the view that negligence liability remains in existence outside the OLA 1957. It is important to note *Murphy* v. *Brentwood District Council* [1991] in this context.

THE OCCUPIERS' LIABILITY ACT 1957

The 1957 Act provides that there are only two categories of person who may enter upon an occupier's premises: (a) lawful visitors; (b) persons who are not lawful visitors, thus outside the scope of the 1957 Act. By s. 2(1) OLA 1957 an occupier owes a single 'common duty of care' to all visitors who enter his premises with his permission.

The duty owed by the occupier under the OLA 1957 Act applies only to dangers arising from the condition of the premises and not to dangers arising from activities carried out at the premises: *see Ward* v. *Tesco Stores Ltd* [1976]. The common duty of care applies not only to injury to persons but also to damage to the visitor's property.

3. What are 'premises'?

Section 1(3) of OLA 1957 defines 'premises' as including any fixed or movable structure; this will include vessels, vehicles and aircraft. It will also include objects one might not otherwise consider to be 'premises': *Wheeler* v. *Copas* [1981] (a ladder), *Bunker* v. *C Brand Ltd* [1969] (tunnelling equipment).

4. Who is an 'occupier'?

Neither the OLA 1957 nor OLA 1984 define an 'occupier' but provide that the rules of the common law shall apply. The test is *occupational control* of the premises: *Wheat* v. *E. Lacon & Co. Ltd* [1966]. Control does not have to be complete or exclusive. In *Wheat* v. *Lacon & Co. Ltd* the defendants owned a public house which was run by a manager. They granted him a licence to use the first floor as his private accommodation, retaining the right to repair. A paying guest of the manager fell down some unlit stairs in the private area of the premises and was killed. The House of Lords held that the defendants had sufficient control over the private accommodation to be occupiers along with the manager.

Lord Denning took the following view:

'In order to be an "occupier" it is not necessary for a person to have active control over the premises. He need not have exclusive occupation. Suffice it that he has some degree of control. He may share control with others. Two or more may be "occupiers". And whenever this happens, each is under a duty to use care towards persons coming lawfully on to the premises, dependent on his degree of control. If each fails in his duty, each is liable to a visitor who is injured in consequence of his failure, but each may have a claim to contribution from the other.'

It should be noted that one consequence of the concept of 'dual occupation' is that it is possible for a person to be a visitor in relation to one occupier yet a trespasser in relation to another: *see Ferguson* v. *Welsh* [1987].

5. Who is a visitor?

The vital issue is to be able to distinguish *visitors* from *non-visitors*. Visitors are persons who have either the express permission of the occupier to visit the premises, or can be said to have an implied permission, i.e. those persons who in common law would be held to be invitees or licensees.

Where a person enters the premises pursuant to a contract, a term is implied into the contract that the person is a visitor to whom the common duty of care is owed (*see* s. 5(1) OLA 1957). Where express permission to enter the premises has not been granted problems may arise. The issue then turns on whether or not permission can be implied. This is essentially a question of fact; can the occupier's conduct be interpreted as the grant of an implied permission to enter? Mere knowledge of entry is not equivalent to consent. In *Lowery* v. *Walker* [1911], members of the public had used a short cut across the defendant's field for many years. The defendant had attempted to prevent this but did not take any legal proceedings. The plaintiff was savaged by a horse and the House of Lords held that he had implied permission to enter the field.

An occupier may set limits on the visitor's permission as to the time, place or purpose of the visit. The common duty of care is specifically restricted to 'the purposes for which the visitor is invited or permitted by the occupier to be there': *see* s. 2(2) OLA 1957 and *Stone* v. *Taffe* [1974] below.

Section 2(2) OLA 1957 requires the occupier to take such care as in all the circumstances of the case is reasonable to see that visitors will be reasonably safe in using the premises for the purposes for which they are invited or permitted by the occupier to be there; lawful visitors, therefore, will only be owed a duty insofar as they remain within the scope of their invitation or permission to be on the premises. A person who exceeds the scope of an invitation becomes a trespasser: *see Mersey Docks and Harbour Board* v. *Proctor* [1923]. Persons who enter the premises as lawful visitors may not remain within that category if they step outside their invitation or permission to be on the premises. Guests at a hotel will be lawful visitors to certain parts of the hotel to which they have been invited, e.g. public rooms, lounge, reception, restaurant and their bedrooms, conveniences, etc., provided for guests' use. Guests will cease to be lawful visitors if they enter parts of the premises such as the kitchen, offices, laundry, etc. which they do not have permission to enter.

These principles are clearly illustrated in *Campbell* v. *Selbourne Hotel Ltd* [1939]. The plaintiff was a guest at the defendants' hotel in London. He had previously stayed at the hotel on 12 or 13 occasions, but had never occupied a room on the ground floor. At about 11.20 pm on the night in question he arrived back in his room and desired to use the lavatory. He had ascertained during daylight that the lavatory was diagonally across the passage from his room door, and, as the passage was now unlit and he was unable to find the electric light switch, he crossed the passage in the dark and by feeling his way came to a door which he believed to be that of the lavatory but was in fact a door leading to the basement. Opening and passing through this door the plaintiff immediately fell down a flight of steps and sustained injury. It was held that the defendants owed to the plaintiff a duty to take all reasonable care to see that the premises were safe and that their failure to light the passage in a London hotel at 11.20 pm, when guests might reasonably be expected to be using the passage, was a breach of that duty which had resulted in injury to the plaintiff. The plaintiff who had not been shown to be contributorily negligent was entitled to recover damages, on the ground of the defendants' negligence. It can be said therefore that the duty owed to a lawful visitor only extends so long as, and so far as, the lawful visitor is making what can reasonably be contemplated as an ordinary and reasonable use of the premises by the lawful visitor for the purposes for which he has been invited.

A further aspect of the problem is that the permission of the occupier may be extended to the visitor for a fixed period of time, thereafter the visitor becomes a trespasser and is outside the scope of the OLA 1957.

In *Stone* v. *Taffe* [1974], Mr Stone was a committee member of a society which regularly met at a public house owned by a brewery and managed by their employee Taffe. Taffe agreed to allow the society, of which he was also a member, to use an upstairs room at the public house for a social occasion. Drinks were served to members of the club by Taffe until the early hours of the morning, without any extension having been granted by the licensing magistrates. Mr Stone, when leaving the premises by a narrow unlit staircase at approximately 1.00 am, fell and was killed. The widow of Mr Stone sued both Taffe and the brewery for damages *inter alia* under s. 2 OLA 1957. It was held that an occupier who intended to permit another person to enter and use his premises for a limited period of time only, had to give a clear indication to the other that the permission was subject to a time limit. Accordingly, at the time of the accident the deceased was a visitor lawfully on the premises since the brewers had not given the deceased any indication that the permission which they had given to him to be on the premises expired at 10.30 pm. It followed that at the time the brewers still owed him the duty of care under s. 2 of the 1957 Act. It should be noted, however, that on the particular facts of the case the deceased was found to be *contributorily negligent*, a deduction of 50 per cent in the damages for which the occupier was liable was therefore made.

Section 2(6) OLA 1957 provides that persons who enter premises for any purpose in the exercise of a right conferred by law are to be treated as visitors for that purpose, whether the occupier has in fact given permission or not. This will include a fireman attending a fire, a policeman executing a warrant, and many other officers of public authorities exercising statutory rights of entry.

6. The common duty of care

By virtue of s. 2(2) of the 1957 Act, the common duty of care is a duty to take such care as in all the circumstances of the case is reasonable to see that the visitor will be reasonably safe in using the premises for the purposes for which he is invited or permitted by the occupier to be there.

It is clear from the provision that it is the *visitor* who must be made reasonably safe; the precautions which an occupier must take will, therefore, vary according to who the visitor is, e.g. a child or an elderly person.

It is also important to note that under s. 2(4)(b) OLA 1957 the duty placed upon the occupier by section 2 is delegable.

7. Children

Section 2(3)(a) OLA 1957 directs that an occupier must be prepared for children to be less careful than adults. Dangers which appear obvious to adults are not necessarily so to children. Additionally, children are naturally more curious and inquisitive than adults and may be lured by objects or situations which are outside the scope of their permission to enter.

In *Glasgow Corporation* v. *Taylor* [1922] a boy aged seven died after eating poisonous berries picked from a shrub in a botanical garden. The defendants knew the berries were poisonous but did not fence off the shrub or give any warning. It was held that the attractive looking berries constituted an 'allurement' to children, for which the defendants were liable. By his acts, the boy had not been trespassing.

Although a minor is a person aged less than 18, older children are treated for the purposes of the OLA 1957 in the same ways as adults: *see Tichener* v. *BRB* [1983]. The problem which young children present is not easily overcome.

In *Phipps* v. *Rochester Corporation* [1955], the defendants were developing a housing estate and had dug a trench two and a half feet wide and eight feet deep. The plaintiff aged five and his sister aged seven crossed the land in order to pick berries. The plaintiff fell into the trench and broke his leg. The trench was neither an allurement nor a concealed danger, but Devlin J accepted that so far as the plaintiff was concerned the danger was 'concealed from his understanding'.

An occupier who tacitly permits the public to use his land must assume that the public may include little children. The occupier is also entitled, when considering what precautions he ought reasonably to take for the safety of such children, to take into account the habits of prudent parents who will not normally allow their young children to go out unaccompanied. This places the primary responsibility for the safety of young children upon parents: *see Simkiss* v. *Rhondda Borough Council* [1982].

8. Skilled visitors

By s. 2(3)(b) OLA 1957, an occupier is entitled to expect that a person entering the premises in the exercise of his calling will appreciate and guard against any special risk which is ordinarily incidental to it, so far as the occupier allows him to do so.

The skilled visitor should be better able to take care of his own safety, but only with respect to the risks associated with his specialism. In *Roles* v. *Nathan* [1963], two chimney-sweeps died from carbon monoxide poisoning while cleaning the flue of a boiler. They had been warned not to continue working while the boiler was alight. The Court of Appeal held that the occupier was not liable because:

(a) the sweeps had been warned; *and*

(b) it is reasonable to expect a specialist to appreciate and guard against the dangers arising from the very defect that he has been called in to deal with.

In *Salmon* v. *Seafarer Restaurants Ltd* [1983] the defendants argued that an occupier's duty to a fireman attending a fire at his premises was limited to protecting him from special or exceptional risks over and above the ordinary risks incidental to fighting fires. Woolf J rejected this contention. The occupier owed the same duty as he did to any other visitor but, in determining whether there was any breach of that duty, a fireman could be expected to exercise the ordinary skills of a fireman. If he did so, but nonetheless suffered injury as a foreseeable consequence of the negligence, the occupier will be liable.

More recently in *Owgo* v. *Taylor* [1987], the House of Lords approved the view taken by Woolf J in *Salmon* v. *Seafarer Restaurants Ltd*, that a fireman foreseeably injured while fighting a fire, caused by the defendant's negligence, had a right to damages; only an outrageous risk taken by the fireman would relieve the owner's liability.

9. Independent contractors

The negligence of an independent contractor in carrying out any work of construction, repair or maintenance for an occupier will not put the occupier in breach of the common duty of care where:

(a) it was reasonable to entrust the work to an independent contractor; *and*

(b) the occupier had taken reasonable care to see that the contractor was competent to carry out the work; *and*

(c) the occupier had taken reasonable care to check that the work was properly carried out.

If these three conditions apply, s. 2(4)(b) OLA 1957 is operative.

The circumstances of the case will determine whether or not it is reasonable for the occupier to depend upon an independent contractor. Specialist skills or expertise on the part of the independent contractor may be required such that the occupier cannot rely upon his own knowledge: *see Haseldine* v. *A. Daw Ltd* [1941] (maintenance of a lift). Simple everyday tasks such as office cleaning are often carried out by sub-contractors and it will be more difficult for an occupier to rely on s. 2(4)(b) to absolve himself from liability in such cases.

It may well be necessary for an occupier to have the work of the sub-contractor independently checked by a professionally or technically competent third party: *see AMF International Ltd* v. *Magnet Bowling Ltd* [1968]; *Ferguson* v. *Welsh* [1987].

10. Persons exercising a right of way

A lawful visitor under the OLA 1957 is anyone who would have been a licensee or invitee before the Act. Such categories did not include a person exercising a public or private right of way; therefore no duty is owed by an occupier to such a person either at common law or under the Occupiers' Liability Act 1957.

In *Greenhalgh* v. *British Railways Board* [1969], the plaintiff pedestrian was injured crossing an accommodation bridge, occupied by the British Railways Board. The bridge constituted a right of way. It was held that the Board owed no duty of care to the plaintiff under OLA 1957.

In *Holden* v. *White* [1982], it was decided that persons using a private right of way were not the visitors of the occupier of the land over which the right of way was exercised. Thus a milkman who was injured by a defective manhole cover could not sue the owner of the land over which the right of way passed under OLA 1957.

The OLA 1984 now makes provision for persons exercising a right of way. Persons exercising a public right of way do not fall under either statute and must therefore bring their action in negligence: *see* e.g. *McGeown* v. *N.I. Housing Executive* [1994].

11. Persons entering under contract

Obligations under a contract depend upon the terms of that contract. Section 5 OLA 1957 therefore provides that the common duty of care is to be implied as a term of the contract in respect of the duty owed by the occupier 'in respect of damages due to the state of the premises or to things done or omitted to be done on them', where such matters are not covered by a term forming part of the contract. The important exception is the case of contracts 'for the hire of, or for the carriage for reward of, persons or goods in any vehicle, vessel, aircraft or other means of transport', and should be noted. The effects of this exception are as follows:

(a) It is necessary to distinguish carefully between vehicles, ships and aircraft constituting exceptions governed by common law rules (*see* below) and vehicles, ships and aircraft which are *premises* governed by the Act.

(b) Implied terms in respect of carriage by vehicles, ships and aircraft constituting exceptions under s. 5 are governed, not by the Act, but by the more onerous common law rules. The effect of these is that the duty of care is not discharged unless all reasonable care and skill have been used to see that the vehicle, ship or aircraft is safe. The effect of this is that the 'occupier' will be liable in respect of the negligence of his independent contractor, contrary to the general rule.

12. Third parties entering under contract

The effect of s. 3(1) OLA 1957 is that, where an occupier is bound by contract to allow persons who are not parties to the contract (s. 3(2) OLA 1957) to enter or use the premises, the occupier cannot by that contract exclude the common duty of care he owes to such third parties as lawful visitors. Such a contract includes the occupier's duty to perform his obligations under it, 'in so far as those obligations go beyond the obligations otherwise involved in that duty'. Furthermore, s. 3(4) OLA 1957 provides that the same principles shall apply where a landlord or tenant is bound by the terms of a tenancy, though not by contract, to allow persons to enter or use premises of which he is the occupier.

13. Warning notices

Warning notices may in certain circumstances absolve the occupier of liability for the visitor's injuries. Section 2(4)(a) OLA 1957 provides that 'Where damage is caused to a visitor by a danger of which he had been warned by the occupier, the warning is not to be treated without more as absolving the occupier from liability, unless in all the circumstances it was enough to enable the visitor to be reasonably safe.'

Not all warnings will, therefore, be sufficient to provide a defence (*see Roles* v. *Nathan* [1963]), only such warnings which enable the visitor to be reasonably safe. An example would be if, on a door to a store-room which contained high voltage electrical equipment involved in the supply of electricity to a building, there was a notice which said 'Danger: Keep Out: High Voltage'. This may not be sufficient if a person who strayed into the store-room and was injured could not read English. A warning notice must be readily understandable and clear symbols explaining the danger required. The warning should give some indication of the nature and location of the danger in order to enable the visitor to avoid it.

14. Where the visitor accepts the risk

Where the visitor to the premises accepts the risk of danger on the premises, s. 2(5) OLA 1957 applies and an occupier has no obligation to the visitor with respect to the risk: *see Simms* v. *Leigh Rugby Football Club* [1969]. This defence is expressly equated to the common law defence of *volenti* (see below).

Mere knowledge of the danger is not to be treated as an acceptance of it by the visitor, unless such knowledge enables the visitor to take precautions to make himself reasonably safe: *see Bunker* v. *C. Brand & Sons Ltd* [1969].

15. Excluding liability

An occupier may 'restrict, modify or exclude his duty to any visitor by agreement or otherwise', insofar as he is free to do so. This is stated in s. 2(1) OLA 1957. A business occupier's ability to restrict or exclude liability for the death of, or personal injury to, a lawful visitor is removed by s. 2(1) Unfair Contract Terms Act 1977. Section 2(1) UCTA 1977 states that 'A person cannot by reference to any contract or to a notice given to persons generally or to particular persons exclude his liability for death or personal injury resulting from negligence.'

The private occupier does still have some freedom to exclude his liability whether by agreement or by a 'notice': *see Ashdown* v. *Samuel Williams & Sons Ltd* [1957]. In *White* v. *Blackmore* [1972], the plaintiff's husband was killed at a jalopy race when a car became entangled in the safety ropes, with the result that stakes holding the ropes were pulled up, and he was catapulted about 6 metres through the air. A notice at the entrance to the race track and at other points about the field specified that the organisers were to be absolved from all liabilities arising out of accidents causing damage or personal injury, 'however caused'. A majority of the Court of Appeal concluded that this was an effective defence. The deceased had entered the premises subject to the conditions of the notice. Of course, the circumstances of this case would now fall squarely within the scope of s. 2(1) UCTA 1977, since the defendant was a 'business occupier' and therefore the exclusion of liability would be ineffective. However, the principle in the case still holds good for 'private occupiers'.

A limitation upon the defendant's ability to exclude liability as an occupier is that, where the plaintiff has no real choice about whether to enter the premises on the terms of an exclusionary notice, there can be no implied agreement that he will be bound by its terms: *see Burnett* v. *British Waterways Board* [1973].

The exclusion of liability does *not* depend upon *actual notice* of the term by the plaintiff. The occupier will have done enough if he takes reasonable steps to bring the condition to the visitor's attention; *constructive notice* will suffice.

It is difficult to imagine circumstances where constructive notice of the exclusion will suffice where the party injured is a child, or an adult acting under disability (e.g. blind or illiterate). Equally, where the plaintiff has no choice but to enter the premises, constructive notice will be insufficient.

CONTRIBUTORY NEGLIGENCE

Where visitors have contributed to the injuries they have sustained due to the defendant's breach of duty under the OLA 1957, then the damages to which they are entitled may be reduced. Section 1(1) of the Law Reform (Contributory Negligence) Act 1945 states: 'Where any person suffers damage as the result partly of his own fault and partly of the fault of any other person or persons, a claim in respect of that damage shall not be defeated by reason of the fault of the person suffering the damage, but the damages recoverable in respect thereof shall be reduced to such an extent as the court thinks just and equitable having regard to the claimant's share in the responsibility for the damage . . .'.

In *Stone* v. *Taffe* [1974] a 50 per cent reduction was made due to the claimant's contributory negligence: *see also Sayers* v. *Harlow UDC* [1958]. For a more recent case example, *see Adams* v. *Southern Electricity Board* [1993].

VOLENTI NON FIT INJURIA

This amounts to the voluntary assumption of the risk of injury. Section 2(5) OLA 1957 provides: 'The common duty of care does not impose on an occupier any obligation to a visitor in respect of risks willingly accepted as his by the visitor . . .'.

It will be a question of fact in each case whether the visitor has voluntarily accepted the risk. Reference should also be made to s. 2(3) UCTA 1977 which provides in relation to exclusion clauses: 'Where a contract term or notice purports to exclude or restrict liability for negligence a person's agreement to or awareness of it is not of itself to be taken as indicating his voluntary acceptance of any risk'. For further discussion *see* Chapter 15.

LIABILITY TO NON-VISITORS

The law at one time did not recognise any liability on the part of an occupier towards persons who were *not* lawful visitors to the occupier's premises.

16. The common law

In *R. Addie & Sons (Collieries) Ltd* v. *Dumbreck* [1929], the view was taken that:

> 'Towards the trespasser the occupier has no duty to take reasonable care for his protection or even to protect him from concealed danger. The trespasser comes on to the premises at his own risk. An occupier is in such a case liable only where the injury is due to some wilful act involving something more than the absence of reasonable care. There must be some act done with the deliberate intention of doing harm to the trespasser, or at least some act done with reckless disregard of the presence of the trespasser.'

This decision was subsequently overruled by the House of Lords in *British Railways Board* v. *Herrington* [1972]. In that case an electrified railway line owned by BRB ran through property open to the public, the fences on either side of the track were in poor repair and in April 1965 children were seen on the line. A particular place in the fence had been used as a route to cross the railway. In June 1965 the plaintiff, a child of six, was severely injured when he stepped on the line, having passed through the broken fence. The plaintiff claimed damages for negligence on the part of BRB due to the disrepair of the fence through which he had passed.

The House of Lords held that whilst occupiers do not owe the same duty to trespassers which they owe to lawful visitors, they owe trespassers a duty to take such steps as common sense or 'common humanity' would dictate, to avert the danger, or warn persons coming onto the premises of its presence. Lord Pearson observed:

> 'In my opinion, the occupier of premises does not owe any such duty to a trespasser: he does not owe to the trespasser a duty to take care, as in all the circumstances of the case it is reasonable to see that the trespasser will be reasonably safe in using the premises for the purposes for which he is trespassing. That seems to me to be the fundamental distinction, and should be fully preserved. It does not follow that the occupier never owes any duty to the trespasser. If the presence of the trespasser is known to or reasonably to be anticipated by the

occupier, then the occupier has a duty to the trespasser, but it is a lower and less onerous duty than the one which the occupier owes to a lawful visitor. Very broadly stated, it is a duty to treat the trespasser with ordinary humanity . . . the occupier is not at fault if he has done as much as is required of him, if he has taken reasonable steps to deter the trespasser from entering or remaining on the premises, or part of the premises, in which he will encounter a dangerous situation. In simple language, it is normally sufficient for the occupier to make reasonable endeavours to keep out or chase off the potential or actual intruder who is likely to be or is in a dangerous situation. The erection and maintenance of suitable notice boards or fencing or both, or the giving of suitable oral warning . . . will usually constitute reasonable endeavours for this purpose'.

Because a trespasser forces himself into a relationship of proximity with the occupier, the trespasser must accept a lower standard of precautions against injury than a visitor – a duty to act humanely is owed by the occupier to a trespasser. Such a duty was only owed when a reasonable man, knowing the facts which the occupier actually knew, would appreciate that a trespasser's presence at the point and time of danger was so likely that in all the circumstances of the case it would have been inhumane not to give effective warning of the danger.

The level of precautions which an occupier was expected to take depended upon the occupiers' knowledge, ability and resources, that is to say it was subjective. Alternatively, in circumstances where the danger arose due to the occupier's actions on the premises the standard of care was objective: see *Southern Portland Cement Ltd* v. *Cooper* [1974].

The vestigial importance of the common law is illustrated in *Revill* v. *Newbery* [1996].

THE OCCUPIERS' LIABILITY ACT 1984

Basing itself upon Law Commission Report No. 75 (Cmnd 6428), Parliament enacted the Occupiers' Liability Act 1984. This legislation is, however, similar to the common law as enunciated by the House of Lords in *BRB* v. *Herrington* in imposing a statutory duty of care on an occupier which is owed to persons 'other than visitors'. The OLA 1984 determines:

(a) whether an occupier of premises owes a duty to persons other than visitors, in respect of any risk of those persons suffering *injury* on the premises by reason of any danger due to the *state of the premises* or to *things done or omitted to be done on them* and

(b) what that duty is.

Terms such as *premises* (*see* ss. 1(2) and (9) OLA 1984) and *occupier* (*see* s. 1(2)(a) OLA 1984) are defined in the same way as under the OLA 1957. One point of difference, however, is the type of loss recoverable under the OLA 1984; there is *no liability* for loss or damage to the *property* of a non-visitor (*see* s. 1(8) OLA 1984), whereas under OLA 1957 such loss is recoverable by a visitor (s. 1(3)(b) OLA 1957).

17. To whom is a duty owed?

An occupier owes a duty under OLA 1984 to 'persons other than his visitors', *see* s. 1(1)(a) OLA 1984 ('non-visitors'). These include:

(a) Trespassers: *see Revill* v. *Newbery* [1996], burglar shot in course of burglary on defendant's premises.

(b) Persons who enter land in the exercise of rights conferred by an access agreement or order under s. 60 National Parks and Access to the Countryside Act 1949

(c) Persons lawfully exercising a private right of way (*see* **10** above).

18. When does the duty exist?

The Occupiers' Liability Act 1984 creates separate tests for *the existence of the duty* owed to the non-visitor and *the content of the duty*, if it is found to exist.
 Section 1(3) states that an occupier owes the statutory duty if:

(a) he is aware of the danger or has reasonable grounds to believe that it exists

(b) he knows or has reasonable grounds to believe that the 'non-visitor' is in the vicinity of the danger concerned or that he may come into the vicinity of the danger (in either case, whether the 'non-visitor' has lawful authority for being in that vicinity or not). Where the occupier had no reason to expect that trespassers were taking shortcuts across his land, no duty arose: *White* v. *St. Albans City and District Council* [1990] (CA).

(c) the risk is one against which, in all the circumstances of the case, he may reasonably be expected to offer the 'non-visitor' some protection.

Where the section states '*he knows or has reasonable grounds to believe*' this applies to the situation where the occupier knows or is aware of the primary facts but fails to draw the reasonable inference that the premises are dangerous or that the non-visitor's presence is likely. In *Harris* v. *Birkenhead Corporation* [1976], Lawton LJ construed the requirement of actual knowledge under *British Railways Board* v. *Herrington* [1972] to include cases where the occupier ignores the obvious or fails to draw reasonable inferences from known facts.
 Whether the risk is one against which the occupier may reasonably be expected to offer some protection will depend upon factors which are more usually taken into account when assessing the standard of care (e.g. the nature and extent of the risk, practicability of precautions and, possibly, the type of entrant). If s. 1(3) OLA 1984 is satisfied, the court will then consider the *content* of the occupier's duty.

19. The content of the duty

Under s. 1(4) OLA 1984, the duty is to take such care as is reasonable in all the circumstances of the case to see that the non-visitor does not suffer injury on the premises by reason of the danger concerned. This is an *objective test* which does not depend upon either the skill or resources of the particular occupier. What constitutes *reasonable care* will, however, vary considerably taking account of 'all of the circumstances of the case'. The circumstances of the case will obviously include the nature of the non-visitor's presence on the premises, his or her age and capabilities. Factors to be considered when applying s. 1(4) OLA 1984 are:

(a) The gravity and likelihood of the probable injury; high risk merits greater precautions.

(b) The nature of the premises.

(c) The foreseeability of the entrant; the more likely the presence of the non-visitor the greater the precautions required.

20. Warning notices

In *appropriate cases* but not in all cases, an occupier may discharge his duty by taking reasonable steps to warn of the danger, or by taking steps to discourage people from incurring the risk (*see* s. 1(5) OLA 1984). Where the non-visitor is a *child* a warning will be inadequate to discharge the duty, further steps should be taken to discourage the person from taking the risk, e.g. fencing. With *adult* non-visitors a warning notice will be sufficient.

21. *Volenti non fit injuria*

Section 1(6) OLA 1984 preserves this defence in relation to non-visitors. The defendant must establish not only that the plaintiff consented to the risk but also that he agreed that if he was injured the loss should be his not the defendant's. The plaintiff should also appreciate both the nature and extent of the risk, not simply the fact that there is some risk.

22. Excluding liability

The OLA 1984 makes no reference to the question of whether an occupier can exclude or restrict his potential liability under the Act. The omission of such a reference suggests that this cannot be a defence under the Act. This view is supported by contrast with the OLA 1957.

Progress test 5

1. How may an occupier be held liable for injury caused to another on the occupier's premises?

2. Who is an 'occupier'?

3. Who is a 'visitor'?

4. What duty is owed by an occupier to a lawful visitor on his premises?

5. How may the standard of care expected of an occupier towards a lawful visitor on his premises vary according to the nature of the visitor?

6. To what extent if at all may an occupier exclude liability to a lawful visitor?

7. In what circumstances and to what extent does an occupier owe a duty of care to a non-visitor on his premises?

6

EMPLOYERS' LIABILITY

INTRODUCTION

The relationship between master and servant, more appropriately referred to as employer and employee, gives rise to specific duties and liabilities. An employer owes a duty to his employees by reason of the fact that he employs them; this duty arises exclusively from the contract of employment between employer and employee. Equally, an employer may be held vicariously liable for the actions of his employees carried out in the course of their employment. It is vital, at the outset, to define clearly the relationship between employer and employee.

THE RELATIONSHIP BETWEEN EMPLOYER AND EMPLOYEE

1. Who is an employee?

The starting point for formulating a definition is the Employment Rights Act 1996: ' "employee" means an individual who has entered into or works under (or, where the employment has ceased, worked under) a contract of employment'.

Such a definition is of little help since it does not enable one to identify immediately a particular relationship as that of employer and employee. A 'contract of employment' is also defined in the Act as a *contract of service*. This takes us little further, hence we must look outside the Act to establish a test to determine whether a person is an employee of another. Various tests have been put forward and these are set out below.

2. The control test

This is the traditional approach. Does the employer have sufficient control over the person to make that person an employee? This approach was first enunciated in *Performing Rights Society Ltd* v. *Mitchell & Booker* [1924]. An employee works sufficiently under the control of another where the other may tell the employee not only what to do but also when and how to do it: *see Yewens* v. *Noakes* (1880). The greater the degree of control exercised the more likely it is that the person subject to control is an employee. A porter or a waitress are clearly employees of a hotel, under the control test. Is the head chef? An employer may use skills of highly trained personnel whom he cannot tell how to perform their work, e.g. head chef. Are such persons still employees? The greater the skill required for an employee's work, the less significant is control in determining whether the employee works under a contract of service: *see Beloff* v. *Pressdram Ltd* [1973].

3. The business integration test

This test considers to what extent the work of the so-called employee is integrated with the work of the employer's business organisation. The test was explained by Denning LJ (as he then was) in *Stevenson, Jordan & Harrison Ltd* v. *Macdonald & Evans* [1952]: '. . . under a contract of service, a man is employed as part of the business, and his work is done as an integral part of the business; whereas, under a contract for services, his work, although done for the business, is not integrated into it but is only accessory to it'.

4. The multiple test

The law evolved in the 1960s and early 1970s to recognise that a single test would not be applicable to all employees. In *Ready Mixed Concrete (South East) Ltd* v. *Minister of Pensions and National Insurance* [1968], Mackenna J said:

> 'A contract of service exists if the following three conditions are fulfilled: (i) the servant agrees that in consideration of a wage or other remuneration he will provide his own work and skill in the performance of some service for the master. (ii) He agrees, expressly or impliedly, that in the performance of that service he will be subject to the other's control in a sufficient degree to make that other master. (iii) The other provisions of the contract are consistent with its being a contract of service.'

The 'multiple test' adopts a broader approach, not determining who is an employee on the basis of a single factor. It contains an element of the control test, but also element (iii) requires all the surrounding circumstances to be taken into account. In *Ferguson* v. *John Dawson & Partners (Contractors) Ltd* [1976], the Court of Appeal approved this threefold approach, taking the view that one can only determine the issue by looking at the whole relationship.

Is a statement by the parties as to their respective positions conclusive in determining whether the relationship is one of employer and employee? In *Ferguson* v. *John Dawson* it was said that a statement by the parties that the relationship was one of contractor and sub-contractor was not conclusive, and on the facts of the case the plaintiff was found to be an employee of the defendants. The label placed on the relationship by the parties themselves is insufficient to determine the true nature of the relationship. In *Massey* v. *Crown Life Insurance Co.* [1978], Denning MR took the view that if the relationship between the parties is ambiguous and is capable of being either one of contractor and sub-contractor or employer and employee, then the ambiguity may be resolved by assessing any label placed upon the relationship by the parties in the contract between them.

Other factors, such as the method of payment, may also help to determine the question of whether or not a particular person is an employee. Particular problems arise in relation to part-time and seasonal workers when determining whether they fall into the category of 'employees': *see O'Kelly* v. *Trusthouse Forte plc* [1984].

Summary

The overall pattern of employment and the nature of employment terms and conditions have changed markedly since the earlier key cases on who is an employee. Guidance has recently been given by the Court of Appeal in *Lane* v. *Shire Roofing (Oxford) Ltd* (1995) where commenting on the control test Henry L.J. opined:

> 'The control test might not be decisive, for instance in the case of skilled employees with discretion to decide how their work should be done. In such cases the question was broadened to whose business was it? Was the workman carrying on his own business, or was he carrying on his employer's?
>
> The answer to that question might involve looking to see where the financial risk lay, and whether and how far the workman had an opportunity of profiting from sound management in the performance of his task'.

It is the question 'whose business is it?' which is increasingly pertinent to a number of employment situations, e.g. persons paid by means of commission only, staff paid per session / shift. Where businesses have been eager to limit their overheads and move persons who were clearly employees to a position where they are separate business entities trading with their former employer – e.g. the position of many milkmen – this test is particularly apposite.

VICARIOUS LIABILITY

5. The nature of vicarious liability

Lord Reid observed, in *Staveley Iron and Chemical Co.* v. *Jones Ltd* [1956], that: 'It is a rule of law that an employer, though guilty of no fault himself, is liable for damage done by the fault or negligence of his servant *acting in the course of his employment.*' This dictum clearly outlines the nature of vicarious liability. It must always be proven so as to render an employer vicariously liable for the torts of his employee, that at the material time the employee was acting in the course of his employment. Recently in *Re Supply of Ready Mixed Concrete (No. 2)* [1995] Lord Templeman has provided useful guidance on the approach to be taken: 'An employee who acts for the company within the scope of his employment is the company'.

Acting in the course of his employment has been given a broad interpretation by the courts, covering not only where the employee is acting upon the employer's instructions but also where he is acting for the employer's benefit yet in an unauthorised manner, or in a way which the employer has sought to prohibit.

6. The courts' interpretation

In *Rose* v. *Plenty* [1976], the plaintiff Rose (a 13-year-old boy) was helping Plenty (a milkman) to deliver milk. Plenty's employer, the local Co-op, expressly forbade him from using the services of children to assist in the delivery of milk to clients. Plenty had employed Rose to help him with his milk round. On an occasion when Rose was assisting Plenty with the milk round, Rose sustained an injury due to an accident caused by Plenty. Rose brought an action for damages against Plenty and his employer, the Co-op. The Co-op defended that action by contesting that Plenty had acted outside the scope of his employment, and thus he alone was liable to damages, and that the Co-op was not vicariously liable for his negligent driving.

It was held by the Court of Appeal that the Co-op was vicariously liable for the actions of Plenty, who had been acting in the course of his employment. Lawton LJ dissented from this view. Lord Denning MR observed: 'In considering whether a prohibited act was within the course of the employment it depends very much on the purpose for which it is done. If it is done for his employer's business, it is usually done in the course of his employment, even though it is a prohibited act.'

Actions prohibited by the employer may still be within the scope of an employee's employment if they were done to further the employer's business.

There does, however, appear to be a further limitation upon this principle, namely where the plaintiff is aware at the time of the incident that the employee's actions are prohibited by the employer.

In *Stone* v. *Taffe* [1974], it was held:

> 'A prohibition by an employer of what his servant might or might not do was not by itself conclusive of the scope of his employment against third parties injured by the servant, but the injured person could not make the employer liable where he himself knew of the prohibition and had had the opportunity to avoid the danger of injury from the prohibited act before he exposed himself to the danger, or where the employer could prove that the prohibition was likely to be known to the injured person.'

On the facts in *Stone* v. *Taffe*, the manager (who was an employee of the brewery) failed to provide adequate lighting on the stairway. The brewery was vicariously liable for this failure on the part of the manager, who was acting within the scope of his employment. The fact that the party injured was present at the licensed premises in direct contravention of a company rule forbidding entertainment and service of alcoholic drinks to customers outside licensing hours did not render the manager beyond the scope of his employment. This prohibition contained in the company rules was not one of which the plaintiff had knowledge. Had the plaintiff colluded with the manager to breach either the licensing laws, or the manager's contractual obligations with the brewery, the brewery would not have been liable to the plaintiff in negligence. The brewery's liability was, on the facts, reduced by 50 per cent due to the plaintiff's contributory negligence.

In *Harrison* v. *Michelin Tyre Co. Ltd* [1985], Comyn J formulated a test to determine whether or not an employee was acting in the course of employment for the purpose of determining vicarious liability. 'Course of employment' cases could, he said, be broadly divided into five categories, though it would be naive to regard these as being totally exclusive: firstly, into the so-called 'vehicle' cases: see *Smith* v. *Stages* [1989], **7** below; secondly, into those that deal with 'incidents' which occurred away from the actual place of work; thirdly, into those concerned with 'incidents' which had been specifically prohibited by the employer; fourthly, into those cases where the conduct was 'of such a bizarre nature that one would not think at first sight any employer could be held liable for and yet in many cases have been'; and, fifthly, into another line of cases dealing with 'completely extraneous activities by employees which it would be hard to categorise as conceivably coming within the scope of employment'.

In *Aldred* v. *Nanconco* [1987], the employee, A, suffered an injury to her back during an incident which occurred at her place of work. She was in the washroom getting ready to leave work at the end of the day when another employee, Miss P, came in and pushed a washbasin that was known to be unsteady against the plaintiff in order to startle her. The push resulted in the rim of the basin striking the upper part of her thigh. She turned round to see what had happened and in so doing twisted her back. A based her claim for damages on two grounds. First, because the washbasin was not as reasonably safe as a reasonable employer should have made it; second because the employers were vicariously liable for the employee's action which led to the injury.

The High Court dismissed A's claim. She appealed to the Court of Appeal. In the Court of Appeal Lawton LJ and Donaldson MR took the view that the correct principle of law to be applied is set out in *Salmond and Heuston, On the Law of Torts* (18th edn) p. 437, where the learned authors write:

> 'It is clear that the master is responsible for acts actually authorised by him: for liability would exist in this case, even if the relation between the parties was merely one of agency, and not one of service at all. But a master, as opposed to the employer of an independent contractor, is liable even for acts which he has authorised that they may rightly be regarded as modes – although improper modes – of doing them. In other words, a master is responsible not merely for what he authorises his servant to do, but also for the way in which he does it. If a servant does negligently that which he was authorised to do carefully, or if he does fraudulently that which he was authorised to do honestly, or if he does mistakenly that which he was authorised to do correctly, his master will answer for that negligence, fraud or mistake. On the other hand, if the unauthorised and wrongful act of the servant is not so connected with the authorised act as to be a mode of doing it, but is an independent act, the master is not responsible: for in such a case the servant is not acting in the course of his employment, but has gone outside of it'.

On the facts of the case, Miss P was in the washroom in the course of her employment, but what she did had nothing whatsoever to do with anything she was employed to do. It was not, said Lawton LJ, an improper way of doing her job – it was something wholly outside her job. Turner J in the High Court was therefore correct in coming to the conclusion he did that the employers were not vicariously liable, though he could perhaps be criticised for not making it clear that the fact that what she was not doing for the purposes of her employer's business was merely one of the many factors to be taken into account in considering whether she was acting outside the scope of her employment.

Donaldson MR referred to the test formulated by Comyn J in *Harrison*, and said that had it been applied to the facts of the instant decision, as it was argued it should be, the plaintiff A would succeed, because Miss P was in the washroom 'in the ordinary context of her employment'. The Master of the Rolls was not sure that she would succeed. A's counsel was '. . . driven to say that arguably, on his interpretation of that test, if instead of rocking the basin she had knifed the plaintiff, that would have given rise to vicarious liability'. That he regarded as '. . . so extreme a proposition as to betray that there must be something wrong in the test if it had been correctly applied'. For a further example of conduct outside employment, *see Makanjuola* v. *Metropolitan Police Commissioner* [1992].

Another interesting decision of the Court of Appeal, reported in *The Independent*, 'Case Summaries', on 25 May 1987 is *Skenner* v. *Taff-Ely Borough Council*. A local authority which allowed the gymnastics coach employed by them at their leisure centre to bring friends and children into the gymnasium to coach them at a time when the centre was closed to the public and when he was not working, was not vicariously liable for the employee's negligence which resulted in one of his friends, the plaintiff, being seriously injured while using the equipment because although the employee was doing acts which he was employed to do, he was not acting in the course of his employment but was engaged on a private venture.

It is not every act of employees which can be said to be within the scope of their employment. Although s. 32(1) of the Race Relations Act 1977 provides that anything done in the course of employment is imputable to the employer, it should encompass the situation where employees racially harassed a fellow worker. However, in *Tower Boot Co.* v. *Jones* [1995], the Employment Appeal Tribunal found that on its facts such behaviour was outside the scope of the employment of the workers who were undertaking the harassment and that the employer was not therefore vicariously liable for their actions.

In *Racz* v. *Home Office* [1994] the House of Lords held that an official who has committed the tort of *misfeasance in office* (this calls for bad faith and / or abuse of public powers) may, depending on the facts of the case, render his employer vicariously liable for his actions.

Immunity may enable an employer to escape liability for an employee failing to protect the plaintiff from harm: *see Osman* v. *Ferguson* [1993] and *Swinney* v. *Chief Constable of Northumbria Police* [1996]. The extent to which police immunity has been utilised to have claims against the police struck out is considered in an article on police immunity in the *Solicitors Journal* (1996, vol. 140, p. 606).

TRAVELLING TO AND FROM WORK

7. *Smith* v. *Stages* [1989]

The courts have been troubled over the years by cases in which the question has arisen whether or not an employee travelling to or from his place of work is acting in the course of his employment. These difficulties were considered by the House of Lords in *Smith* v. *Stages* [1989].

In *Smith* v. *Stages* Mr Machin was employed by D.I. Co. Ltd. (the second defendants) as a peripatetic lagger; his job was to install insulation at power stations. In August 1977 he and Mr Stages (the first defendant), who was also employed as a lagger by the second defendants, were taken away from work in Staffordshire and ordered to do urgent work at Pembroke Power Station in Wales. They were to start work at Pembroke at 8.00 am on Tuesday 23 August and return to Staffordshire and report for work at 8.00 am on Wednesday 31 August. They were paid to work for an eight-hour day to cover the journey to Pembroke, and for a further eight-hour day for the return journey to Stafford-shire. They were also given the equivalent of a rail fare as travelling expenses, but there was no requirement made that they should travel by rail. Both Machin and Stages travelled to Pembroke in Stages' car, did the work, and to complete the assignment worked for an uninterrupted period of 24 hours, finishing at 8.30 am on Monday 29 August. They then decided to drive straight back to Stafford-shire without any sleep and on the way the car, driven by Stages, left the road and crashed into a brick wall. Both men were seriously injured.

Machin brought proceedings against Stages for damages and later joined the second defendants alleging that they were vicariously liable for Stages' negligence. In 1979, Machin died from unrelated causes and the action was continued by his widow and administratrix, Mrs Smith. Stages was uninsured.

The trial judge held that the accident had been caused by Stage's negligence but that the second defendants were not liable because Stages had not been 'acting in the course of his employment.' On appeal, the Court of Appeal [1988] ICR 201, reversed the decision and held that the second defendants were vicariously liable.

The second defendants appealed to the House of Lords. In the House of Lords Lord Goff opined:

'The fundamental principle is that an employee is acting in the course of his employment when he is doing what he is employed to do, to which it is sufficient for present purposes to add, or anything which is reasonably incidental to this employment . . .

'We can begin with the simple proposition that, in ordinary circumstances, when a man is travelling to or from his place of work, he is not acting in the course of his employment. So a bank clerk who commutes to the City of London every day from Sevenoaks is not acting in the course of his employment when he walks across London Bridge from the station to his bank in the City. This is because he is not employed to travel from his home to the bank. He is employed to work at the bank, his place of work, and so his duty is to arrive there in time for his working day. Nice points can arise about the precise time, or place, at which he may be held to have arrived at work; but these do not trouble us in the present case. Likewise, of course, he is not acting in the course of his employment when travelling home after his day's work is over. If, however, a man is obliged by his employer to travel to work by means of transport provided by his employer, he may be held to be acting in the course of his employment when so doing.

'These are the normal cases. There are, however, circumstances in which, when a man is travelling to (or from) a place where he is doing a job for his employer, he will be held to be acting in the course of his employment. Some of these are listed by Lord Atkin in *Blee* v. *London and North Eastern Rly Co.* [1937] 4 All ER 270 at 273, [1938] AC 126 at 131–2.

'How do we distinguish the cases in this category in which a man is acting in the course of his employment from those in which he is not? The answer is, I fear, that everything depends on the circumstances. As Sir John Donaldson MR said in *Nancollas* v. *Insurance Officer* [1985] 1 All ER 833 at 836, the authorities: 'approve an approach which requires the court to have regard to and to weigh in the balance every factor which can be said in any way to point towards or away from a finding that the claimant was in the course of his employment. In the context of the present appeals, there are a number of such factors to which we must have regard, but none is of itself decisive'.

'For example, the fact that a man is being paid by his employer in respect of the relevant period of time is often important, but cannot of itself be decisive ...

'I have it very much in mind that Mr Machin and Mr Stages were described by counsel for the employers as peripatetic laggers working at such sites as were available. This may well be an accurate description of their work. If so, their contracts of service may have provided at least an indication as to how far they would be acting in the course of their employment when changing from one power station to another.

'I turn to Mr Stages' journey back. Another ordinary working day, Tuesday 30 August, was made available for the journey, with the same pay, to enable him to return to his base in the Midlands to be ready to travel to work on the Wednesday morning. In my opinion, he was employed to make the journey back, just as he was employed to make the journey out to Pembroke. If he had chosen to go to sleep on the Monday morning and afternoon for eight hours or so, and then to drive home on the Monday evening so that he could have Tuesday free, that would not have detracted from the proposition that his journey was in the course of his employment. For this purpose, it was irrelevant that Monday was a bank holiday. Of course, it was wrong for him to succumb to the temptation of driving home on the Monday morning, just after he had completed so long a spell of work; but once again that cannot alter the fact that his journey was made in the course of his employment.'

For those reasons, Lord Goff dismissed the appeal.

Lord Lowry took a similar but distinct view:

'The paramount rule is that an employee travelling on the highway will be acting in the course of his employment if, and only if, he is at the material time going about his employer's business. One must not confuse the duty to turn up for one's work with the concept of already being 'on duty' while travelling to it.

'It is impossible to provide for every eventuality and foolish, without the benefit of argument, to make the attempt, but some prima facie propositions may be stated with reasonable confidence:

(1) An employee travelling from his ordinary residence to his regular place of work, whatever the means of transport and even if it is provided by the employer, is not on duty and is not acting in the course of his employment, but, if he is obliged by his contract of service to use the employer's transport, he will normally, in the absence of an express condition to the contrary, be regarded as acting in the course of his employment while doing so.

(2) Travelling in the employer's time between workplaces (one of which may be the regular workplace) or in the course of a peripatetic occupation, whether accompanied by goods or tools or simply in order to reach a succession of workplaces (as an inspector of gas meters might do), will be in the course of the employment.

(3) Receipt of wages (though not receipt of a travelling allowance) will indicate that the employee is travelling in the employer's time and for his benefit and is acting in

the course of his employment, and in such a case the fact that the employee may have discretion as to the mode and time of travelling will not take the journey out of the course of his employment.

(4) An employee travelling in the employer's time from his ordinary residence to a workplace other than his regular workplace or in the course of a peripatetic occupation or to the scene of an emergency (such as a fire, an accident or a mechanical breakdown of plant) will be acting in the course of his employment.

(5) A deviation from or interruption of a journey undertaken in the course of employment (unless the deviation or interruption is merely incidental to the journey) will for the time being (which may include an overnight interruption) take the employee out of the course of his employment.

(6) Return journeys are to be treated on the same footing as outward journeys.

'All the foregoing propositions are subject to any express arrangements between the employer and the employee or those representing his interests. They are not, I would add, intended to define the position of salaried employees, with regard to whom the touchstone of payment made in the employer's time is not generally significant.'

Lord Keith and Lord Griffiths agreed with Lord Lowry's speech, whilst Lord Brandon agreed with the speeches of both Lord Goff and Lord Lowry. The appeal was therefore dismissed and the second defendants held to be vicariously liable for Stages' negligence.

RES IPSA LOQUITUR

This is a rule of evidence which has the effect of reversing the burden of proof in negligence cases. The principle was first established in the case of *Scott* v. *London & St Katherine Docks Co.* [1861–73]. The plaintiff was passing under a loading bay to a warehouse when six heavy sacks of sugar fell from the loading bay on the upper floor of the warehouse onto the plaintiff, who sustained injuries. There was no clear explanation as to how this had come about. Allowing the plaintiff's claim it was *held* that: 'There must be reasonable evidence of negligence, but, where the thing is shown to be under the management of the defendant, or his servants, and the accident is such as in the ordinary course of things does not happen if those who have the management of machinery use proper care, it affords reasonable evidence, in the absence of an explanation by the defendant, that the accident arose from want of care'.

The principle was again considered by Megaw LJ in *Lloyde* v. *W. Midland Gas Board* [1971].

'It means that a plaintiff prima facie establishes negligence where: (*i*) it is not possible for him to prove precisely what was the relevant act or omission which set in train the events leading to the accident; but (*ii*) on the evidence as it stands at the relevant time it is more likely than not that the effective cause of the accident was some act or omission of the defendant or of someone for whom the defendant is responsible, which act or omission constitutes a failure to take proper care of the plaintiff's safety.'

In *Ng Chun Pui and Others* v. *Lee Chuen Tat and Another* [1988], the Privy

Council approved the above dictum. Megaw LJ and Lord Griffiths took the view that it was misleading to talk of the burden of proof shifting to the defendant in a *res ipsa loquitur* situation because the burden of proving negligence rested throughout the case with the plaintiff. An oft-cited example of the operation of *res ipsa loquitur* is the case of *Ward* v. *Tesco Stores Ltd* [1976]. In that case yoghurt was spilt on the floor of the defendants' store. The plaintiff sustained injury having slipped on the yoghurt which had been left on the floor and not mopped up by the defendants' staff. There was no explanation of how the yoghurt came to be on the floor of the shop. It was held that *res ipsa loquitur* applied and since the defendants were unable to discharge the evidential burden placed upon them by the operation of that rule, and thereby show that the accident did not occur as a result of want of care on their part, the defendants were liable in negligence to the plaintiff.

For an interesting discussion of the use of *res ipsa loquitur* as a tactical tool in litigation, see '*Res ipsa loquitur*: the defendant's friend' in the *Solicitors Journal* (1996, vol. 140, p. 824).

AN EMPLOYER'S COMMON LAW DUTY OF CARE

8. The general situation

The common law duties owed by an employer to his or her employees are primarily to be found in the tort of negligence, and in particular in the area of *employer's liability*. However, much of the common law has been superseded by the statute and the victim of an accident at work may sue for breach of the specific statutory duty imposed upon the employer or occupier of the work-place.

Not all persons who may be at the work-place are employees; sub-contractors (e.g. window cleaners, service engineers, decorators and repair men) and other lawful visitors (e.g. postman, butcher's delivery man) may also be present and could sustain injury. In the problem context it is important, therefore, to consider safety at work in a slightly broader aspect than simply the duties owed by employers to their employees. Although the law in this area stems from the law of torts it is worthy of note that the contract of employment as between the employer and the employee contains an implied term as to safety at work.

In *Smith* v. *Baker* [1891], Lord Herschell observed: 'It is quite clear that the contract between employer and employed involves on the part of the former the duty of taking reasonable care to provide appliances, and to maintain them in a proper condition, and so to carry on his operations as not to subject those employed by him to unnecessary risk. Whatever the dangers of the employment which the employed undertakes, amongst them is certainly not to be numbered the risk of the employer's negligence and the creation or enhancement of danger thereby engendered.'

Applying this principle it would seem that an employee may sue an employer for breach of an implied term of his contract of employment, namely to take reasonable care to ensure the employee's safety at work.

9. Negligence liability

At common law an employer is under a duty to take reasonable care to ensure the health and safety of his employees. This duty is derived from the general duty owed to one's neighbour as laid down by Lord Atkin in *Donoghue* v. *Stevenson* [1932]. The duty set out in *Donoghue* v. *Stevenson* is a general duty owed to those persons who one might reasonably foresee as being injured by one's actions. The scope of the duty owed covers not only employees but also other visitors to the premises; however, where the plaintiff is an employee who is injured at his employer's premises, he may consider a claim based either upon *employers' liability* or upon *occupiers' liability*, depending upon how his injury was sustained.

10. An employer's liability to employees

Whilst this tort is derived from the general tort of negligence, it gives rise to a special form of duty owed by an employer to his employees. In the nineteenth century the courts denied employees a right of action against their employers for injuries sustained at work: *see Priestly* v. *Fowler* [1835–42]. By the twentieth century, the House of Lords' decision in *Wilsons & Clyde Coal Co. Ltd* v. *English* [1937] recognised such a right of action. This duty of care is owed personally by an employer to his employees and cannot be delegated to another person, e.g. a manager. The duty is owed by the employer to each employee as an individual; this gives rise to two issues. Firstly, each individual employee therefore has a potential right of action against the employer for breach of duty. Secondly, the duty owed will vary according to the individual nature of each employee. If an employee is particularly young or inexperienced, or he is disabled or mentally sub-normal in some way, the standard of care required of the employer to fulfil his duty towards that particular employee may be higher than that required in relation to a 'normal' employee.

In *Paris* v. *Stepney Borough Council* [1951], the plaintiff, Mr Paris, was employed by the defendant as a garage hand. His job involved general manual work in preparing vehicles for service, dismantling, etc. It was not customary to provide garage hands with goggles to wear in the course of their work. However, Mr Paris was blind in one eye. In the course of his work he hit a bolt on the underside of a vehicle causing a metal splinter to fly into his good eye, with the disastrous consequence that he became totally blind. Mr Paris alleged that his employer had breached the duty of care owed to him by failing to provide him with goggles. It was held that the defendants had breached their duty of care towards Mr Paris. Lord Simmonds stated: 'I will say at once that I do not dissent from the view that an employer owes a particular duty of care to each of his employees. His liability in tort arises from his failure to take reasonable care in regard to the particular employee and it is clear that, if so, all the circumstances relevant to the employee must be taken into consideration.'

The fact that the duty is a personal one owed by the employer to each individual employee raises two further practical points. An employer who employs a person whom he knows to be illiterate will owe that person a higher duty. A mere written notice will not be sufficient to communicate safety procedures, etc.; the employer will have to take further steps. Similarly, where the employee does not have a good command of English, e.g. a non-English speaking immigrant labourer, the duty owed to such a person will be higher than that owed to other employees who have a full command of the English language. The only case in this area is *James* v. *Hepworth & Grandage Ltd* [1967] where the employee was illiterate and unable to read the employer's notice. It was held, however, that the employer had done sufficient to bring the need for safety clothing to his attention.

It is of vital importance that the person to whom the duty is owed is an employee of the defendant. If the plaintiff is not an employee no duty is owed and the defendant will have a complete answer to the plaintiffs claim.

11. The scope of the employer's duty

The employer owes a duty to take such precautions for the safety of his or her employees as would be taken by a reasonably prudent employer in the same circumstances. Therefore, this is not an absolute duty; rather it is one tempered by reasonable foreseeability of injury to the employee. If, therefore, an employer does not know of the danger, and could not reasonably be expected to know of it in the light of current knowledge, or the employer did not foresee a potential hazard and could not reasonably be expected to foresee it, the employer will not be liable to the employee. However, if a danger is appreciated the employer must take those steps which all reasonably prudent employers would take to protect the employee from the danger: *see Latimer* v. *AEC Ltd* [1953]. Such a duty is non-delegable: *see McDermid* v. *Nash Dredging* [1987] and *Square D. Ltd* v. *Cook* [1992].

The duty owed by an employer to his employees is said to be threefold, though each element can be said to form part of a single more general duty to take reasonable care of the health and safety of the employee.

11(i). Equipment

There is a duty to provide employees with safe plant, machinery and tools with which to carry out their work. The failure of an employer to provide any equipment, or the provision of inadequate or defective equipment, will constitute a breach of his duty towards his employees. Hence, if a cook is burned in the hotel kitchen when a defective chip fryer malfunctions, the cook has a potential right of action against his employer, the proprietor of the hotel, under this principle. However, if an employer purchases equipment from a reputable supplier, and has no knowledge of any defect in it, he will have done sufficient to discharge the duty owed to his employees: *see Davie* v. *New Merton Board Mills Ltd* [1959]. Therefore, if, in the example cited above, the hotel proprietor has been given no reason to suspect that the fryer was in any way defective, then he will have done sufficient to discharge the duty of care which he owes to the cook.

The employee does, however, have a remedy against the employer by virtue of the Employers' Liability (Defective Equipment) Act 1969, which reverses *Davie* v. *New Merton Board Mills*.

Section 1(1) of the 1969 Act states:

'Where . . . (a) an employee suffers personal injury in the course of his employment in consequence of a defect in *equipment* provided by his employer for the purposes of the employer's business; and (b) the defect is attributable wholly or partly to the fault of a third party (whether identified or not), the injury shall be deemed to be also attributable to negligence on the part of the employer (whether or not he is liable in respect of the injury apart from this subsection), but without prejudice to the law relating to contributory negligence and to any remedy by way of contribution or in contract or otherwise which is available to the employer in respect of the injury.'

Therefore in circumstances such as those in the above example, the injured employee would sue the employer for his 'deemed' negligence, and the employer would attempt to recover the amount of damages he has paid out to the employee from the third party who was truly at fault.

In *Coltman* v. *Bibby Tankers Ltd* [1988] the House of Lords held that the word 'equipment' in s. 1(1) of the Act includes a ship provided by the employers for the purposes of business. The case arose from the sinking of the *Derbyshire* with all hands off the coast of Japan in 1980. It was alleged that due to the manufacturer's negligence the ship was defectively constructed and designed rendering it unseaworthy and that these were defects in 'equipment' deemed under the Act to be attributable to the negligence of employers. It was held that 'equipment' covers all forms of defective plant with which an employee is compelled to work. In *Knowles* v. *Liverpool City Council* [1993] 'equipment' was held to cover a defective flagstone which broke whilst being handled by the employee.

11(ii). System of work

There is a duty to provide a safe system of work for each employee. The employer is responsible for the layout of the work-place, the training and supervision of staff and the methods of working adopted. The employer's responsibilities also cover the provision of protective clothing and instructions for their use where necessary. Whether by taking the precautions which the particular employer has taken he or she has established a safe system of work is a question of fact in each case. How much must be done by the employer to establish a safe system of work will depend upon the risk of injury involved and the likely gravity of the injury which may be sustained.

In *McDermid* v. *Nash Dredging and Reclamation Co. Ltd* [1987], the House of Lords had an opportunity to consider the 'safe system of work doctrine'. The facts of the case were that Mr McDermid (P) was employed by the defendants as a deck hand. In the course of his employment he worked on board a tug, the *Ina*, owned by a Dutch company, Stevin Baggeren BV, and under the control of a Dutch captain, Captain Sas. P's work included untying ropes mooring the *Ina* fore and aft to a dredger. The system used by the captain was that when P untied the ropes and it was safe to move the tug, P would give a double knock on the wheelhouse. At the time in question P was under orders to untie so that the *Ina* could go astern. He had safely untied the aft rope and stowed it inboard the *Ina*, but was still in the course of untying the forward rope when the captain, without waiting for P's signal and without giving any warning, put the tug hard astern. As a result, the rope snaked around P's leg, pulling him into the water and causing him injuries which involved the amputation of his leg. Damages were assessed at £178,450.05 by Staughton J, to whom the case had been remitted for this purpose by the Court of Appeal.

This case raised important questions concerning the existence, in the particular circumstances, of a safe system of work and whether or not the employer's prime duty to ensure that there was such a safe system was one which was delegable. This latter issue raises questions of vicarious liability and the complementary matter of whether or not the plaintiff's employers were vicariously or personally liable for the negligence of another of the actors. The third issue concerned the vexed question of limitation of liability consequent upon the construction of the Merchant Shipping Act 1894 and the Merchant Shipping (Liability of Shipowners and Others) Act 1958.

P's claim against the defendants alleged, *inter alia*, negligence. The High Court held that P's injuries had been caused by the captain's negligence, and that the defendants were vicariously liable for that negligence because, following e.g. *Wilsons and Clyde Coal Co. Ltd* v. *English* [1937], that duty was non-delegable. Nonetheless, the High Court then went on to find that the system of work provided for P was not unsafe. The task was, said Staughton J, '. . . a simple one and well within his capabilities. Given due care and attention on the part of himself and Captain Sas, there was nothing unsafe about it'. P therefore succeeded on the ground that the defendants were vicariously liable for the captain's negligence, but failed on the second ground – the failure of the defendants to provide a safe system of work.

The defendants appealed to the Court of Appeal. The Court of Appeal dismissed the defendants' appeal on the liability question, but allowed the cross-appeal on the limitation on damages point under the Merchant Shipping Acts. In the course of the leading judgment Neill LJ analysed the legal principles governing the pertinent question of when an employer may be held liable for the acts or omissions of a person not their servant. Neither case law nor other authorities, he said, were able to suggest any general principle providing any sure guide to the limits of vicarious liability in tort.

Upon a further appeal to the House of Lords, Lord Brandon took the view that the real question was whether the defendants were in breach of the duty of care which they owed to P in not devising and operating a safe system of work for him. Lord Brandon considered the system of work which was operated was unsafe. He opined:

'A statement of the relevant principle of law can be divided into three parts. First, an employer owes to his employee a duty to exercise reasonable care to ensure that the system of work provided for him is a safe one. Secondly, the provision of a safe system of work has two aspects: (a) the devising of such a system and (b) the operation of it. Thirdly, the duty concerned has been described alternatively as either personal or non-delegable. The meaning of these expressions is not self-evident and needs explaining. The essential characteristic of the duty is that, if it is not performed, it is no defence for the employer to show that he delegated its performance to a person, whether his servant or not his servant, whom he reasonably believed to be competent to perform it. Despite such delegation the employer is liable for non-performance of the duty.'

Walker v. *Northumberland County Council* [1995] is a landmark decision for office-based workers. Earlier cases on 'safe system' were confined to physical injury at the work-place primarily in factory premises, building sites and other 'high risk' settings. The harm in *Walker* was stress-induced psychological injury, a different sort of harm from personal injury caused by an incident at work, e.g. a scalding with boiling liquid, a burn, a broken limb. The *Walker* decision turns on the knowledge on the part of the employer of the risk of psychological injury to Mr. Walker, by reason of his having previously suffered stress-related illness caused by his work. The 'safe system' should have eliminated or prevented the known risk occurring. It was within the power of the employer to transfer the plaintiff to another job, or provide additional support and assistance as he had requested and been promised.

The impact of this decision is not entirely clear; it may be wide-ranging, more likely it will be confined in its scope by the fact that potential plaintiffs bringing claims of stress-induced injury at the work will need to establish that this specific risk was known to the employer (as it was in *Walker*). It may also prove difficult for plaintiff's to show that the psychological harm was caused entirely by stress at work; it may well be that there are other contributing factors, e.g. stress from financial problems, marital discord, medical conditions, etc..

As outlined in Chapter 1, two areas of tortious liability may often arise from one factual situation. In *Ferguson* v. *Welsh and Others* [1987], the issues of occupiers' liability and the duty owed by an employer to his employee arose. A local authority which engaged the services of an independent contractor to demolish a building was held not liable to a workman (employed by operators whom the contractor had allowed on the site) who was injured as a result of the adoption by those operators of an unsafe system of work. Nor were the local authority, as occupiers of the premises, liable under s. 2 of the Occupiers' Liability Act 1957.

11(iii). Staff

An employer is under a duty to provide a reasonably competent staff with whom the employee will be required to work. If an employer engages an incompetent employee whose actions thereafter cause an injury to another employee, the employer will be liable to the injured employee for failing to take reasonable care in the selection of the employee's colleagues. In *Hudson* v. *Ridge Manufacturing Co. Ltd* [1957], the employer was held liable where a fellow employee injured the plaintiff whilst carrying out a practical joke. In such circumstances, and after due warning, the employer should dispense with the services of a practical joker who proved to be a menace to himself and to others to prevent injury being caused to others. The employer should, therefore, at the time of appointing staff be mindful as to whether the employee's lack of experience, personality, etc. will expose other employees to danger and create a risk of injury. Hence, the employer should always ensure that where inexperienced staff are allocated work which could give rise to danger, either to the employee or to others, the employee is given proper training and is adequately supervised. An employer will therefore be liable for the acts of an employee, which are done in the course of his employment and which cause injury to another employee.

12. Limitations upon the employer's liability

A primary limitation upon the liability of an employer towards his employees is that the employer is only required to do that which *is reasonably practicable* to ensure the safety of the employee. This principle can be most clearly seen in the case of *Latimer* v. *AEC Ltd* [1953]. In that case the employers had done all that was practicable, save to shut down the premises and exclude the workforce. The House of Lords held that the employers were not liable for the plaintiff's injuries. Just what is required of an employer to satisfy the standard of care is a question of degree, to be decided according to the facts of each particular case. Hence employers may deny negligence on their part simply by establishing that they took those steps which a reasonably prudent employer would take in the circumstances: e.g. *Brown* v. *Rolls Royce Ltd* [1960]. Equally, employers may argue that the actions which they took were not the cause of the employee's injury, and therefore they are not liable. If the employee has contributed by his actions to the injuries which he has sustained, the employer may have a defence of contributory negligence based on the Law Reform (Contributory Negligence) Act 1945. If the employee is the sole cause of his own injuries, the employer will have a complete defence to the employee's action under the principle of *volenti non fit injuria*. This may, however, be extremely difficult to establish.

The employee will be required in each case to prove that the injury was due to the negligence of the employer. In other words employees must establish, firstly that the employer owed them a duty of care, secondly that the employer acted in breach of that duty, and thirdly that as a result of that negligence they suffered injury. A recent case example illustrating how far the duty of care of an employer extends is *Hewett* v. *Alf Brown's Transport Ltd* [1992]. In that case, the plaintiff's husband was employed as a lorry driver carrying loads of lead oxide waste. The plaintiff banged the dust from his overalls and washed them each day. She became ill and was found to have lead poisoning. She brought an action against her husband's employers for personal injury on the grounds of negligence and breach of statutory duty under the Control of Lead at Work Regulations 1980. The Court of Appeal held that, although the illness was directly attributable to exposure to lead, no liability arose. During the course of his employment Mr. Hewett's exposure to lead oxide dust had been 'insignificant' within the terms of the 1980 regulations (reflecting the employer's duty of care). If the employer owed no duty of care to the employee none could arise with respect to the plaintiff. Had the husband's exposure been 'significant' there was every likelihood that the employer would have owed the plaintiff a duty of care.

There are a number of rules of evidence which help employees to prove their cases. For instance, to ensure that the full facts are available to the employees so that they can more easily establish their cases the court may order the disclosure of documents in the employer's possession or an inspection of the premises. A most useful rule of evidence to the employee in establishing his case is *res ipsa loquitur* (*see* p. 101).

STATUTORY DUTIES

Parliament has laid down a number of duties which an employer must adhere to with regard to the safety of work premises, e.g. Factories Act 1961, and Health and Safety at Work etc. Act 1974: *see* e.g. *R.* v. *Associated Octel Ltd* [1994] (CA). Whilst these are primarily concerned with the enforcement of appropriate safety standards through the imposition of criminal sanction, such statutes may also give rise to civil liability. Full guidance on these issues is given in Chapter 10, breach of statutory duty, to which you should refer.

Progress test 6

1. Who is an employee? What is the significance of determining whether a person is or is not an employee?

2. Explain the circumstances in which an employer may be vicariously liable for the negligence of his employees.

3. Of what significance is the House of Lords decision in *Smith* v. *Stages* [1989]?

4. What is the utility of *res ipsa loquitur*? Where may it apply?

5. Outline the duty owed by an employer to his employees.

6. Of what significance is the decision in *Walker* v. *Northumberland County Council* [1995]?

7. What limitations are there upon the scope of an employer's liability to his employees?

7

BUSINESS AND ECONOMIC TORTS

BUSINESS AND ECONOMIC TORTS IN THE CONTEXT OF TORTS IN GENERAL

We have seen from Chapters 2–4 that the basic requirement for negligence liability is that A by his wrongful act should cause loss to B. A's wrongful act may be deliberate or negligent. B's loss may amount to physical injury, or alternatively, injury to his economic or business interests. If the circumstances were appropriate B might claim that physical injury had resulted in economic loss.

There are, therefore, a number of permutations which may arise. We are interested in this chapter in a situation where A's act is deliberate, and B's loss is of an economic nature. This arises most commonly where A's economic or business activities cause damage to B's economic or business interests. It is the task of the law to decide which activities should be deemed wrongful, and therefore tortious, and which amount to the justifiable pursuit of self-interest in the business world. This decision may turn on a number of factors, for example the number of parties involved in the activities; whether they result, and are calculated to result, in the breach of legally enforceable agreements; or the decision may turn on the intimidatory tactics inherent in the activities. The role of the law in this area is to mark out limits of acceptable competition and provide suitable remedies for unacceptable behaviour.

1. The requirement of an unlawful act

In order to succeed in a tort action which alleges damage to economic or business interest, the plaintiff will have to show that his loss or damage has been caused by an unlawful or wrongful act on the part of the defendant. In the leading case, *Allen v. Flood* [1898], Allen, a trade union official, told the employers that unless certain shipwrights were dismissed other employees who were employed on a daily basis would stop work. The shipwrights, Flood and Taylor, were lawfully dismissed and took action against Allen. The House of Lords held that in the absence of any unlawful act by Allen, the action must fail. *Malice* towards those ultimately affected did *not* make what was essentially a lawful act, unlawful.

Similarly, in *Mogul SS Co. Ltd* v. *McGregor Gow and Co.* [1892], the Court of Appeal was not prepared to hold 'unfair' methods of competition, calculated to drive the plaintiffs out of business, to be unlawful. The position was concisely summarised by Lord Atkin in *Ware and De Freville Ltd* v. *Motor Trade Association* [1921], when he said: 'The true question is, was the power of the plaintiff to carry on his trade . . . interrupted by an act which the law deems wrongful?'

2. What is a wrongful act?

How do we decide what is wrongful? The difficulty in answering this question derives primarily from the type of relations which this area of the law seeks to regulate. Business is by its nature productive of competition and conflict. Indeed we often hear the metaphor 'cut throat' applied to describe the activities of industry and commerce. The courts, in the last 150 years or so, have defined certain circumstances in which individuals and bodies are to be taken to have acted wrongfully, by going further than is acceptable in the furthering of their interests. These may be categorised as conspiracy, inducement to breach of contract, unlawful interference with business, intimidation, injurious falsehood, and passing off, and are considered below.

CONSPIRACY

3. The legal nature of conspiracy

In *Quinn* v. *Leathem* [1901], it was held that the doing of an act which in itself is lawful will become unlawful if done by two or more parties together and if intending to and actually causing damage to someone else. This is the tort of *conspiracy*. The facts of the case were: members of a trade union were in dispute with their employer, a butcher, over his employment of non-union labour. In order to pressurise the employer into respecting their desired 'closed shop' arrangement, the union threatened industrial action against one of his customers. They thereby successfully compelled him to sever dealings with the butcher. On the principle already established in *Allen* v. *Flood* and *Mogul SS Co. Ltd* v. *McGregor Gow and Co.* the result contrived at (the discontinuance of a trading contract between one of these parties and his employer) was quite lawful, whether any of these parties suffered disadvantage or not. What made the action unlawful was the fact that this result was achieved by two parties, i.e. it was *conspired at*.

Why should an act which causes economic loss to A but is not actionable at his suit if done by B alone become actionable because B did it pursuant to an agreement between B and C? This question, posed by Lord Diplock in the House of Lords in *Lonrho Ltd* v. *Shell Petroleum Co. Ltd* [1981], can be answered by referring back to *Mogul SS Co. Ltd* v. *McGregor Gow and Co.* [1892] where Bowen LJ took the view that: 'a combination may make oppressive or dangerous that which if proceeded only from a single person would be otherwise, and the very fact of the combination may show that the object is to do harm, and not to exercise one's own just rights'. This anomalous approach taken in the tort of civil conspiracy to injure appears now to be too well established to be discarded – *see* Lord Diplock's speech in *Lonrho Ltd* v. *Shell Petroleum*.

4. Legitimate interests as a defence

In *Crofter Hand Woven Harris Tweed Co. Ltd* v. *Veitch* [1942], it was held that there could be a defence to the tort of conspiracy if the purpose of the two or more parties was to further a *legitimate interest* – in that case, the protection of the legitimate interests of the conspirators from competition. The further importance of this case was that the protection of a 'closed shop' agreement was seen as legitimate, where it was not seen as such in *Quinn* v. *Leathem*. Other legitimate interests include limiting competition, increasing profits, and raising wages: *see Crofter Hand Woven Harris Tweed Co. Ltd* v. *Veitch*. Non-financial interests are also capable of providing a justification. In *Scala Ballroom (Wolverhampton) Ltd* v. *Ratcliffe* [1958] the defendant organised a boycott of a dance hall operating a colour bar. It was held that the opposition of racism was a legitimate interest.

It was stated in the *Crofter* case that even if the damage caused in the pursuit of a legitimate interest was disproportionately severe, it did not necessarily make the conspirators liable. However, disproportionate damage may clearly cast doubt on the genuineness of the claim that legitimate self-interest is the only motive. Action is not legitimate if it simply constitutes a vindictive show of strength, *see Huntley* v. *Thornton* [1957], or an unnecessary continuation of a boycott after a trade dispute has ended, *see also Hutchinson* v. *Aitchison* (1970).

5. Mixed motives

Where the motives of the parties are mixed, one looks to the predominant motive. If each individual has a different motive, as long as the predominant motive of each person is legitimate, they are all protected. Should one of those involved have a predominantly malevolent motive, he will be liable, if damage results. If his purpose is known to the others, who assist in its attainment, they will also lose protection.

6. Conspiring to commit an unlawful act

Until the case of *Lonrho Ltd* v. *Shell Petroleum Co. Ltd* [1981], it was considered that legitimate self-interest could not protect itself. However in this case it was held that the defence could succeed where the defendants had caused damage to the plaintiffs by evading a government oil embargo, and prolonging sanctions against South Africa. However it is thought that the defence could not be used in more serious cases, where the unlawful means is constituted by a breach of contract or a criminal or tortious act. In any case where unlawful means are employed, there will be alternative heads of liability for the plaintiff to claim under, e.g. Inducement to breach of contract, and Unlawful interference with business.

In *Metall und Rohstoff AG* v. *Donaldson Lufkin & Jenrette Inc.* [1989] the Court of Appeal sought to resolve conflicting views as to the scope of unlawful means to conspiracy. The Court of Appeal did so by basing their decision upon the predominant purpose of the defendant, i.e. whether or not it was the defendant's purpose to cause injury to the plaintiff's interests. This decision may be contrasted with *Derby & Co.* v. *Weldon (No. 3)* [1989].

In *Lonrho plc* v. *Fayed* [1989](CA), [1991](HL) the House of Lords explained its previous decision in *Lonrho Ltd* v. *Shell Petroleum Co. Ltd* [1981] and overruled in part the Court of Appeal's decision in *Metall und Rohstoff AG* v. *Donaldson Lufkin & Jenrette Inc.* [1989]. The facts in *Lonrho plc* v. *Fayed* were that following the Secretary of State's reference of the plaintiff's proposed takeover of a public company to the Monopolies and Mergers Commission and the commission's subsequent report, the plaintiff gave an undertaking to the Secretary of State not to acquire more than 30 per cent of the company's equity. While that undertaking was still in effect, thereby effectively blocking the plaintiff's proposed acquisition of the target company, the fourth defendant, a company (H. Ltd) controlled by the first three defendants, acquired most of the plaintiff's shares in the target company with the intention of acquiring a controlling interest, which in turn gave rise to a new takeover situation, which was not, however, referred by the Secretary of State to the commission. H. Ltd then made a bid for the company while the plaintiff was still subject to its undertaking and acquired more than 50 per cent of the shares in the company. A few days later the plaintiff was released from its undertaking.

The plaintiff brought an action against the first four defendants, the merchant bankers who had advised them on the takeover and a director of the bankers, alleging that the Secretary of State had been induced not to refer H. Ltd's takeover of the company to the commission by false and fraudulent misrepresentations made to him by the first four defendants about themselves, their commercial background and the source of their finance for the acquisition. The plaintiff alleged that the intention was both to benefit the first three defendants and H. Ltd by furthering their interest in the takeover of the target company and to injure the plaintiff by preventing it from acquiring that company, and that the plaintiff had lost the opportunity to acquire the target company without competition from the first three defendants and H. Ltd and had thereby suffered damage. The plaintiff claimed that those facts gave rise to, *inter alia*, the torts of wrongful interference with the plaintiffs trade or business and conspiracy to injure.

On the defendants' application, the judge struck out the claim as disclosing no reasonable cause of action. The plaintiff appealed to the Court of Appeal, which allowed its appeal in relation to the cause of action founded on the tort of unlawful interference with trade or business but it was accepted by the plaintiff that the court was bound by a previous decision to hold that, because the statement of claim had not alleged that the predominant purpose of the alleged conspiracy was to injure the plaintiff, the pleaded cause of action in conspiracy could not succeed. The defendants appealed against the reinstatement of the cause of action founded on unlawful interference with trade or business, while the plaintiff cross-appealed on the conspiracy issue.

113

The House of Lords held that the tort of conspiracy to injure could be established either by showing that an intention to injure the plaintiff in his trade or business was the predominant purpose of the conspirators, even though the means used to inflict damage on the plaintiff were lawful and would not have been actionable if done by an individual, or by showing that unlawful means were used. But when the conspirators intentionally injured the plaintiff and used unlawful means to do so, it was no defence for them to show that their primary or predominant purpose had been to further or protect some legitimate interest of their own: it was sufficient to make their action tortious that they had used unlawful means. It followed that although the plaintiff had not pleaded that the defendants' intention to cause injury to the plaintiff was the predominant purpose of their alleged unlawful action that was not a ground for striking out the cause of action in conspiracy.

Furthermore, since the cause of action as pleaded was founded upon unlawful interference with trade or business and the cause of action in conspiracy stood or fell together with it, it would be inappropriate to strike out the statement of claim and the case should therefore proceed to trial. The appeal was therefore dismissed and the cross-appeal allowed.

INDUCEMENT TO BREACH OF CONTRACT

7. Definition

This tort consists in A, intentionally and without justification, inducing or procuring B to breach his contract with C, thereby causing loss to C. In *Lumley* v. *Gye* (1853), a famous opera singer was contracted to sing exclusively for the plaintiff. The defendant persuaded her to break her contract with the plaintiff and perform in his hall instead. The defendant was held to have committed the tort of inducement to breach of contract.

8. Knowledge and intention

No malice or malevolent motive is necessary to constitute this tort. All that is required is the knowing violation of a legal right, i.e. the right to expect performance of contractual obligations: *see* Lord McNaughten in *Quinn* v. *Leathem*. So for the plaintiff to succeed, the defendant must *know* of the contract (or turn a convenient blind eye to it) and *intend* to breach it: *see Emerald Construction Co. Ltd* v. *Lowthian* [1966]. If A asks B to come and work for him without knowing that he works for someone else, then unless there were circumstances which should have put him to enquiry, he cannot be said to have induced a breach of contract. Even if he does know that he works for someone else, A may believe, with justification, that B will give the requisite notice – most employers will specifically ask the period of notice required on an application form.

It will not always be a sufficient defence to claim a lack of *actual* knowledge of the contract, and consequently an absence of any intention to breach it. The courts are prepared to construe the presence of knowledge, and consequent intention to breach the contract where any reasonable person would see this as being the inevitable result of their actions: *see White* v. *Riley* [1921]. For instance if one knows the way in which business is conducted in a particular trade or profession, one cannot conveniently fail to realise that a particular action will almost certainly result in a breach of contract: *see McMahon (James) Ltd* v. *Dunne* [1965].

9. Types of contract covered

The tort covers inducing a breach of a contract which involves an ongoing course of dealing, as well as contracts to do a particular act: *see National Phonograph Co. Ltd* v. *Edison-Bell Phonographic Co. Ltd* (1908), and also covers contracts other than contract of service. In *Temperton* v. *Russell* [1893] the defendant trade union officials induced the breach of a contract for the sale of building materials, by threatening the buyer with industrial action if he went ahead with the purchase. This case made it clear that although the subject matter of *Lumley* v. *Gye* was a contract of service, the principle was wider. It is not, however, a tort to induce a person not to enter into a contract: *see* Lord Herschell's remarks in *Allen* v. *Flood*. This is simply a restatement of the *Allen* v. *Flood* policy discussed earlier, that competition, however ruthless, does not become unlawful unless it violates a legal right (e.g. induces the breach of a contract), or is conspired at: *see Quinn* v. *Leathem.*

10. Damage

For a claim to succeed, damage to the plaintiff must result from the breach of contract. In *Jones Brothers (Hunstanton) Ltd* v. *Stevens* [1955], the defendant continued to employ a servant, despite knowing that by working for him he had broken his contract of service with the plaintiff. It was held that as the servant would not have resumed his employment with the plaintiff, the latter had suffered no damage.

One of the leading cases in this area, *Thomson (D.C.) & Co. Ltd* v. *Deakin* [1952], has established that the breach induced need not be material to give rise to an action. Indeed, as shown below, mere *interference* with contractual relations, without an actual breach occurring, may be sufficient to ground an action.

11. Void, voidable and unenforceable contracts

It is not a tort to induce a *breach* of a void contract (e.g. a contract promoting sexual immorality, prejudicial to the administration of justice, or in restraint of trade) as in theory there is no contract to be broken. It is probably not tortious either to induce the breach of an unenforceable contract, for example a contract covered by the Law of Property Act 1925 s. 40: *Smith* v. *Morrison* [1974]. The position of voidable contracts is less certain. There have been suggestions that if a party has the *right* to set aside a contract, then it has not been broken, and consequently a breach has not been induced: *see McManus* v. *Bowes* [1938]. The

115

contrary argument runs that simply because there is no liability between A and B in the circumstances, it does not mean that C will not be liable for his interference. *See Salmond and Heuston, On The Law of Torts*, p. 406; *Merkur Island Shipping Corp.* v. *Laughton* [1983]; and *Daily Mirror Newspapers Ltd* v. *Gardner* [1968]. The whole question of liability for *interference* as opposed to *inducement* of actual breach is discussed below, *see* Unlawful interference with business, p. 118.

12. The scope of inducement to breach of contract

The tort is generally recognised as being capable of arising in the following ways:

(a) *Direct persuasion of one of the contracting parties to breach his contract.* Examples would be *Lumley* v. *Gye* (*see* 7), or where a trade union, by means of picketing or otherwise, successfully persuades a trader to break a contract of supply with another person, or persuades employees to break their contract of employment. (The detailed nature of trade union immunities from liability in such circumstances is beyond the scope of this book.)

(b) *Physical interference in the contract.* This may arise in two ways:

(*i*) Where A makes it impossible for B to fulfil his contract with C by, for example, physically restraining him, or breaking his tools or machinery, A would be liable to B for assault or intimidation. To be liable to C for inducing the breach of contract, he must also have had knowledge of the contract, and the intention to break it (*see* 8).

(*ii*) Where A interferes in a contract without the knowledge of either of the contracting parties, B and C (and almost certainly contrary to their wishes). In *GWK Ltd* v. *Dunlop Rubber Co. Ltd* (1926), the plaintiff had a contract with a car manufacturer binding them to use his tyres on their cars. Dunlop, a rival tyre manufacturer, removed the plaintiff's tyres from a display car and replaced them with their own. Dunlop was liable to GWK for inducing a breach of contract. Again the requisite knowledge and intention is required, although it is fairly readily implied in the case of such blatant action.

(c) *Indirect inducement.* This occurs where A does not exert the pressure directly on B to break his contract with C. Rather, he secures his aim by inducing a breach of another contract, which necessarily results in the breach of the contract between B and C. A typical scenario is where A (the trade union) induces its members to break their contract with B so that B will not be able to fulfil his contract with C (e.g. by not being able to supply the goods he is contracted to supply to C). In addition to the normal requirement that A must have knowledge of, and the intention to break, the contract between B and C, the means by which the breach of the principal contract is induced must be *unlawful*. This requirement will normally be satisfied where the means involves the breaking of employment contracts. It is not satisfied simply by A (the trade union) saying to its members 'Black C's goods'. The members may well react perfectly lawfully, i.e. they may find a way of following the instructions without breaking their contracts of employment, or their employer B may not insist on their dealing with C's goods. In such a case they would not have broken their employment contracts, and the inducement would not be occasioned by unlawful means. In *Thomson (D.C.) & Co. Ltd* v. *Deakin* [1952], a trade union was in dispute with a printer. They approached the printer's suppliers of paper and told them that their employees (trade union members) would object to delivering paper to the printers. The paper suppliers ceased deliveries and did not require their employees to make any deliveries. Consequently the employees had not broken their employment contracts, the inducement had not been brought about by unlawful means, and the trade union was not liable.

In *Stratford (J.T.) and Son Ltd* v. *Lindley* [1965], the union was in dispute with the plaintiffs. They persuaded their members, who worked for the customers of the plaintiffs, not to return hired barges to the plaintiffs. This refusal to return the barges was a breach of their employment contracts (an unlawful act), which resulted in a breach of the hire contract between their employer and the plaintiffs. The plaintiffs were therefore able successfully to sue the trade union for indirectly inducing a breach of contract of hire between themselves and one of their customers.

For other examples *see Falconer* v. *ASLEF* [1986]; *News Group Newspapers* v. *SOGAT '82* [1987] and *Middlebrook Mushrooms Ltd.* v. *TGWU* [1993].

(d) *Dealings inconsistent with an existing contract.* This occurs where A has dealings with B which he knows are at odds with a contract which B has with C, e.g. by purchasing a car from B in the knowledge that the purchase breaches a contractual agreement disallowing the sale of new cars: *see BMTA* v. *Salvadori* [1949]. These actions probably also amount to the tort of conspiracy committed by A and B.

13. Justification as a defence

The nature and extent of this defence is very unclear. In *Glamorgan Coal Co.* v. *South Wales Miners' Federation* [1903], Romer LJ said that the issue turned on the circumstances of each case and would include the type of contract; the reason for the breach; the means adopted; the relationship of the parties; and the aim contrived at. The pursuit of a particularly *laudable* aim will not guarantee a defence because it is very unlikely (particularly in industrial relations) that there would be agreement as to what is laudable.

There have only been few cases where justification has succeeded as a defence. In *Brimelow* v. *Casson* [1924], a theatrical company had paid their chorus girls such low wages that they were forced into prostitution. This was held to justify the inducement of a breach of the girls' contracts of employment. In *Church of Scientology* v. *Kaufman* [1973], inducement to breach of contract was held to be justified to expose the activities of a religious sect. In the *South Wales Miners'* case it was held that inducement to breach of contract could not be justified by the claim that an organisation (here a trade union, but presumably also including a business organisation) was duty bound to protect its members' interests. This provides an interesting contrast with the decision discussed above in the *Crofter Hand Woven Tweed* case, to the effect that trade union objects are legitimate.

The Court of Appeal in *Edwin Hill (a firm)* v. *First National Finance Corporation plc* [1988] reviewed the authorities on justification when applying them to the position of a mortgagee exercising his power of sale in possession.

UNLAWFUL INTERFERENCE WITH BUSINESS, AND INTIMIDATION

14. Unlawful interference

In *Torquay Hotel Co. Ltd* v. *Cousins* [1969], the defendants sought to disrupt fuel supplies to the plaintiff's hotel. The contract for the supply of fuel contained a *force majeure* clause which protected the supplier from liability for breach of contract. However it was held that it was a tort to interfere unlawfully with contractual performance, even in circumstances where a breach is not actually induced.

The Court of Appeal's decision in this case was confirmed by the House of Lords in *Merkur Island Shipping Corp.* v. *Laughton* [1983]. The interference in question need not relate to an actual contract for liability to arise. Other interferences with business relations have been held to suffice. In *Prudential Assurance Co. Ltd* v. *Lorenz* [1971], interference with the equitable duty of an insurance agent to account to his principal for money in his possession was held to be an instance of this tort.

Reference should also be made to the trilogy of leading decisions with regard to unlawful interference with another's business, namely: *Hadmor Productions Ltd* v. *Hamilton* [1982](HL), *Lonrho plc* v. *Fayed* [1991](HL), and *Associated British Ports* v. *TGWU* [1989](CA).

15. Intimidation

This tort may take two forms:

(a) *Intimidation of the plaintiff in order to influence his behaviour*. This would occur where A, by threatening an illegal act against B, compels him to do something which causes him loss. Examples would include a threat of violence to obtain money, or to stop trading; or a threat that money owed will not be paid unless a lower amount is accepted: *see D. and C. Builders* v. *Rees* [1966]. In keeping with the principle in *Allen* v. *Flood* (*see* Inducement to breach of contract, p. 114), the threat must be to do something unlawful.

(b) *Intimidation of other parties causing injury to the plaintiff*. The essence of liability is that by means of the same type of illegal threat discussed in **(a)**, A compels B to do an act which he is entitled to do, but which damages C. In the leading case of *Rookes* v. *Barnard* [1964], the defendants (the trade union) threatened BOAC that their members would strike (an unlawful breach of their employment contracts), if the company did not dismiss the plaintiff, a non-union member. He was properly dismissed with full notice *lawfully*, but was able successfully to sue the union representatives who had *unlawfully* intimidated his employers into this lawful action. The real significance of the case was that it proceeded on the assumption that a threat to break a contract could amount to unlawful means for the purpose of this tort.

For a more recent case, involving threats of violence, *see Godwin* v. *Uzolgwe* (1993).

INJURIOUS FALSEHOOD

This tort arises where a false statement is made maliciously by A about B's person, property or goods, with the result that other people are deceived and damage is caused to B. Injurious falsehood may be classified into three categories: slander of title; slander of goods; and false statements which damage the plaintiff's trade or business.

16. Slander of title and goods

These two types of injurious falsehood are appropriately conjoined because they are of common origin. The action originally lay for damage to the plaintiff arising from aspersions cast upon his title to land. It was later extended to cover similar cases involving:

(a) The plaintiff's personal and incorporeal property (e.g. patents and copyrights).

(b) The quality of his goods, stock-in-trade or products.

At common law the action will not succeed unless the plaintiff can prove *actual damage*.

In *White* v. *Mellin* [1895], the defendant, a retail chemist, without the plaintiff's permission, labelled the plaintiff's baby food to the effect that the defendant's baby food was superior to all other such products. It was held that the plaintiff was not entitled to an injunction as the statement neither injured nor was calculated to injure him.

(a) *Effect of Defamation Act 1952, s. 3.* This section alters the common law rule by providing that, in an action for malicious falsehood, the plaintiff need not prove special damage if:

(*i*) the statement was published in writing or other permanent form, and was calculated to cause pecuniary damage to the plaintiff

(*ii*) the statement was calculated to cause pecuniary damage to the plaintiff in respect of any office, profession, calling, trade, or business held or carried on by him at the time of the publication: *see Calvet* v. *Tomkins* [1963].

(b) Mere puffing is not actionable. It is not an injurious falsehood to say, in general terms, that one's goods are superior to those of one's competitors, even if it is untrue and maliciously motivated. This is to prevent the courts being used 'in trying the relative merits of rival productions': *White* v. *Mellin* per Lord Herschell LC. Where a statement disparages a rival product, the test of whether

119

it is slander of goods or a mere puff is whether or not a reasonable person would take the statement seriously: *De Beers Abrasive Products Ltd* v. *International General Electric Co. of New York Ltd* [1975].

17. False statements which damage the plaintiff's trade or business

Such a statement is actionable even though it does not fall within the scope of slander of title, slander of goods, or passing off. In *Ratcliffe* v. *Evans* [1892], the defendant, the proprietor of a newspaper, maliciously and falsely implied in a published article that the plaintiffs had gone out of business and their trade suffered in consequence. It was held that the action for malicious falsehood would succeed.

In *Kaye* v. *Robertson* (1991) the plaintiff, an actor, was photographed in a hospital bed recovering from severe injuries. This was done without his consent. The newspaper printing the photograph and story presented it as having been obtained with Mr Kaye's authority. As a result, Mr Kaye was denied an opportunity to market his own account of events. This was held sufficient to constitute injurious falsehood.

In *Joyce* v. *Sengupta* [1993] the defendant newspaper published an article implying that the plaintiff, as maid to the Princess Royal, had abused her position to steal her employer's personal letters. The plaintiff claimed that the article would prejudice her future employment prospects and succeeded in her claim of injurious falsehood. Both this case and *Kaye* illustrate the essence of the tort: that the defendant's lies should have caused economic damage to the plaintiff.

For an action for malicious falsehood to succeed, the plaintiff has to prove that he suffered monetary loss as a result of the publication. It is insufficient to show that the newspaper in question published falsely and with malice: *see Allason* v. *Campbell* [1996].

PASSING OFF

Passing off consists of a misrepresentation by A about his own goods or services to prospective customers or consumers, which leads as a *foreseeable consequence* to damage to the business or goodwill of B. B will normally be required to prove that a significant number of ordinary customers or consumers will be misled by A's misrepresentation, though it is unnecessary for B to prove that he has suffered any actual damage. This tort may be constituted in the following ways:

18. Marketing goods under the plaintiff's trade name

If goods have been marketed under a particular name for so long that it has become generally recognised that such goods are those of the plaintiff, it is actionable if another markets goods under the same or a closely similar name. For an action to succeed:

(a) The public must have been misled.

(b) The name must be a *trade name,* i.e. not a mere general description of a class of goods.

The protection is not confined to business stock-in-trade, e.g. a performer may bring a passing off action in respect of his stage name: *see Hines* v. *Winnick* [1948].

In *Reddaway* v. *Banham* [1896], a machine belting called 'camel-hair belting' was generally acknowledged in the trade to be that manufactured by the plaintiff. The defendant marked his goods 'camel-hair belting' and an injunction was granted to prevent this practice unless the defendant clearly differentiated his belting from that of the plaintiff. In *Bollinger (J.)* v. *Costa Brava Wine Co. Ltd* [1961], an injunction was granted to forbid the use of the misleading description 'Spanish Champagne', genuine champagne being manufactured from grapes grown in the Champagne district of France by the champenoise method. Similarly, in *Walker (John) and Sons Ltd* v. *Henry Ost and Co. Ltd* [1970], it was held that 'Scotch' was restricted to whiskies distilled in Scotland. In *Vine Products Ltd* v. *Mackenzie and Co. Ltd* [1969], it was held that the use of the name 'Sherry' was restricted to fortified wine made in Jerez de la Frontera. In *Erven Warnink BV* v. *Townsend and Sons* [1979], the House of Lords (reversing the Court of Appeal) held that the name 'Advocaat' when used to describe a drink made from dried eggs and sherry constituted passing off as against importers of Advocaat made in Holland from eggs and grain spirit.

For a highly publicised case of passing off *see Taittinger* v. *Allbev Ltd* [1993], when the defendants marked a soft drink under the name 'Elderflower Champagne'.

19. Illicitly using the plaintiff's trade mark, or an imitation of it, with intent to deceive the public

Registered trade marks are protected by the Trade Marks Act 1938; unregistered trade marks by a common law action for passing off.

20. Imitation of the appearance or presentation of the plaintiff's goods with intent to deceive

Examples are imitation of the coke bottle: *Coca Cola* v. *Barr* [1961]. In the famous 'Jif lemon' case, *Reckitt & Coleman* v. *Borden Inc.* [1990], the House of Lords, affirming the decision of the Court of Appeal, held that the trial judge had been correct in restraining by injunction the sale of the competitor's lemon juice in plastic lemon-shaped squeeze containers.

Progress test 7

1. What is the scope of the tort of conspiracy?

2. How is inducement to breach of contract committed?

3. Explain the importance of *Allason* v. *Campbell* [1996]

4. How may the tort of passing off be committed?

8

NUISANCE

CLASSIFICATION OF NUISANCE

The law attaches the term *nuisance* to a variety of different situations. In only certain of these situations will liability in tort arise. The classification of the differing types of nuisance recognised by the law is as follows.

1. Private nuisance

The essence of the tort of private nuisance was, until recently, that the plaintiff is adversely affected in his use or enjoyment of land or of some right over interest in land. In *Cunard* v. *Antifyre* [1933], it was said that 'private nuisances, at least in the vast majority of cases, are interferences for a substantial length of time by owners or occupiers of property with the use or enjoyment of neighbouring property'. In *Butler* v. *Standard Telephone and Cables Ltd* [1940], it was held that tree roots growing under neighbouring land amounted to a nuisance. In *Lemmon* v. *Webb* [1894], the same principle was applied to overhanging tree branches. Other typical instances of the commission of the tort are incursions by smoke, *Crump* v. *Lambert* (1867); destructive animals, *Farrer* v. *Nelson* (1885); unreasonable noise, *Christie* v. *Davey* (1893); vibration, *Hoare & Co.* v. *McAlpine* [1923]; water, smell, fumes, gas, heat, electricity and vegetation. The list is by no means exhaustive and the constantly developing use and adaptation of the environment will always make the creation of an exhaustive list impossible. See the judgment of Hardie Boys J in *Bank of New Zealand* v. *Greenwood* [1984]. Another example of a private nuisance arose in the case of *Carr-Saunders* v. *Dick McNeil* [1986], where the plaintiff had an easement for the access of light to his building. Two rear rooms were lighted by two rear windows which faced the defendants' premises. The defendants then added two storeys to their premises. It was held that the plaintiff was entitled to such access of light as would render his premises adequately lit for all ordinary purposes for which they were used or might reasonably be expected to be used, including an alteration in their internal arrangement. The plaintiff obtained damages for obstruction of light to his rear windows, caused by the addition of the extra two storeys to the defendant's premises.

Only in 1993, in the judgment of *Khorasandjian* v. *Bush* [1993], did the Court of Appeal allow a claim in private nuisance by a plaintiff lacking any proprietary interest in the property where she was subjected to the nuisance. This case is discussed further below.

2. Public nuisance

A public nuisance is an act or omission which has a material effect on the reasonable comfort and convenience of a class of people and amounts to a criminal offence. An action may also be brought by the Attorney-General or a local authority to bring an end to the nuisance. In *Attorney-General for Ontario* v. *Orange Productions Ltd* [1971], it was held that the offence of public nuisance was constituted by the organisation of a rock festival which generated excessive noise, traffic and apprehension. Another example of this crime is obstruction of the highway, such that the public are prevented from 'passing and repassing', and this is typically used against pickets and demonstrators: *see Hubbard* v. *Pitt* [1976] and *Thomas* v. *NUM* [1986] (the latter arising from the 1984–5 miners' strike). It is a question of fact as to whether the number of persons affected by the nuisance is sufficiently large to constitute a class. In the leading case of *Attorney-General* v. *PYA Quarries Ltd* [1957], blasting and other quarrying operations gave rise to a widespread nuisance. Romer LJ said that the law had to determine whether the nuisance was 'so widespread in its range or indiscriminate in its effects that it would not be reasonable to expect one person to take steps to put a stop to it'.

The circumstances of a public nuisance are *not of themselves* a tort. A tort is only committed where, as a result of the public nuisance, *particular damage* is caused to an individual, over and above that suffered by the public at large. The remedy in tort in such a case is an action for *private nuisance*; the only head of tortious liability in this context is *private nuisance*. In *Campbell* v. *Paddington Corp.* [1911], the Corporation committed the public nuisance of obstructing the highway with a grandstand from which to view a procession and thus prevented the plaintiff from letting her windows to view the procession. It was held that she was entitled to damages for the tort of private nuisance.

3. Statutory nuisance

Certain nuisances are proscribed by statute, examples of which are sections 79 and 80 of the Environmental Protection Act 1990.

ENVIRONMENTAL PROTECTION ACT 1990

Statutory Nuisances

79.—(1) Subject to subsections (2) to (6) below, the following matters constitute "statutory nuisances" for the purpose of this Part, that is to say –

(a) any premises in such a state as to be prejudicial to health or a nuisance;
(b) smoke emitted from premises so as to be prejudicial to health or a nuisance;
(c) fumes or gases emitted from premises so as to be prejudicial to health or a nuisance;
(d) any dust, steam, smell or other effluvia arising on industrial, trade or business premises and being prejudicial to health or a nuisance;
(e) any accumulation or deposit which is prejudicial to health or a nuisance;
(f) any animal kept in such a place or manner as to be prejudicial to health or a nuisance;

123

(g)   noise emitted from premises so as to be prejudicial to health or a nuisance;

(ga) noise that is prejudicial to health or a nuisance and is emitted from or caused by a vehicle, machinery or equipment in a street;

(h)   any other matter declared by any enactment to be a statutory nuisance;

and it shall be the duty of every local authority to cause its area to be inspected from time to time to detect any statutory nuisances which ought to be dealt with under s. 80 below and, where a complaint of a statutory nuisance is made to it by a person living within its area, to take such steps as are reasonably practicable to investigate the complaint.

. . .

(4)   Subsection (1)(c) above does not apply in relation to premises other than private dwellings.

. . .

(7) . . .   "person responsible", in relation to a statutory nuisance, means the person to whose act, default or sufferance the nuisance is attributable;

. . .

(9)   In this Part "best practicable means" is to be interpreted by reference to the following provisions—-

(a)   "practicable" means reasonably practicable having regard among other things to local conditions and circumstances, to the current state of technical knowledge and to the financial implications;

(b)   the means to be employed include the design, installation, maintenance and manner and periods of operation of plant and machinery, and the design, construction and maintenance of buildings and structures;

(c)   the test is to apply only so far as compatible with any duty imposed by law;

(d)   the test is to apply only so far as compatible with safety and safe working conditions, and with the exigencies of any emergency or unforeseeable circumstances;

and, in circumstances where a code of practice under s. 71 of the Control of Pollution Act 1974 (noise minimisation) is applicable, regard shall also be had to guidance given in it.

80.—(1)   Where a local authority is satisfied that a statutory nuisance exists, or is likely to occur or recur, in the area of the authority, the local authority shall serve a notice ("an abatement notice") imposing all or any of the following requirements –

(a)   requiring the abatement of the nuisance or prohibiting or restricting its occurrence or recurrence;

(b)   requiring the execution of such works, and the taking of such other steps, as may be necessary for any of those purposes,

and the notice shall specify the time or times within which the requirements of the notice are to be complied with.

(2)   The abatement notice shall be served –

(a)   except in a case falling within paragraph (b) or (c) below, on the person responsible for the nuisance;

(b)   where the nuisance arises from any defect of a structural character, on the owner of the premises;

(c)   where the person responsible for the nuisance cannot be found or the nuisance has not yet occurred, on the owner or occupier of the premises.

(3)   The person served with the notice may appeal against the notice to a magistrates'

court within the period of twenty-one days beginning with the date on which he was served with the notice.

(4) If a person on whom an abatement notice is served, without reasonable excuse, contravenes or fails to comply with any requirement or prohibition imposed by the notice, he shall be guilty of an offence.

(5) Except in a case falling within subsection (6) below, a person who commits an offence under subsection (4) above shall be liable on summary conviction to a fine not exceeding level 5 on the standard scale together with a further fine of an amount equal to one-tenth of that level for each day on which the offence continues after the conviction.

(6) A person who commits an offence under subsection (4) above on industrial, trade or business premises shall be liable on summary conviction to a fine not exceeding £20,000.

(7) Subject to subsection (8) below, in any proceedings for an offence under subsection (4) above in respect of a statutory nuisance it shall be a defence to prove that the best practicable means were used to prevent, or to counteract the effects of, the nuisance.

(8) The defence under subsection (7) above is not available –

(a)   in the case of a nuisance falling within paragraph (a), (d), (e), (f) or (g) of s. 79(1) above except where the nuisance arises on industrial, trade or business premises;

(b)   in the case of a nuisance falling within paragraph (b) of s. 79(1) above except where the smoke is emitted from a chimney; and

(c)   in the case of a nuisance falling within paragraph (c) or (h) of s. 79(1) above.

Where a person on whom an Abatement Notice been properly served contravenes or fails to comply with any requirement or prohibition imposed by the Notice, he is guilty of a criminal offence – see section 80(4). In dealing with this offence the court may make a compensation order against the person found guilty of committing the crime: *see Herbert* v. *Lambeth L.B.C.* [1992]. A court may make a compensation order against anyone guilty of a statutory nuisance: *see Botross* v. *Hammersmith & Fulham L.B.C.* (1994).

PRIVATE NUISANCE

Private nuisance occurs where the plaintiff suffers damage in consequence of an unlawful interference with his use or enjoyment of land which he owns or occupies.

In order to understand fully the nature of the tort it is necessary to analyse in closer detail the following:

(a) In what ways use or enjoyment of land may be interfered with

(b) What makes the interference unlawful

(c) What heads of damage may be claimed

(d) Who can sue and who can be sued.

4. Modes of interference

Traditionally two types of interference are recognised as capable of giving rise to an action in nuisance. These are:

(a) Interference with the plaintiff's beneficial use of the premises

125

(b) Physical injury to the premises or to the plaintiff's property situated on the premises.

Examples of **(a)** would be excessive noise: *see Christie* v. *Davey* [1893], or smells emanating from a pig farm: *see Bone* v. *Seale* [1975]. The basic criterion is that the interference should substantially detract from the plaintiff's comfort or convenience in the use of his property causing him personal discomfort. Examples of **(b)** include causing damage to the plaintiff's land by vibrations from engines: *see Meux's Brewery Co.* v. *City of London Electric Lighting Co.* [1895], or allowing sewage or flood water to collect on it. Clearly certain types of interference (e.g. vibrations) would be capable of falling into either category. The distinction between categories is, however, important as the burden of proof on the plaintiff varies depending under which category he is claiming.

5. What makes the interference unlawful?

The interference will be unlawful only if it is unreasonable; for 'a balance has to be maintained between the right of the occupier to do what he likes with his own land, and the right of his neighbour not to be interfered with'; this view was taken in *Sedleigh-Denfield* v. *O'Callaghan* [1940], by Lord Wright. However, interference will not be unreasonable unless it is substantial, 'not merely according to elegant or dainty modes and habits of living, but according to plain and sober and simple notions among the English people': *see Walter* v. *Selfe* [1851] per Knight-Bruce VC. The requirement of reasonableness in this context is not the same as that of reasonable care in negligence. One who takes reasonable (or even extreme) care may nevertheless commit nuisance if, despite this care, another's use or enjoyment of his land is adversely affected.

6. Reasonableness: a question of fact

The reasonableness of an act is a question of fact to be determined in accordance with the circumstances, e.g. time, place and manner of commission, the presence or absence of malice, whether the effects are transitory or permanent, and the state of scientific knowledge at the time. In *Manchester Corp.* v. *Farnworth* [1930], a case involving the escape of fumes, Lord Dunedin said: 'The onus of proving that the result is inevitable is on those who wish to escape liability for nuisance, but the criterion of inevitability is . . . what is possible, according to the state of scientific knowledge at the time, having also in view a certain common-sense appreciation, which cannot be rigidly defined, of practical feasibility in view of situation and of expense.'

In *St Helens Smelting Co.* v. *Tipping* [1865] there was physical damage to property by the emission of fumes and Lord Westbury took the view that: 'The law does not regard trifling inconveniences; everything must be looked at from a reasonable point of view . . . the time, locality and all the circumstances should be taken into consideration.'

The question of reasonableness was discussed at both Court of Appeal and House of Lords level in the case of *Cambridge Water Company* v. *Eastern Counties Leather* plc [1994].

In this case the plaintiff was suing the defendants for polluting the plaintiff's water supply. The pollution had arisen through the leakage of chemicals on the defendant's land which seeped through the ground and polluted the underground water supply. The plaintiff lost at first instance, having based its claim on nuisance, negligence and *Rylands* v. *Fletcher* (see Chapter 9). The Court of Appeal determined the appeal by looking at nuisance and arguing that liability could be strict if there was an interference with natural rights, such as water. In the House of Lords, their Lordships considered that in private nuisance:

> 'Liability has usually been regarded as strict, at least in the case of a defendant who has been responsible for the creation of the nuisance, even so that liability has been kept under control by the principle of reasonable user ... the effect is that, if the user is reasonable, the defendant will not be liable for consequent harm to his neighbour's enjoyment of his land; but if the user is not reasonable, the defendant will be liable, even though he may have exercised reasonable care and skill to avoid it.'

The concept of reasonable user is thus the significant test. This is considered further in Chapter 9.

The law of nuisance is in essence a restriction on the use which one can make of one's own property. If you cannot keep a hundred goats on your land without causing nuisance to your neighbours, the law says that you cannot keep them there.

What of the situation where the law permits you to do something, but the doing of it causes a nuisance? For example, you have planning permission to build pig-styes and keep pigs on your land. The thing which has been authorised can only be done insofar as it causes the minimum harm consistent with it being done. Where a defendant in a nuisance case has acted under statutory authority, the common law of nuisance can only require that he has acted reasonably so as to minimise the harm. Proof of reasonable care will provide him with a defence. The burden of proving that he took reasonable care is on him.

A case which illustrates this point is *Wheeler* v. *Saunders* [1995]. In that case the defendant was prevented from using pig-styes which had been erected in accordance with the necessary permissions, because the smell from them was intolerable at the plaintiff's home which was very close by and at holiday cottages on the plaintiff's land.

7. Abnormal sensitivity

Abnormal sensitivity of property or persons is immaterial to the question of reasonableness. In *Robinson* v. *Kilvert* (1889), the defendant heated a cellar, thereby damaging the plaintiff's unusually sensitive brown paper on the floor above. The heat would not have damaged paper generally and it was held that there was no nuisance.

In *Heath* v. *Mayor of Brighton* (1908), the incumbent of a church alleged nuisance by noise from the adjacent power station. The noise was not excessive and the congregation had neither diminished nor complained. It was held that there was no nuisance and an injunction was therefore refused. It is important to distinguish the effect of abnormal sensitivity before and after nuisance has been established for, once the nuisance has been established, the remedies of damages and injunction will extend to abnormally delicate or sensitive operations; this is illustrated by the growing of orchids in the case of *McKinnon Industries Ltd* v. *Walker* [1951] (PC).

8. Duration of the interference

The duration of the interference is relevant, in conjunction with the other circumstances, to whether or not it was substantial. In general, the fact that the interference was merely temporary or intermittent will be evidence (but no more) that it was reasonable. However, a permanent or continuous interference may be lawful, and a transitory or intermittent (even a momentary) interference may be a nuisance. Most private nuisances, in fact, consist of a lengthy interference with the enjoyment of property.

In *Leeman* v. *Montague* [1936], cocks crowed for weeks in a residential area and this was held to be a nuisance, meriting damages and an injunction. In *Castle* v. *St Augustine's Links* (1922), golf balls were repeatedly hit into the highway. This was held to be a public nuisance and the plaintiff, who had lost an eye, recovered for private nuisance. In *Bolton* v. *Stone* [1951], cricket balls were hit into the highway about six times in thirty years and this was held not to constitute a nuisance. In *Dollman* v. *Hillman Ltd* [1941], the plaintiff was injured by slipping on a piece of fat outside the defendant's shop. It was held that, although a single occurrence, the defendant was liable in nuisance and negligence. In *Midwood* v. *Mayor of Manchester* [1905], the defendant corporation allowed gas to accumulate and it was held that the resultant explosion was a nuisance, but for such a single occurrence to be a nuisance, it must be a state of affairs arising from the condition of the defendant's land or premises and the activities thereon and not merely an isolated event; for further details *see SCM (UK) Ltd* v. *W.J. Whittal & Son Ltd* [1970].

9. Malice in nuisance

An act not otherwise a nuisance may become one if done *maliciously* in order to annoy the plaintiff. In *Christie* v. *Davey* [1893], the defendant created a din whenever his neighbour gave music lessons. This was held to be a nuisance, because the defendant acted deliberately and maliciously to annoy the plaintiff. An injunction was granted. In *Hollywood Silver Fox Farm Ltd* v. *Emmett* [1936], the defendant, out of spite, fired guns near the fox farm, thereby causing harm to breeding vixens. It was held that although the defendant fired the guns on his own land, he was liable in nuisance because he acted maliciously. Damages and an injunction were granted. In *Palmer* v. *Loader* [1962], a perpetual injunction was granted to restrain noise maliciously intended to interfere with the plaintiff's enjoyment of her flat. In *Stoakes* v. *Brydges* [1958], the defendant, because of a grievance against the plaintiff, persistently telephoned the latter. This was held to be a nuisance, for 'you are not entitled to abate a nuisance by creating another', per Bramwell B in *Barnford* v. *Turnley* (1862).

At first sight, these cases may seem difficult to reconcile with *Bradford Corp.* v. *Pickles* [1895], in which it was held that a malicious motive does not make a lawful act unlawful; but in the above cases the effect of the defendant's malice was to make his conduct unreasonable and, therefore, a nuisance.

ACTION IN PUBLIC AND PRIVATE NUISANCE

10. What damage is actionable?

A plaintiff in an action for nuisance may recover for actual but not potential damage to land and chattels. Damages for personal injuries may be recovered where caused by a public nuisance, although it is uncertain what the position is with private nuisance. Although there is a basic requirement of actual damage, if the damage is clearly imminent as a result of the defendant's activities, the court may order the cessation of these activities by the use of a *quia timet* injunction.

11. Who can sue?

Up until 1993 the general principle was that only a plaintiff with an interest in the land affected could sue in private nuisance. This was a logical position given that private nuisance protected interests in land. It was said that 'the plaintiff in order to maintain an action must show some title to the thing to which the nuisance is alleged to be': *Cunard* v. *Antifyre Ltd.* [1933].

In *Khorasandjian* v. *Bush* [1993] the Court of Appeal appeared to abolish this long-standing principle. The plaintiff lived with her mother and was being harassed by persistent and abusive phone calls from a former lover. The Court of Appeal held that such intrusive conduct was capable of amounting to 'substantial interference' with enjoyment of property. The legal owner of the property could obtain an injunction in private nuisance to restrain such activity. The Court proceeded to go one step beyond the traditional approach by allowing the daughter to obtain an injunction to her own right. Dillon LJ stated that the Court must reconsider earlier decisions in the light of changed social conditions and, citing Canadian authority allowing a wife with no proprietary interest to sue in private nuisance, stated '. . . if the wife of the owner is entitled to sue in respect of harassing telephone calls, then I do not see why that should not also apply to a child living at home with her parents.'

The decision in *Khorasandjian* suggests that any occupant of premises now has a right to bring an action in private nuisance.

In *Hunter* v. *Canary Wharf Ltd* [1996] the Court of Appeal had to consider an action in nuisance brought by occupants of the area in which a massive office development was built. The office development blocked the reception of television programmes by local residents and the building of the roads surrounding the development caused damage to properties by means of the dust generated by their construction.

This case posed the question: is the interference with television reception capable of constituting an actionable private nuisance? The trial judge at first instance held that it did. However, Pill L.J. took the view in the Court of Appeal that it was not stating:

> 'I accept the importance of television in the lives of very many people. However, in my judgment the erection or presence of a building in the line of sight between a television transmitter and other properties is not actionable as an interference with the use and enjoyment of land'.

He continued:

> 'The loss of a view, which may be of the greatest importance to many householders, is not actionable and neither is the mere presence of a building in the sight line to the television transmitter'.

Crucial to the determination of this case was the question: is it necessary to have an interest in property to claim private nuisance?

Lord Justice Pill opined:

> 'A substantial link between the person enjoying the use and the land on which he or she is enjoying it is essential but, in my judgment, occupation of property as a home does confer upon the occupant a capacity to sue in private nuisance'.

Lord Justice Pill cites the judgment of Dillon L.J. in *Khorasandjian* v. *Bush* [1993] with approval.

12. Who can be sued?

(a) *The creator of a nuisance*. One who creates a nuisance by misfeasance is strictly liable in respect of its creation and continuance, even if not in occupation of the land from which it emanates. It is no defence that he could not abate the nuisance without trespassing; nor is it a defence to a continuing nuisance that all possible care and skill had been directed to its prevention: *see Rapier* v. *London Tramways Ltd* [1893].

(b) *The occupier*. It is a general principle that an occupier is responsible for all nuisances existing on his premises during his occupancy whether created by himself or others. In *Laugher* v. *Pointer* (1826), Sir Charles Abbott CJ said, 'I have the control and management of all that belongs to my land or my house, and it is my fault if I do not so exercise my authority as to prevent injury to another.'
By way of qualification, the test (whether he is not the creator of the nuisance) seems to be whether the occupier knew or reasonably should have known of the actual or potential nuisance. If so, he must take reasonably prompt and efficient action to abate the actual or potential nuisance. This test must be applied to the normal circumstances that may be anticipated in which the occupier does not actually create the nuisance.
In *R.* v. *Shorrock* [1993] the defendant was prosecuted for public nuisance when he hired his land to others who then held an acid house party. He was held liable as he ought to have known that there was a real risk of a nuisance occurring.

13. Nuisance created by trespasser or natural causes

In *Sedleigh-Danfield* v. *O'Callaghan* [1940], a trespasser laid a pipe in a ditch in such a way that the grating became choked with leaves and adjoining land was flooded. The defendants knew of the pipe and it was held that they should have foreseen the possibility of a flood. As they had taken no action over a period of three years they were liable for both *continuing* and *adopting* the nuisance. They had continued the nuisance by taking no steps to abate it and they had adopted it by using the pipe to drain their own land. In *Goldman* v. *Hargrave* [1967] and *Leakey* v. *National Trust* [1980], it was held that the same criteria apply where the nuisance is created by natural causes.

14. Nuisance created by independent contractors

One who orders work to be done which is likely to cause nuisance cannot, by employing another, exempt himself from his responsibility to take reasonable steps to prevent the nuisance. This is one of the exceptions to the general rule that a person is not responsible for the torts of his independent contractor, and applies particularly to dangerous or extraordinary interferences with highways, creating a risk clearly greater than those arising from normal repairs.

In *Hole* v. *Sittingbourne Railway* (1861), the railway company had statutory authority to build a swing bridge but their independent contractor built it so badly it would not open. It was held that the railway company was liable. *Matania* v. *N.P. Bank Ltd* [1937] involved nuisance from building operations carried on by the defendant's independent contractor. It was held that the defendant was liable; 'Unless precautions were taken there was a great and obvious danger that nuisance would be caused', *per* Finlay J.

Note that an occupier has an absolute right to lateral support from his neighbour's building; therefore the neighbour is liable if his contractor infringes the right: *see Bower* v. *Peate* (1876). There must be knowledge of the risk, and failure to take action to abate it, such that the nuisance is continued and/or adopted.

15. Nuisance created by predecessors in title

One who acquires land from which a nuisance emanates will be liable only if he knew of or ought reasonably to have discovered the nuisance. In *St Anne's Well Brewery Co.* v. *Roberts* [1929], an adjoining building collapsed because of ancient excavations which the present owner could not reasonably have discovered. It was held that he was not liable. Liability would only arise if the party acquiring the land continued or adopted the nuisance.

16. Nuisance caused by latent defect

The occupier will only be liable if he knew of the defect or reasonable care on his part would have revealed it. In *Sedleigh-Denfield* v. *O'Callaghan* [1940], Lord Atkin said that 'the occupier or owner is not an insurer'. *See also Toff* v. *McDowell*

[1993]. In *Noble* v. *Harrison* [1926], there was a latent defect in a tree which caused a branch to fall off and damage a coach on the highway below. It was held that the defect could not have been discovered by a reasonably careful inspection and the occupier was therefore not liable.

17. Natural hazards on land

If the occupier takes no reasonable steps to obviate a natural hazard of which he is aware, he will be liable in nuisance. In *Leakey* v. *National Trust* [1980], earth movements caused a steep, natural hill to collapse causing damage to the plaintiffs' land. The occupier was held liable in nuisance. The Court accepted that an occupier of land is under a duty to abate a naturally occurring nuisance on his property once the risk has become patent but held that the duty was subjective – the occupier's duty was to do what was reasonable in the light of his personal capacity to deal with the nuisance. In such circumstances, where an occupier finds himself being responsible for a potential danger which he played no part in creating, less may therefore be expected of him, in terms of time and money, to obviate the danger to others.

18. Extent to which knowledge of danger necessary

One view of the law is that an occupier (and sometimes an owner) may be liable due to failure to repair premises adjoining a highway whether or not he knew or ought to have known of the danger. In *Wringe* v. *Cohen* [1940], part of the respondent's house which adjoined the highway collapsed due to disrepair and damaged the appellant's property. The respondent was held liable even though he neither knew nor had the means of knowing of the disrepair. Whether or not this imposes strict liability on the occupiers of premises adjoining the highway is not clear. In *Spicer* v. *Smee* [1946], Lord Atkinson said that the lack of knowledge in such circumstances could not be relied upon because of the duty to inspect a house to prevent it becoming dangerous. It is still not clear, however, whether there need to be circumstances which suggest that it would be prudent to inspect and examine property – in other words does the occupier or owner need to be put to inquiry? This seems to have been the view taken by the House of Lords in *Cominer* v. *Northern and London Investments Trust Ltd* [1949]. Here it was held that the respondent was not liable when an elm tree fell from his land on to the appellant's car because a prudent landowner would not have been put to inquiry and foreseen any danger.

19. Landlord and tenant

The general rule is that the tenant, as occupier, is liable for a nuisance on the premises, but the landlord will be liable in the following circumstances:

(a) Where he knew or ought to have known of the nuisance at the commencement of the tenancy: *see Bowen* v. *Anderson* [1894]. A landlord cannot avoid liability by taking a repairing covenant from the tenant: *see Brew Brothers Ltd* v. *Snax (Ross) Ltd* [1970].

(b) If he has covenanted to repair: *see Payne* v. *Rogers* (1794).

(c) If he has reserved the right to enter and repair.

(d) If he has authorised the nuisance: *see Harris* v. *James* (1876). A more recent example is *Tetley* v. *Chitty* [1986], where the leasing of land for go-kart racing was held to authorise by implication the nuisance which arose as a natural consequence. On the other hand in *Smith* v. *Scott* [1973], a landlord was not responsible for the nuisance caused by tenants known to be unruly, as a result of a clause in the lease prohibiting the commission of a nuisance.

(e) He is strictly liable for nuisance due to want of repair of premises adjoining a highway where he has
   (*i*)   covenanted to repair; or
   (*ii*) reserved the right to enter and repair.

Furthermore, the landlord is liable even though he did not know of the nuisance, *but* note that the liability will not arise unless the nuisance arose from want of repair. *See Cushing* v. *Peter Walker & Son* [1941], where the dangerous condition was due to enemy action. *See also Toff* v. *McDowell* [1993].

Much of the older case law in this area has been incorporated into section 4 of the Defective Premises Act 1972. As a result, a landlord who has sufficient control over tenanted property to be under a duty to neighbouring owners with respect to nuisances created by failure to maintain or repair it will be liable only for those defects of which he ought reasonably to be aware.

EFFECTUAL DEFENCES

20. Rebuttal

It is an adequate defence against an action for nuisance to prove that the activity complained of is not a nuisance, i.e. not an unreasonable interference with the use or enjoyment of land, or with health or comfort.

21. Consent

The consent of the plaintiff is a good defence, provided the defendant was not negligent. But it is no defence that the plaintiff came to the nuisance, i.e. consent will not be implied by his coming to the premises with knowledge of the nuisance, unless the interference is with comfort and the nature of the locality may be relevant – 'What would be a nuisance in Belgrave Square would not necessarily be so in Bermondsey': *Sturges* v. *Bridgman* (1879).

22. Prescription

A private nuisance is legalised after twenty years, but time begins to run only when the plaintiff becomes aware of the nuisance.

In *Sturges* v. *Bridgman* (1879), the defendant for more than twenty years caused noise and vibration, which were not, however, complained of as a nuisance. Then his neighbour, a physician, built a consulting room adjacent to the site of the noisy operations, which the physician now alleged were a nuisance. It was held that a prescriptive right had not been established, as the activity was not previously a nuisance. An injunction was granted.

23. Statutory authority

Activities which would be a nuisance at common law may be sanctioned by statute. Authority will be lost, however, if the conduct goes beyond the limits permitted by the statute. By way of a case example, *see Gillingham Borough Council* v. *Medway (Chatham) Dock Co. Ltd* [1992].

24. Other defences

The following defences have also succeeded against a plea of nuisance:

(a) Contributory negligence by the plaintiff: *Trevett* v. *Lee* [1955].

(b) Inevitable accident: *Esso Petroleum Co. Ltd* v. *Southport Corp.* [1956].

(c) Act of a stranger, of which the plaintiff had neither actual nor constructive notice: *Sedleigh-Denfield* v. *O'Callaghan* [1940].

(d) Act of God – in the sense of wholly exceptional natural events.

INEFFECTUAL DEFENCES

25. Public benefit

If the nuisance injures the plaintiff, it is no defence that it benefits the public generally, even if the public benefit is substantial and the injury to the plaintiff relatively slight: *see Adams* v. *Ursell* [1913]. Occasionally public interest may be taken into consideration and damages awarded in lieu of an injunction prohibiting the activity. In *Miller* v. *Jackson* [1977], the Court of Appeal refused to grant an injunction closing a cricket field and awarded damages instead. However, such decisions are rare and in a subsequent Court of Appeal decision *Kennaway* v. *Thompson* [1981], *dicta* in *Miller* v. *Jackson* were criticised and the decision of the trial judge to refuse an injunction on the grounds of public interest was reversed.

26. Use of all possible care and skill by defendant

Nuisance is not merely a branch of negligence, therefore the defendant cannot excuse himself by showing that he took reasonable (or even extreme) care – although proof of care may have evidential value in determining whether an ordinary user of land is actionable as a nuisance.

In *Adams* v. *Ursell* [1913], a fried fish shop was held to be a nuisance in a residential street. It was no defence:

(a) that it benefited the poor

(b) that all possible care and 'the most approved appliances' were used.

At common law an activity which cannot be prevented from being a nuisance cannot be carried on at all, except by the consent of those affected. Note, however, that many common law nuisances are authorised by statute.

In *Powell* v. *Fall* (1880), nuisance was caused by sparks from a traction engine. They could not be prevented and there was no consent or statutory authority. It was held that the machine could not lawfully be operated.

27. *Volenti non fit injuria*

It is well established that it is no defence that the plaintiff came to the nuisance. In *Bliss* v. *Hall* (1838), the plaintiff took a house near a tallow chandlery, which emitted fumes and smells. It was held to be no defence that these activities had been carried on for three years before the plaintiff's arrival. In *Miller* v. *Jackson* [1977] escaping cricket balls were held to be a nuisance to occupiers of newly built adjacent houses. It was no defence that they had 'come to the nuisance'. However, the nature of the locality is relevant to the application of this rule. For instance, one who chooses to reside in a manufacturing district cannot expect more immunity from its disadvantages than the other inhabitants. The local standard approach is confined to nuisance causing personal discomfort, and has no application to cases involving damage to property. In *St. Helens Smelting Co.* v. *Tipping* [1865], the appellant's house was in a manufacturing district, and his vegetation was damaged by fumes. It was held to be a nuisance, the situation of the house being no defence.

28. Suitable place

It is no defence that the place from which the nuisance emanates is a suitable one for the purpose of carrying on the activity complained of, and that no other place is available. If the business cannot be carried on without creating a nuisance, then it cannot be carried on at all, except by consent of those affected or by statutory authority.

29. Reasonable use of property

Reasonable use of his own property cannot be a defence to the creator of a nuisance, since the creation of a nuisance is unreasonable by definition. 'If a man creates a nuisance he cannot say that he is acting reasonably. The two things are self-contradictory': *A.-G.* v. *Cole* [1901] *per* Kekewich J.

The nature of the defendant's act cannot be tested by enquiring whether he could foresee the damage. The matter must be looked at from the point of view of the victims of the alleged nuisance: the criterion is – was the activity to which the victim was exposed tolerable in all the circumstances of the case?

THE RELATIONSHIP OF NUISANCE TO OTHER TORTS

30. Trespass

Nuisance and trespass are mutually exclusive. Trespass lies only for *direct* interference with land and nuisance only for *indirect* interference.

31. Negligence

In the sense that nuisance may be committed by an inadvertent or negligent action, as well as by a deliberate action, the same behaviour may give rise to claims under nuisance and negligence. On the other hand, negligent action which injures someone within the defendant's own land will not give rise to an action in nuisance. The appropriate action in such circumstances will be for negligence or breach of statutory duty.

32. *Rylands* v. *Fletcher*

Liability for nuisance and liability under *Rylands* v. *Fletcher* both require an escape from the defendant's land to the plaintiff's land, and in this sense are analogous. They differ, however, in that for liability to arise under the *Rylands* v. *Fletcher* principle there must have been a non-natural use of the land, *see* 9:3. A defendant may, however, be liable in nuisance for damage resulting from natural use of the land, para. 17 above, and in particular refer to *Leakey* v. *National Trust* [1980].

Progress test 8

1. Explain the difference between public and private nuisance.

2. Give some examples, from decided cases, of actionable nuisances.

3. Of what significance is the decision of the Court of Appeal in *Hunter* v. *Canary Wharf Ltd* [1996]?

4. How does 'reasonableness' affect liability in nuisance? Is this the same as 'reasonable care' in negligence?

5. What is the effect on liability for nuisance of abnormal sensitivity of persons or property?

6. Which defences are effective against an action in nuisance?

9

STRICT LIABILITY

THE NATURE AND EXTENT OF STRICT LIABILITY

In order to appreciate properly the nature and extent of strict liability it is crucial to realise it is a fringe form of liability. Its recognition is an exception to the general rule that liability in tort requires either a deliberate or negligent act, i.e. some element of fault.

1. Strict but not absolute

Although in principle no fault is required, the imposition of strict liability tends to be hedged with restrictions and exceptions. This means that it would be misleading and indeed incorrect to refer to absolute liability. Absolute liability implies unavoidable liability in a given set of circumstances. The exceptions to the rule clearly demonstrate that is not the case.

2. *Rylands* v. *Fletcher* (1868)

The most common example of strict liability is the rule in *Rylands* v. *Fletcher* (1868). It was originally formulated by Blackburn J when the case was heard in the Court of Exchequer Chamber in 1866 (*sub nom. Fletcher* v. *Rylands*) in the following terms: 'The person who for his own purposes brings on his land and collects and keeps there anything likely to do mischief if it escapes, must keep it in at his peril and, if he does not do so, he is *prima facie* answerable for all the damage which is the natural consequence of its escape'. This was approved by the House of Lords when the case was finally settled in 1868.

The defendant employed an independent contractor to construct a reservoir on his (the defendant's) land. The defendant did not know of, and could not reasonably have discovered, the existence of disused mine shafts on the site. When the reservoir was filled, the plaintiff's adjoining coal mine was flooded. Despite the absence of negligence on the part of the defendants they were held liable. It is clear that one of the essential requirements for liability is that the phenomenon causing the damage must have been *artificially* accumulated on the land, and so the rule does not apply to things naturally on the land. In the course of the development of the rule by the courts this point of distinction has given rise to difficulties. However, it is possible at this stage to illustrate the basic distinction by way of example. In *Smith* v. *Kenrick* [1849], the defendant's ordinary mining operations caused water to flow into an adjoining mine causing damage. The defendant was not liable under the *Rylands* v. *Fletcher* principle as the water had not been artificially accumulated on the land. The House of Lords decision in *Cambridge Water Co. Ltd.* v. *Eastern Counties Leather plc* [1994] provides a further example of non-natural user. The case concerned the pollution of a borehole used by the plaintiff to extract water for domestic use. The pollution was traced to repeated spillages of solvents at the defendants' tanning works. Lord Goff in his speech stated that the storage of chemicals on industrial premises was a 'classic case of non-natural use'. This case is therefore significant in opening up *Rylands* to perform an effective role in protecting the environment. The plaintiff's claim for compensation however failed on the basis that the defendant could not have foreseen the type of damage suffered by the plaintiff as a result of the spillages. The House of Lords refused to impose strict tortious liability for 'historic pollution', i.e. the cost of repairing environmental damage which was not appreciated when done.

The other factor which must be present for the *Rylands* v. *Fletcher* principle to apply is that the thing brought on to the land must be likely to do mischief. Again this requires closer analysis, but the general policy of the two elements of the rule is clear from Lord Blackburn's judgment in the House of Lords in *Rylands* v. *Fletcher*:

> 'It seems but reasonable and just that the neighbour who has brought something on his own property which was not naturally there, harmless to others so long as it is confined to his own property, but which he knows to be mischievous if it gets on his neighbour's, should be obliged to make good the damage which ensues if he does not succeed in confining it to his own property. But for his act in bringing it there no mischief could have occurred, and it seems but just that he should at his peril keep it there so that no mischief may accrue, or answer the natural and anticipated consequences. And upon authority, this we think is established to be the law whether the things so brought be beasts or water, or filth, or stenches.'

There is strict liability for the escape, resulting in damage, of potential hazards brought on to land. However, closer analysis is necessary in order to be able to predict with some degree of certainty when liability will arise.

3. Things brought on to the land

The requirement that the phenomena in question must have been brought on to the land by the defendant was further refined by Lord Cairns in his judgment in the House of Lords in *Rylands* v. *Fletcher*. The refinement lay in requiring that there be a *non-natural use* of the land, the ascertainment of which will depend on policy considerations such as the benefit to the community of the use to which the land is being put. In *Rickards* v. *Lothian* [1913], Lord Moulton said: 'It must be some special use bringing with it increased danger to others and must not merely be the ordinary use of land or such a use as is proper for the general benefit of the communities.'

What is considered to be natural may also vary with changing social circumstances. In *Read* v. *Lyons & Company Ltd* [1947], a munitions factory (albeit in war-time) was held to be a natural use of land. The approach in *Read* v. *Lyons* should be contrasted with *Rylands* v. *Fletcher* itself where a dam was held to be a non-natural use.

The following are uses which the courts have held to be natural: in *Rickards* v. *Lothian* [1913], the bringing of water into a cistern in a house; in *Miller* v. *Addie & Sons Collieries* (1934), a landlord laying gas pipes for supply to dwelling houses; in *British Celanese Ltd* v. *A. H. Hunt Capacitors Ltd* [1969], the manufacture of electrical or electronic components; and in *Collingwood* v. *Home and Colonial Stores* [1936], wiring for domestic *or* trade purposes.

The following have been held to constitute non-natural use: in *North Western Utilities* v. *London Guarantee Company* [1936], electricity carried in bulk for non-domestic purposes; in *Musgrove* v. *Pandelis* [1919], the storage of a motor vehicle with a tank full of petrol in a garage; in *Smeaton* v. *Ilford Corp.* [1954], the collection in a sewer of a large amount of noxious and intrinsically dangerous sewage; and in *Cambridge Water Co. Ltd* v. *Eastern Counties Leather plc* [1994], the storage of chemicals on industrial premises (*per* Lord Goff). Obviously in the 1990s some if not all of these cases are open to doubt, in particular *Musgrove* v. *Pandelis* [1919].

4. Things likely to do mischief if they escape

(a) *A question of fact.* Whether a 'thing' which has been brought and kept on the defendant's land is one which is likely to do mischief if it escapes is a question of *fact*. Consequently, a particular 'thing' may come within the rule in one case but not in another. This has applied, *inter alia*, to trees, water, motor vehicles and guns; whilst electricity and chemicals have always been held to come under the rule.

(b) *What is a 'thing'?* Again, it is a question of fact in each case for such a wide variety of animate and inanimate objects and phenomena have been held to come under the rule that neither a concise nor exhaustive definition is possible. Examples would include:

(*i*) Electricity: *Eastern and South African Telegraph Co.* v. *Cape Town Tramways Co.* [1902].

(*ii*) Gas: *North Western Utilities Ltd* v. *London Guarantee and Accident Co.* [1936].

(*iii*) Sewage: *Jones* v. *Llanrwst UDC* [1911].

(*iv*) Vibration: *Hoare and Co.* v. *McAlpine* [1923].

(*v*) Projecting poisonous trees: *Crowhurst* v. *Amersham Burial Board* (1878).

It is impossible to say with certainty when such an object will give rise to liability, but it will do so if it is *dangerous* or *potentially dangerous*. These descriptions, although often invoked, are difficult to define and have been much criticised. An object is dangerous if, having been brought and kept upon the defendant's land, it will *do damage if it escapes therefrom*. Thus anything which will do damage if it escapes, even if harmless while confined, comes under the rule. There must be some knowledge, based on 'the common experience of mankind' (*Crowhurst* v. *Amersham Burial Board* (1878)) of the likelihood that the thing will do harm should it escape. This means an element of foreseeability in relation to the dangerous propensity of the thing, though it does not mean that there need be any foreseeability about the *likelihood* of the thing escaping. It is no defence to claim that all reasonable precautions were taken to prevent the escape; this is a point of distinction between strict liability and negligence liability.

5. What constitutes an escape?

The rule in *Rylands* v. *Fletcher* is analogous with nuisance to the extent that the thing doing the damage must escape from *the land* of the defendant. Thus, damage occurring *outside* the boundaries of the land from which the thing doing the damage emanated is actionable in nuisance or *Rylands* v. *Fletcher*, but damage caused wholly *within* the land or premises concerned is not, the appropriate action being, for example, for negligence or breach of statutory duty.

Thus, in *Read* v. *J Lyons & Co. Ltd* [1947], it was said that 'escape' for the purposes of applying the proposition in *Rylands* v. *Fletcher* means 'escape from a place where the defendant has occupation of or control over land to a place which is outside his occupation or control': *per* Lord Simon; and 'there must be the escape of something from one man's close to another man's close': *per* Lord Macmillan. In *Read* v. *J. Lyons & Co. Ltd* [1947], the plaintiff, a munitions inspector of the Ministry of Supply, was injured while on the defendant's premises by the explosion of a shell in process of manufacture. She did not allege negligence but sued in *Rylands* v. *Fletcher*. It was held that *Rylands* v. *Fletcher* did not apply as there had been no escape of a dangerous thing *from the premises*. Lord Macmillan said that: 'The doctrine of *Rylands* v. *Fletcher* . . . derives from a conception of mutual duties of adjoining or neighbouring landowners and its congeners are trespass and nuisance.' In *Cambridge Water Company* v. *Eastern Counties Leather plc* [1994] the Court of Appeal drew a distinction between liability for *escape*, held to fall within *Rylands* liability, and liability for *actions* where liability under *Rylands* would not arise. This has been questioned by some academics and is potentially likely to be a very fine distinction in some cases. The simplest explanation when looking at the element of escape is to see the tort as part of private nuisance and therefore based upon interference with another person's land. If this is accepted, the claim in *Read* should have been based in personal injury.

6. Who may sue?

An initial restriction on who is entitled to bring an action is imposed by the rule expressed above in *Read* v. *Lyons and Co. Ltd* that the escape must have been from a place under the defendant occupier's control to a place outside his control. This means that if, as in *Read* v. *Lyons*, the plaintiff is on the defendant's land at the time injury is suffered, their action on the *Rylands* v. *Fletcher* principle will fail. As noted above, the more appropriate action would be negligence in such circumstances.

Secondly, the action is probably only open to those who have some interest in the land which has been affected. There is *obiter dicta* to the contrary in *Perry* v. *Kendrick's Transport Ltd* [1956] and *British Celanese Ltd* v. *A. H. Hunt* [1969]. In a New Zealand case, *N.Z. Forest Products Ltd* v. *O'Sullivan* [1974], it was said that 'liability under *Rylands* v. *Fletcher* requires proof of interference with the use of the land of another'. The person whose land is affected need not be the owner. It is sufficient if he is the occupier, defined in *Benning* v. *Wong* [1969], as a person who has 'some right or interest in land beyond that of a mere gratuitous licensee'. This clearly includes tenants and licensees in exclusive occupation.

7. What damage may be claimed?

Apart from claiming for the damage caused to the land, the plaintiff may also claim for damage to chattels, *see Jones* v. *Festiniog Railway Co.* (1868), but not for personal injury.

Following *Cambridge Water Co. Ltd* v. *Eastern Counties Leather plc* [1994] it should be noted that the correct test for liability is the *Wagon Mound* test of reasonable foresight and not a test of directness.

DEFENCES

In the following instances the occupier is not liable under the rule in *Rylands* v. *Fletcher* – although he may be liable for negligence:

    Consent of the plaintiff.
    Default of the plaintiff.
    Statutory authority.
    Act of a stranger.
    Act of God.

8. Consent of the plaintiff

(a) If the plaintiff expressly or impliedly consented to the defendant's bringing and keeping the dangerous thing on his premises, the latter will not be liable in the absence of negligence. Thus, the tenants of lower floors in a building may be taken to have impliedly consented to damage by water which escapes, without the occupier's negligence, from the upper floors – for the water is there by the implied consent and for the common benefit of the various occupiers.

(b) The defence will *not* apply, however, to an extraordinary use, or quantity, of water, for the defendant's own purposes. *See Western Engraving Co.* v. *Film Laboratories Ltd* [1936], where there was an escape of an excessive quantity of water accumulated by defendants for washing film.

9. Default of the plaintiff

This may arise where the plaintiff causes his own injury or where it arises through the special sensitivity of his own property.

(a) *Plaintiff causes own injury*. If the plaintiff himself caused his injury he cannot recover under the rule. In *Rylands* v. *Fletcher* itself Lord Blackburn specifically made reference to the fact that the defendant could 'excuse himself by showing that the escape was due to the plaintiff's default'. The Law Reform (Contributory Negligence) Act 1945 will apply to reduce damages awarded where the plaintiff's conduct is part of the reason for or cause of the damage suffered.

(b) *Special sensitivity.* By analogy with the similar rule in nuisance, a plaintiff cannot recover for damage arising from the special sensitivity of his property.

10. Statutory authority

The defendant may plead that he is exempt by statutory authority from *Rylands* v. *Fletcher* liability: but the success of the plea will depend on the construction of the statute in question; if, for example, the statute in question does not contain provision making the undertaker liable in nuisance it will be necessary to prove negligence to establish liability.

In *Green* v. *Chelsea Waterways Co.* (1894), the defendants' water main burst, flooding the plaintiff's premises. The defendants had statutory authority to lay the main and a statutory duty to supply water, and they had not been negligent. It was held that they were not liable in *Rylands* v. *Fletcher*. This was re-affirmed by the Court of Appeal in *Dunne* v. *North Western Gas Board* [1964], although the relevant statute expressly preserved liability in nuisance. Such cases should be contrasted with *Charing Cross Electricity Supply Co.* v. *Hydraulic Power Co.* [1914], in which, on similar facts, the defendants were held liable in *Rylands* v. *Fletcher*. In this case, however, the defendants, although they had *statutory powers* to lay mains and supply water, were under no *statutory obligation* to do so.

A defendant with statutory exemption from *Rylands* v. *Fletcher* liability may nevertheless be liable if there was negligence. In *Hardaker* v. *Idle District Council* (1896), the defendants had statutory authority to supply gas. Gas escaped into the plaintiff's house because of the negligence of the council's independent contractor. It was held that the council were liable in *Rylands* v. *Fletcher*.

11. Act of a stranger

The occupier will not be liable in *Rylands* v. *Fletcher* where the escape of the dangerous thing arose from the act of a stranger over whom the occupier had no control.

In *Box* v. *Jubb* (1879), a third person discharged water into the defendant's reservoir, so that it overflowed and damaged the plaintiff's property. It was held that there was no liability in *Rylands* v. *Fletcher*. In *Rickards* v. *Lothian* [1913], water was caused to escape from a lavatory on the upper storey of a block of flats, by the malicious act of a third party. The occupier of the upper flat was held not liable in *Rylands* v. *Fletcher* to the occupier of the lower flat which was damaged. The onus is on the *defendant* to show:

(a) that the escape was due to the act of a stranger

(b) that he had no control over that stranger

(c) that he could not reasonably have guarded against the act.

Note also that an occupier may be liable in *negligence* for the act of a stranger when the circumstances are such that the occupier ought to have taken reasonable steps to guard against it. In *Jaundrill* v. *Gillet* [1996] the malicious release on the road of horses kept by the defendant by a 'stranger' did not render the defendant liable in damages for injuries sustained by the plaintiff when the horses collided with his car. In *North Western Utilities* v. *London Guarantee and Accident Co.* [1936], a Privy Council case, gas was being carried at high pressure underground by the appellants. It escaped as a result of a leak caused by third parties, and caused the destruction of a hotel insured by the respondents. The appellants were held liable in negligence because of the conspicuous nature of the third parties' activities which were foreseeable and could have been prevented. A *stranger* for these purposes is a trespasser; or a person who causes the escape, although he did not himself come upon the land. It is important to distinguish strangers from employees for whom an occupier is vicariously liable. An occupier will also be liable for escapes resulting from the acts of his independent contractor. In *E. Hobbs (Farms) Ltd* v. *The Baxenden Chemical Co. Ltd* [1992] it was held that the landowner's liability extended not only to escapes from his land caused by the negligence of an independent contractor but also those caused by the negligence of the manufacturer whose materials the independent contractor used.

12. Act of God

The possibility that an act of God might provide a defence was expressly recognised in *Rylands* v. *Fletcher* by Lord Blackburn. There is, however, conflicting subsequent authority as to whether or not this is the case. In *Nichols* v. *Marsland* (1876), the damming of a stream on the defendant's land had created artificial pools; the embankments were efficiently constructed and secure against ordinary eventualities. A storm, described by witnesses as the most severe in living memory, broke down the embankments and caused damage to bridges. It was held by the Court of Appeal that the defendant was not liable as the escape had been caused by an act of God. In *Greenock Corporation* v. *Caledonian Railway Company* [1917], however, despite similar circumstances where the rain fell in an 'extraordinary and it may be said an unprecedented spate', the defence failed.

Although *Nichols* v. *Marsland* does not appear to have been followed since, the modern trend is to require that there be at least some degree of foreseeability as a pre-requisite of liability (although not the foreseeability required for a negligence action to succeed). This trend would seem to support the view that the defence should be available, albeit in wholly exceptional circumstances. If it is to be established, it must be shown that the escape in question was the result of a wholly unforeseeable natural event against which it was impossible to provide any precautions. Showing that it would not be reasonably possible to guard against the risk will not be enough.

13. The role of *Rylands* v. *Fletcher* today

It has been argued that *Rylands* v. *Fletcher* has no defined role nowadays given the number of exceptions and defences applicable to it. A further factor is the use of private and public nuisance which deal with many similar situations in a perfectly satisfactory manner. It could be said that the tort is only suitable in cases where there is a non-continuous escape from land resulting from non-natural use damaging the use of the land and affecting only a small part of the public.

The *Cambridge Water* case has however highlighted the possibility of using the tort, even if in limited circumstances, as a means of obtaining a remedy for environmental damage. This will be an interesting development to observe.

LIABILITY FOR ANIMALS

Liability for damage caused by animals is in some circumstances strict. In most circumstances however it will depend on proof of a knowledge that the animal was dangerous for the establishment of a general action in trespass, nuisance or negligence.

14. The common law position

(a) *Strict liability*. Under the Animals Act 1971 a person who is the keeper of an animal classed as *ferae naturae* (fierce by nature) is strictly liable for damage caused by the animal, knowledge of its dangerous propensity being presumed.

(b) *The scienter action*. Prior to the 1971 Act a person in charge of an animal classed as *mansuetae naturae* (tame by nature) was only liable for damage caused by the animal if:

(*i*) *Scienter* or knowledge of its dangerous propensity could be proved, e.g. by proving it had previously manifested behaviour of the type complained of or had displayed a general vicious propensity, or

(*ii*) He could be made liable in trespass, nuisance, negligence, contract, or another general head of liability.

The classification of a species as *ferae naturae* or *mansuetae naturae* was a question of law. Examples of the former are lions, tigers and gorillas, and of the latter, dogs, cats and camels.

THE ANIMALS ACT 1971

This Act retains the distinction between dangerous and non-dangerous animals and simplifies the common law position.

15. Strict liability

Section 2(1) of the Act retains the common law rule of strict liability for dangerous animals.

16. Dangerous animals defined

Section 6 defines a dangerous species as:

(a) 'one which is not commonly domesticated in the British Islands' and

(b) 'whose fully grown animals normally have such characteristics that they are likely, unless restrained, to cause severe damage or that any damage they may cause is likely to be severe'.

The definition is not confined to animals likely to attack humans but includes those which pose a danger to property only or which may spread disease.

17. Nature of the liability

The Act imposes liability on the *keeper*. Section 6(3) provides that a person is a keeper of an animal if (a) he owns the animal or has it in his possession; or (b) he is the head of a household of which a member under the age of sixteen owns the animal or has it in his possession. Section 6(3) also provides that if an animal ceases to be owned or possessed by its keeper, that person shall continue to be liable until another person owns or possesses the animal.

Section 6(4) provides that a person is not the keeper of an animal which he has taken into his possession solely in order to prevent it causing damage or to return it to its owner.

An animal may therefore have more than one keeper. In this situation there would be joint liability on the keepers.

18. Liability for animals not belonging to a dangerous species

Section 2(2) imposes strict liability, subject to certain provisions, on keepers of animals which do not belong to a dangerous species. These provisions are:

(a) The damage is of a kind which the animal, unless restrained, was *likely* to cause or which, if caused by the animal, was likely to be severe; *and*

(b) *The likelihood* of the damage or its being severe was due to characteristics of the animal which are not normally found in animals of the same species or are not normally so found except at particular times or in particular circumstances; *and*

(c) Those characteristics were known to that keeper or were at any time known to a person who at that time had charge of the animal as that keeper's servant or, where that keeper is the head of a household, were known to another keeper of the animal who is a member of that household and under the age of sixteen.

In *Cummings* v. *Grainger* [1977], a young woman entered a scrap yard in which an Alsatian dog with a known propensity to attack people was allowed to roam loose. It attacked the plaintiff, who sued under s. 2(2) of the Act. It was held that it was unreasonable to keep a dog of that character, roaming loose in a yard in a well-populated area, particularly as members of the public had a licence to enter the yard. The defendant could not rely on the defences provided by s. 5 of the Act and the plaintiff succeeded; but her damages were reduced by half because she was a trespasser.

In *Smith* v. *Ainger* [1990] (CA), the plaintiff was injured when the defendant's dog, in making an attack on the plaintiff's dog (which was on a lead held by the plaintiff), came into contact with the plaintiff and knocked him over. 'Likely' in s. 2(2)(a) was interpreted by the court as covering things which might happen, thus being broader in meaning than things which were more probable than not.

In another Court of Appeal case, *Curtis* v. *Betts* [1990], the plaintiff was injured when bitten by the defendant's bull mastiff. The Court of Appeal again considered s. 2(2) of the Animals Act 1971, and rejected the view that under the second limb of s. 2(2)(a) the animal in question had to have abnormal characteristics for its species which rendered it likely that, if it caused damage, such damage would be severe. Section 2(2)(a) could apply without such abnormal characteristics being present. In relation to s. 2(2)(b) Stuart-Smith LJ stated:

> 'To my mind the difficulty in the subsection arises from the first three words, "the likelihood of". Without these words, it would be plain that para. (b) was concerned with causation of damage. The plaintiff would have to prove that the damage of one of the types in para. (a) was caused either by a permanent or temporary characteristic specified in para. (b). This makes good sense. But the first three words seem to connote a concept of foreseeability and not causation. This would have remarkable consequences . . . Although I find difficulty in giving content to the words "the likelihood of", I am satisfied that there must be a causal link between the characteristic in question and the damage suffered. In particular, where the case falls under the second limb, the temporary characteristic, the time or circumstances in which the damage is caused, must be those during which particular characteristics are or were prone to be exhibited.'

See also Jaundrill v. *Gillett* [1996] (CA).

19. Defences to actions under s. 2

Section 5 provides that a person is not liable under s. 2:

(a) for any damage which is due wholly to the fault of the person suffering it

(b) for any damage suffered by any person who has voluntarily accepted the risk thereof, e.g. by intervening in a fight between animals (i.e. *volenti non fit injuria* is a good defence)

(c) for any damage caused by an animal kept on any premises or structure to a person trespassing there, if it is proved either that the animal was not kept there for the protection of persons or property; or, if the animal was kept there for that purpose, that keeping it there was not unreasonable.

TRESPASSING LIVESTOCK

Section 4 imposes strict liability on a person in possession of livestock where:

(a) Damage is done by the livestock to the land or to any property on it which is in the ownership or possession of the other person; *or*

(b) Any expenses are reasonably incurred by that other person in keeping the livestock while it cannot be restored to the person to whom it belongs or while it is detained in pursuance of s. 7 of the Act, or in ascertaining its owner.

Note that, although the liability is strict, i.e. no fault need be proved, the tort is not, as it was at common law, actionable *per se*, because damage must be proved consequent upon the entry.

20. Who can sue?

Action under s. 4 can be brought by the person in possession of the affected land or by the owner not in possession if the action is for damage to chattels on it (which presumably includes other animals), and for expenses incurred in keeping livestock until it can be returned to its owner. But he cannot recover under s. 4 for his personal injuries.

21. Cattle trespass

The Act makes the following changes from the common law position:

(a) Although liability for cattle trespass remains strict, it is no longer actionable *per se*; but damage consequent upon entry must be proved.

(b) The plaintiff can no longer recover for personal injuries through cattle trespass, but must establish negligence or liability under s. 2.

(c) There is no longer liability, under s. 4, in respect of damage by trespassing cattle to the chattels of a person not in occupation of the land.

22. Detention of animals

Section 7 abolishes the old common law right to seize and detain animals by way of distress damage feasant, and replaces it by the right of an occupier of land to retain livestock straying on to the land, subject to certain time limits and the provisions as to settlement of claims under s. 4. The occupier is given the right to sell detained animals after fourteen days unless proceedings are pending for the return of the animals or for a claim under s. 4. The detaining occupier can be made liable for damage caused by failure adequately to care for or feed the animals.

ANIMALS STRAYING ON TO THE HIGHWAY

23. Liability under the 1971 Act

Here we must consider liability: (*i*) under the Act; (*ii*) at common law, in negligence and nuisance.

(a) Section 8(1) abolishes the rule in *Searle* v. *Wallbank* [1947], which was that the occupier of land was under no duty to fence his land so as to keep his animals

147

off the highway; therefore he was not liable, save in exceptional circumstances, for damage done by his domestic animals which strayed on to the highway.

(b) Section 8(1) provides that an occupier of land now owes a duty of care in respect of his non-dangerous animals which stray from his land on to the highway. However, s. 8(2) provides that a breach of duty is not committed by a person by reason only of the fact that he placed an animal on land which is common land or a town or village green, provided he had the right to place the animal on that land.

In *Davies* v. *Davies* [1974], the defendant had the right to graze cattle and sheep on land registered as common under the Commons Registration Act 1965. The common was unfenced and adjoined a road. The plaintiff drove into the defendant's sheep which had strayed from the common on to the road. The plaintiff sued for damage to his car, alleging negligence by the defendant in not fencing his land. It was held that because the land was common and the defendant had a right to place animals on it, s. 8(2) of the Animals Act 1971 provided a good defence and the plaintiff could not rely on the duty in s. 8(1) to prevent animals from straying on to a highway. The plaintiff therefore failed. *See also Jaundrill* v. *Gillett* [1996]: runaway horses maliciously released on to the highway by other persons.

24. Liability in negligence and nuisance

The Act does not affect liability under these heads, so that persons who bring or drive animals on the highway incur a duty to take reasonable care to avoid damage to persons and property. In *Gomberg* v. *Smith* [1962], the defendant's St Bernard dog ran out of a shop, damaged the plaintiff's van on the highway and the plaintiff sued in negligence. It was held that he could succeed. The defendant had brought the dog on to the highway and therefore had a duty to take reasonable care to control it.

A person who takes an animal on the highway discharges his duty by taking reasonable care. In *Haimes* v. *Watson* [1981], the County Court judge had held that a rider whose horse shied into a car was under an absolute duty to control the horse at all times. The Court of Appeal declined that interpretation of the law and affirmed that a person alleging damage by a tame animal cannot succeed unless he proves negligence by the person in charge of the animal.

A person in charge of a tame animal is not negligent merely because he 'failed to provide against the possibility that a tame animal of mild disposition will do something contrary to its ordinary nature': *see Aldham* v. *United Dairies (London) Ltd* [1940].

There is liability, probably in nuisance, for large numbers of animals which stray on to the highway and obstruct it, or make its use dangerous: *see Cunningham* v. *Whelan* (1917).

DAMAGE BY DOGS

Section 3 replaces liability under the Dogs Acts 1906 and 1928 and provides that 'Where a dog causes damage by killing or injuring livestock, any person who is keeper of the dog is liable for the damage, except as otherwise provided by the Act.' The relevant provisions are that there is no liability for damage due:

(a) wholly to the fault of the person suffering it; *or*

(b) 'if the livestock was killed or injured on land on to which it had strayed and either the dog belonged to the occupier or its presence on the land was authorised by the occupier': s. 5(4).

THE CONSUMER PROTECTION ACT 1987

25. Product liability

A new form of strict liability was imposed by the Consumer Protection Act 1987. Sections 2(1), 2(2) and 2(3) impose strict liability for damage caused wholly or partly by a defect in a product to:

(a) The producer of the product.

(b) Any person who, by putting his name on the product or using a trademark or other distinguishing mark in relation to the product, has held himself out to be the producer of the product.

(c) Any person who has imported the product into the European Community in order to supply it to another.

(d) A supplier who having received a request by the person suffering the damage to name a person falling under **(a)**, **(b)** or **(c)** fails within a reasonable time to do so.

26. What is a defect?

Section 3 of the Consumer Protection Act 1987 says that there is a defect if the safety of the product is not such as persons are generally entitled to expect. In determining what persons are entitled to expect all the circumstances and particularly the following are to be taken into account:

(a) The manner in which and purposes for which the product has been marketed, its get-up, the use of any mark in relation to the product and any instructions for, or warnings with respect to, doing or refraining from doing anything with, or in relation to, the product. One might ask whether the product is aimed at children or adults; amateurs or professionals; and whether it contained safety catches or similar devices.

(b) What might reasonably be expected to be done with, or in relation to, the product. So the manufacturer may for instance be expected to provide warnings to guard against foreseeable misuses of the product.

(c) The time when the product was supplied by the producer to another.

27. What is 'damage'?

Section 5 defines damage as covering:

(a) Death or personal injury.

(b) Loss or damage to any property including land. There are three restrictions on liability for damage to property:

(*i*) There is no liability for loss of or damage to the product itself (this would require an ordinary contractual claim). Nor is there any liability for any loss or damage to the whole or part of a product comprised in it. This means that if a car is supplied with a defective steering wheel and this causes the car to crash there is no liability under the Act for damage to the car or the steering wheel. If, however, the steering wheel was supplied separately as a replacement there would be liability for damage to the car although not for the steering wheel.

(*ii*) If the product at the time it is damaged is not of a description of property ordinarily intended for private use, occupation or consumption and intended by the person suffering the loss or damage mainly for his own private use, occupation or consumption, then there is no liability under the Act.

(*iii*) For there to be liability under Act the damage suffered to the property must exceed £275.

28. Did the damage 'cause' the defect?

This question is answered by applying the normal rules of causation which apply in tort.

29. Defences

The following defences are open to defendants under s. 4:

(a) That the defect is attributable to compliance with any statutory requirement or community obligation.

(b) That the person proceeded against did not at any time supply the product to another. This will cover instances of mistaken identity or where goods are stolen from the producer and then supplied by the thief to someone else.

(c) That the supply of the product was not in the course of a business and the person was not a producer, own brander or European Community importer (*see* Product liability, **25** above) or if he was, that the activity was not carried out with a view to profit. The defence in general will cover both private sales (e.g. of a car) or sales by producers not intended to make a profit (e.g. sale of home baking at a church fete).

(d) That the defect did not exist in the product at the relevant time. *What is the relevant time*? This is defined by s. 4(2) and varies depending on who the defendant is. If the defendant is a producer, own brander or Community importer the relevant time is when the product was supplied by them to another.

They are not responsible for defects caused by those succeeding them in the chain of distribution. If the defendant is the supplier or retailer, the relevant time is when the product was last supplied by a producer, own brander or Community importer, i.e. when it was supplied to the supplier or retailer. So if the product is not defective when a manufacturer supplies it to the retailer, and it is rendered defective by the retailer, neither the manufacturer nor the retailer are liable under the Act. The retailer may of course be liable in negligence or breach of contract.

(e) That the state of scientific and technical knowledge at the relevant time was not such that a producer of products of the same description as the one in question might be expected to have discovered the defect had it existed in his products while they were under his control.

The 'relevant time' when the state of knowledge is to be assessed is when it is *supplied* by the producer (not when it is *manufactured*). This means he must keep up to date with new developments until he supplies the goods.

(f) That the defect constituted a defect in a subsequent product in which the product in question had been comprised and was wholly attributable to the design of the subsequent product, or to compliance by the producer with instructions given by the producer of the subsequent product.

Progress test 9

1. State the rule in *Rylands* v. *Fletcher* in the words of Blackburn J.

2. What is a thing naturally brought on to the land?

3. When is the occupier not liable under the rule in *Rylands* v. *Fletcher*?

4. What is the significance of the decision of the House of Lords in *Cambridge Water Co. Ltd*. v. *Eastern Counties Leather plc* [1994]?

5. What are the conditions of liability under the Animals Act 1971?

6. Who may be liable and for what under the Consumer Protection Act 1987?

10

BREACH OF STATUTORY DUTY

FUNDAMENTAL CONSIDERATIONS

For over a century it has been a vexed question as to whether breach of a statutory duty by the defendant which caused loss to the plaintiff should give the plaintiff the right to an action in tort independent of any statutory remedy he may have. Assuming that the plaintiff is able to prove that the breach has actually caused the loss or damage alleged, the task of the court is to ascertain exactly what Parliament's intention was. This is normally done by asking two questions: (1) was the plaintiff a person or a member of a class intended to be protected by the statute; and (2) was the injury alleged of the type which the statute was designed to prevent?

The leading decision on breach of statutory duty is that of the House of Lords in *X* v. *Bedfordshire C.C.* [1995]. The opinion of Lord Browne-Wilkinson in this decision is referred to below in this chapter. The opinion of Lord Jauncey provides a useful introduction to the ambit of breach of statutory duty. Lord Jauncey explains the scope of the tort of breach of statutory duty:

> 'Where a statute confers a private law right of action a breach of statutory duty howsoever caused will found the action. Where the statute authorises that to be done which will necessarily cause injury to someone no action will lie if the act is performed with reasonable care. If, on the other hand, the act is performed carelessly whereby unnecessary damage is caused a common law action will lie. This because the act would, but for the statute, be actionable at common law and the defence which the statute provides extends only to the careful performance of the act. The statute only authorises the invasion of private rights to the extent that the statutory powers are exercised with reasonable and proper regard for the holders of such rights. The careless performance of an authorised act, rather than amounting to breach of a new duty, simply ceases to be a defence to a common law right of action.'

1. Does the statute aim to protect that person or class?

A statute may criminalise a particular act without intending to protect a specific class of people. In *Lonhro* v. *Shell Petroleum* [1981], a sanctions order made it a criminal offence to supply oil to Rhodesia. The sole purpose of this prohibition was to undermine the illegal government in Rhodesia. Commission of the offence by unlawful trading did not, therefore, give a right of action in tort to anyone occasioning loss because breach of the order prolonged the regime. If, however, the criminalisation of a particular act or omission by a statutory provision is intended to protect a particular person or class of persons, then a person belonging to that class will have an action in tort if injured in consequence of a breach of the provision. In *Groves* v. *Wimborne (Lord)* [1898], an employer failed in his statutory duty to fence dangerous machinery. An employee who was injured as a result of this criminal offence was able to recover damages.

(a) Often a statute will lay down general guidelines relating to the allocation, for example, of services and facilities to the public. Those responsible for these services and facilities are often given considerable discretion in the manner of provision and generally cannot be made liable in tort for loss which results from their failure to carry out adequately their statutory duties. However, if the plaintiff can show that he belongs to a class of people that these statutory duties were intended to protect, then he will have a claim in tort if the breach of duty causes him loss. In *Thornton* v. *Kirklees M.B.C.* [1979], it was held that local authority duties under the Housing (Homeless Persons) Act 1977 were clearly intended to benefit homeless people who would consequently have a right of action in tort should a breach of duty cause them loss or damage.

An example of the impact of a statutory duty owed by a local authority can be seen in the House of Lords decision in *X* v. *Bedfordshire C.C.* [1995]. An authority must make particular provision for children with special educational needs, such as those affected by dyslexia; no action in damages lies against the authority for breach of this duty: *see also E* v. *Dorset C.C.* [1994]. By way of contrast, the same legislation requires that safety in schools be reasonably assured; a child who injures herself on unsafe equipment, or who cuts herself on a thin pane of glass, can recover for her injuries: *see Reffell* v. *Surrey C.C.* [1964]. A further recent example is *Richardson* v. *Pitt-Stanley* [1995], regarding breaches of the Employer's Liability (Compulsory Insurance) Act 1969, whether an individual director can be liable in civil law for breach of this legislation in which he had connived with others.

(b) The court may conclude that, even though the injured party was someone the Act intended to protect, the remedy or penalty provided in the statute was the only one intended, thereby precluding an action in tort. In the leading case of *Atkinson* v. *Newcastle & Gateshead Water Co.* (1877), the plaintiff's timber yard was destroyed by fire because of the defendants' failure to discharge their duty under the Waterworks Clauses Act 1847, to maintain minimum pressures in water mains. The statute provided for a penalty of £10 for each day that the pressures were not maintained. It was held that on the true construction of the Act this was intended to be the only penalty available. The plaintiff could not, therefore, recover damages in tort for breach of the duty. This approach has been followed in more recent cases concerning public authority liability: *Re HIV Haemophiliac Litigation* [1990]; *R.* v. *Knowsley B.C., ex parte Maguire* [1992]; *Wentworth* v. *Wiltshire C.C.* [1993]

(c) By way of qualification of **(b)** above, it should be stressed that there is *no general presumption against civil liability* simply because a specific remedy is provided for in the statute. It is a matter of interpreting the intention of Parliament in each case. A useful guide to Parliament's intention is the extent of detail in which the duty is couched in the statute. The more *specific* the duty is, the more likely the court is to hold that a *tort action is available* for damage caused by breach. In *Monk* v. *Warbey* [1935], the defendant lent his car to a person who was uninsured against third party risks. The borrower drove negligently and injured the plaintiff. The plaintiff was held to be entitled to sue the owner directly for breach of his duty under the Road Traffic Act in force at the time. If this had been held otherwise the clear object of the statute (to protect those injured by impecunious drivers) would have been defeated. Where, however, the duty is couched in more general terms such as in the Motor Vehicles (Construction and Use) Regulations 1966, breach is unlikely to give rise to any liability in tort.

(d) It may be that the statute did not intend breach of duty to give rise to an action for breach of the statutory duty itself, but that the appropriate remedy is an action for negligence at common law. In *Knapp* v. *Railway Executive* [1949], an engine driver was injured when a car ran into level crossing gates, which had not been maintained in accordance with the relevant statute. It was held that the purpose of the Road Traffic Act was to protect *road* users only and so the engine driver did not come within its scope. In *Wentworth* v. *Wiltshire County Council* [1993] a plaintiff seeking to recover for damage to his business caused by disrepair of the adjacent highway failed in his claim. The duty to maintain the highway existed to protect users against personal injury and not to safeguard the profits of traders.

The House of Lords decisions in the cases of *Hague* v. *Deputy Governor of Parkhurst Prison* [1991] and *Weldon* v. *Home Office* [1992] have served to show the approach taken by their Lordships to breach of statutory duty. From those cases it is clear that in determining whether a plaintiff is entitled to damages for breach of statutory duty the test is whether the legislature intended to confer on the plaintiff a private law cause of action for breach of statutory duty and not whether the plaintiff belongs to a class which the statutory provision is intended to protect and as a result of a breach of that provision has suffered damage of a kind against which the provision was intended to protect him.

These actions, based upon segregation within prisons in breach of Rule 42 of the Prison Rules 1964, were dismissed by their Lordships, the House of Lords taking the view that the breaches of the Prison Rules did not give rise to an action for breach of statutory duty.

A further issue raised by these cases is the tort of trespass to the person – *see* p. 173.

For further illustrations of the Courts' approach in cases of breach of statutory duty *see West Wilts D.C.* v. *Pugh & Others* [1994] where Merritt J held that a district auditor owes a statutory duty under the Local Government Finance Act 1982 to a local authority whose accounts he audits, that duty being enforceable by an action for damages by the local authority; and *R.* v. *Associated Octel Ltd* [1994] (CA), a prosecution under the Health and Safety at Work Act 1974.

The interplay between the imposition of a statutory duty and the common law was discussed at length by their Lordships in *X* v. *Bedfordshire C.C.* [1995].

This consolidated appeal dealt with the issues concerning a local authority's powers in relation to child abuse and special educational needs. Lord Browne-Wilkinson took the view that with regard to child abuse, the relevant statutory duties do not give rise to an action for damages where they are breached. On the facts he considered that the local authority's actions were within their discretion and therefore did not found the basis for a claim. He concluded that it would not be just and reasonable to overlay a further common law duty, nor appropriate given the House of Lords approach to the extension of duty of care in negligence as set out in *Caparo Industries plc* v. *Dickman* [1990]. On the ground of public policy, Lord Nolan concurred with Lord Browne-Wilkinson that the social workers involved did not owe a personal duty of care to the plaintiffs; hence their employers could not be vicariously liable for their actions. As to education, the House held, in the absence of an appeal from the Court of Appeal's decision as to breach of statutory duty, that the authority owed no common law duty of care in the exercise of its powers and discretion with regard to children with special educational needs.

2. Is the injury alleged of the type the statute was designed to prevent?

In *Gorris* v. *Scott* (1974), the plaintiff's sheep were washed overboard because the defendant failed in his statutory duty to provide pens on the ship's deck. There was no action in tort for breach of this statutory duty as the object of the duty was to prevent the spread of disease and not to prevent sheep being washed overboard. As long as the damage caused comes within the risk contemplated by the duty there may be an action for breach of the duty even though the circumstances were not exactly as contemplated by the statutory duty. So if in *Gorris* v. *Scott* the sheep as a result of not being properly penned had contracted some previously unheard of disease, this would have fallen within the risk contemplated by the imposition of the duty, and there would have been an action in tort open to the plaintiff.

Similarly, in *Wentworth* v. *Wiltshire County Council* [1993] the duty imposed on highway authorities to repair the roads in order to protect users from injury was held not to include loss to profit to a local trader.

In *Donaghey* v. *Boulton and Paul Ltd* [1968], the statutory regulation in question was intended to prevent men working on a roof from falling to the ground. The plaintiff was able to claim in tort for breach of the regulation even though he fell through a hole in the roof and not though fragile roofing material.

There may be a significant degree of uncertainty in any particular case as to whether or not an action for breach of a statutory duty is available. The basic test relating to the intention of Parliament in each situation appears straightforward but the approach adopted by the courts to ascertain this intention lacks uniformity. The modern and preferable trend is for Parliament to specify in the statute whether an action for breach of statutory duty will be *available* (as in the Sex Discrimination Act 1975, s. 66(1), the Race Relation Act 1976, s. 57(1), and the Consumer Safety Act 1978, s. 6) *or not* (as in the Safety of Sports Grounds Act 1975, s. 13 and the Guard Dogs Act 1975, s. 5).

BREACH OF DUTY AND THE MATTER OF FAULT

3. Whether or not fault is required to constitute breach of duty

Once it has been decided on the above rules whether or not there is a claim in tort for breach of statutory duty it is a question of construction as to whether the duty is absolute or whether there requires to be proof of fault.

An example of an absolute statutory obligation is s. 14 of the Factories Act 1961 which requires every dangerous part of machinery (excepting prime movers and transmission machinery) to be securely fenced unless it is in such a position or so constructed that it is safe as if it was fenced. This duty, however, is not as absolute as it may appear. For instance, for machinery to be dangerous it must be shown that it could possibly cause injury to anyone acting as they might reasonably be expected to act in reasonably contemplated circumstances. There is, therefore, an element of reasonable foreseeability in the determination of whether the duty has been broken, and it needs to be decided what type of behaviour and in what circumstances could reasonably have been foreseen. However, in *Summers (John) & Sons Ltd* v. *Frost* [1955], it was made clear that it may be necessary to foresee careless as well as careful conduct. An example of breach of the *absolute* duty to fence dangerous machinery is *Groves* v. *Wimborne, see* **1** above.

4. Reasonably practicable steps

In many cases (e.g. Health and Safety at Work, etc. Act 1974) the duty will be to take all reasonably practicable steps to avoid a particular risk. This is not an absolute duty and requires a balancing of the risk against the practicability of the measures needed to avoid it. Practicability is assessed with regard to the time, trouble and efficiency (but not cost) that would be occasioned by remedial measures. These measures must also be practicable according to relevant knowledge and resources at the time.

In *Adsett* v. *K. and L. Steelfounders and Engineers Ltd* [1953], Singleton LJ remarked that: 'In deciding whether all practicable measures were taken one must have regard to the state of knowledge at the material time and particularly to the knowledge of scientific experts.'

See also *R.* v. *Associated Octel Ltd* [1994] (CA) where it was held that the question of degree of control held by an employer over the actions of an independent contractor was relevant to what was reasonably practicable. What was reasonably practicable was said to be a question of fact and degree in each case.

5. Exercise of a discretionary power

Where a local authority exercises a discretionary statutory power, it thereby assumes a duty of care in respect of the exercise of the power, to persons subsequently affected by the authority's negligence in so doing. An example is

Anns v. *Merton London Borough Council* [1978], where the discretionary power was to inspect buildings under the Public Health Act 1936.

6. Statutory negligence

(a) *Scope of statutory duties.* In some instances, e.g. many of the duties imposed by the Factories Acts and the Health and Safety at Work Act, the statutory duty *includes* the duty to take care not to cause harm. In other statutes, e.g. the Road Traffic Acts, this is not the case. The former type of duty was described by Lord Wright, in *Lochgelly Iron & Coal Co.* v. *McMullan* [1934], as 'statutory negligence' – which has been taken to mean that in these cases the criteria of common law negligence and breach of statutory duty largely coincide. Lord Wright subsequently made it clear, however, in *London Passenger Transport Board* v. *Upson* [1949], that he regarded negligence and breach of statutory duty as distinct torts. This is generally accepted – the differences being as follows:

(*i*) In negligence the standard of care is decided by the court; but in breach of statutory duty it is laid down in the statute.

(*ii*) The application of *volenti non fit injuria* differs in the two cases.

(*iii*) In practice and pleading they are treated as distinct and separate causes of action.

(*iv*) A defendant alleged to be in breach of his statutory duty need not necessarily prove, in order to avoid liability, that he did not break his common law duty.

(b) *Overlapping.* The two torts do coincide, firstly to the extent that, when a plaintiff has pleaded both, his success in the one claim usually also settles the other. Secondly if, as in *American Express Co.* v. *British Airways Board* [1983], the statute confers immunity from *proceedings in tort*, this will apply to potential common law and statutory torts.

7. The burden and standard of proof

The plaintiff is required to prove on the balance of probabilities that the breach of duty caused the loss or injury alleged. In *Bonnington Castings Ltd* v. *Wardlaw* [1956], the plaintiff, because of the defendants' breach of the Factories Acts with respect to ventilation, was injured by inhaling silica dust. The defendants admitted the breach but denied it caused the plaintiff's injury. The House of Lords rejected this plea but nevertheless emphasised the obligation to prove causality. Lord Reid stressed that an employee cannot succeed *merely* because there was a breach of duty which could *possibly* have caused his injury, but that he must prove *causation*: 'The employee must, in all cases, prove his case by the ordinary standard of proof in civil actions; he must make it appear at least that, on a balance of probabilities, the breach of duty caused, or materially contributed to, his injury.'

In *Cummings (or McWilliams)* v. *Sir William Arrol & Co. Ltd* [1962], a steel erector was killed by falling seventy feet. A safely belt would have saved him, but belts were not available, contrary to statutory regulations. However it was the practice of steel erectors never to wear safely belts. It was held that even if belts had been available it was very improbable that the deceased would have worn one, so the claim failed: '. . . If I prove that my breach of duty in no way caused or contributed to the accident I cannot be liable in damages', *per* Lord Reid.

DEFENCES

8. *Volenti non fit injuria* (or consent)

Because contracting out of a statutory duty is forbidden as against public policy, the consent of the plaintiff cannot be a defence to a breach of statutory duty whereby he was injured.

For the same reason, however, employees who injure themselves and each other by embarking on a joint enterprise in breach of a statutory duty imposed upon them, cannot make their employer vicariously liable for such breach; for it would be clearly against public policy if an employee could evade the legal consequence of his own breach by causing a fellow employee to join him in it.

In *ICI Ltd* v. *Shatwell* [1964], two qualified shot-firers were injured through testing a circuit without taking shelter, although they knew it was dangerous and against both the company's orders and statutory regulations. It was held that *volenti non fit injuria* was a complete defence to the company in respect of its alleged vicarious liability.

9. Contributory negligence

Contributory negligence is a good defence to an action for breach of statutory duty: *see Caswell* v. *Powell Duffryn Collieries Ltd* [1940] The damages may be apportioned under the Law Reform (Contributory Negligence) Act 1945. Note that the relevant part of the decision in *Caswell* v. *Powell Duffryn etc.* although unanimous was also *obiter*.

Contributory negligence may not be easy to establish where a workman sues his employer for breach of statutory duty, for the standard to be expected is only that of an *ordinary prudent workman*; 'It is not for every risky thing that a workman in a factory may do . . . that the plaintiff ought to be held guilty of contributory negligence.' *See Flower* v. *Ebbw Vale Iron & Steel Co.* [1936], *per* Lawrence J.

If the workman has been manifestly careless this will reduce or negate the employer's liability. In *Norris* v. *W. Moss & Sons Ltd* [1954], a workman repaired scaffolding in a manner described by the court as 'fantastically wrong'. He was held personally responsible for the resulting injuries.

As in negligence, the onus is on the *defendant* to prove the plaintiff's contributory negligence. A plaintiff who has established that the breach caused injury need not show exactly how the accident happened.

10. Delegation of the statutory duty

In case of the breach of an *absolute* statutory duty it is no defence that it was delegated to a reasonably competent person. Furthermore, although delegation is still in theory a defence where the delegation was to the plaintiff himself, who was injured solely because of his own disobedience, the defence is in practice obsolete. The modern test is – was the plaintiff's own negligence so great as to absolve the defendant altogether? If not, then the damages are apportioned under the Law Reform (Contributory Negligence) Act 1945.

This position should be contrasted with that in which two or more servants are involved: *ICI Ltd* v. *Shatwell* [1964], *see* 8.

11. Effect of plaintiff's conduct

Where an employee sues his employer for breach of statutory duty, a good defence is that the employee's conduct was the sole cause of the accident. This will not succeed if the employer failed to instruct the employee properly as to the statutory rules involved.

In *Boyle* v. *Kodak Ltd* [1969], an absolute statutory duty to secure a ladder was laid on both employer and employee. The employee was injured through his failure to observe the regulations with regard to ladders. The House of Lords held that the employers (by their failure adequately to instruct their employee about the regulations) had contributed to the accident. Damages were reduced by half.

Progress test 10

1. How is it decided whether a particular statute is intended to protect a certain class of people?

2. How is it decided whether the injury was of a type intended to be guarded against by the statute?

3. 'I detect a considerable reluctance on the part of the courts to impose upon local authorities any liability for break of statutory duty other than that expressly imposed in the statute': Scott-Baker J in *T.* v. *Surrey C.C.* [1994]
   Explain this statement and the issues which underly judicial attitudes.

4. What defences are open to a defendant against whom breach of statutory duty is alleged?

5. Explain the significance of the House of Lords decision in *X* v. *Bedfordshire C.C.* [1995].

11

TRESPASS TO LAND

UNLAWFUL ENTRY AND POSSESSION

Trespass to land is constituted by any unlawful incursion on to land or buildings in the *possession* of another. Even a person in wrongful possession may bring an action against anyone without a better title to the land (*see* Title to sue, p. 165). Possession means the *right to exclude others* whether or not the possessor is physically present. A possessor would therefore include an absent owner or a tenant but not a landlord (during the lease) or a person with no more than mere use of the land (*see* Title to sue p.165).

1. What amounts to an unlawful incursion?

The incursion may arise either **(a)** by entering upon land in the possession of the plaintiff; **(b)** by remaining on the land in possession of the plaintiff; **(c)** by placing or projecting any object upon the land without the permission of the plaintiff (*see* generally *Barker* v. *The Queen* [1983]) or some other lawful authority, e.g. arrest and search powers under the Police and Criminal Evidence Act 1984 (*see* Defences, **16** below).

2. Entering land in the plaintiff's possession

This may be done by personal entry or by procuring the entry of another person, object or animal. The slightest incursion is sufficient, e.g. it would be trespass to put one's hand or head through an open window; to sit on a boundary fence; or to throw a boomerang which entered the defendant's land only momentarily, before returning. The most readily imaginable example of procuring the entry of a person, object or animal is where the person, object or animal is propelled in some way on to the land (as with the example of the boomerang or where someone is pushed on to land; or, as in *Rigby* v. *Chief Constable of Northamptonshire* [1985], where a gas canister was fired by the police). It can also be trespass, however, where a substance is deliberately so situated by the defendant that the forces of nature will inevitable carry it on to the plaintiff's land. In *Esso Petroleum Ltd* v. *Southport Corporation* [1956], oil was released and carried naturally by the wind and waves to the foreshore of the Corporation. This was held to amount to a trespass.

The object of the trespass need not be as tangible as persons, objects, animals or even oil. In *McDonald* v. *Associated Fuels* [1954], it was held that the release of gas into the plaintiff's land could amount to trespass.

3. Direct and indirect incursion

Although the incursion need not be by a tangible substance it must be by some kind of *substance* and not simply be noise or vibrations. The latter amounts to indirect incursion and at most would give rise to action in nuisance. The distinction between direct and indirect incursion is illustrated by a series of American blasting cases where damage caused by flying rocks amounted to trespass and damage by vibrations or concussion amounted only to nuisance.

4. Entry must be voluntary

To be liable in trespass the defendant must have entered the land voluntarily. By way of illustration, if A pushes B on to C's land it is A and not B who is liable in trespass to C. However a person entering the land voluntarily will be liable in trespass regardless of whether he is aware that he is trespassing (because he believes it to be his own land or land on which he has a right of way for example). In *Basely* v. *Clarkson* (1681), it was held to be a trespass to mow grass on the plaintiff's land even though the defendant honestly believed it to be his own land.

It is uncertain whether a trespasser is strictly liable for any damage resulting from his presence on the land. Although this was the traditional view, it is arguable that, as trespass appears now to be based on fault, there should be liability for foreseeable consequences. In a New Zealand case, *Mayfair* v. *Pears* [1986], a car was parked without permission (amounting to trespass). It unexpectedly caught fire and caused unforeseeable damage to a garage. It was held that there could only be liability for foreseeable consequences.

5. No need for damage

As long as the intrusion is voluntary there is no need to prove damage. In *Entick* v. *Carrington* (1765), it was stated that: 'Every invasion of property, be it ever so minute, is a trespass.' In a situation where the intrusion is voluntary, though mistaken, and no damage is caused it is likely that only nominal damages will be awarded.

6. Accidental trespass

It is debatable whether accidental incursion amounts to trespass. The Statute of Limitations 1623 s. 5 appeared to assume so, as it gave a defendant an opportunity to offer amends for accidental trespass before an action was brought. However, inevitable accident appears now to be recognised as a good defence to an action for trespass to the person and trespass to goods (*see* Chapters 12 and 13).

Given the general trend towards requiring fault in a trespass action, it would be rather anomalous if the same rule did not apply to trespass to land: *see League Against Cruel Sports* v. *Scott* [1986].

TRESPASS BY ABUSE OF AUTHORITY

7. Trespass by contravening particular purpose

A person with authority to enter land for a *particular purpose* becomes a trespasser if he goes beyond that purpose. In *Barker* v. *R.* [1983], entering for the purpose of stealing rather than looking after a neighbour's house was held to amount to trespass. It may also be a trespass to take undercover pictures in a bar to establish that short measures are being served: *see Savoy Hotel* v. *BBC* [1983].

The main application of this rule can be seen in cases involving abuse of public and private rights of way. A public highway, for example, will be vested either in the local authority or adjoining landowners, and subject to a public right of way. This right of way involves the right of passage and purposes incidental thereto such as resting or parking temporarily, *see Rogers* v. *Ministry of Transport* [1952], or stopping to make sketches, *see Liddle* v. *Yorkshire (North Riding) C.C.* [1934]. If the highway is used for other purposes, e.g. depositing cattle on the highway, this will amount to trespass. In *Hickman* v. *Maisey* [1900], the plaintiff owned the soil of the highway and occupied adjoining land, where racehorses were trained. The defendant traversed the highway for two hours in order to observe the form of the horses. It was held that this was not an ordinary and reasonable use of the highway and amounted to trespass. The distinction between reasonable and unreasonable use of the highway was succinctly drawn by Paull J in *Iveagh* v. *Martin* [1961], when he said: 'I may stoop to tie up my shoe lace but I may not occupy a pitch and invite people to come upon it and have their hair cut.' If the act carried out while on the land in question is within the allowed purpose, then any motive for being there is irrelevant. So it is not trespass to walk across a public park, intending to commit a crime on reaching the other side. If a crime is committed while in the park itself, it is only trespass if the park was entered with this *criminal act in mind*, e.g. A goes to the park to assault B or to sell him illegal drugs. If A did not enter the park with any illegal purpose in mind, he is not a trespasser unless the doctrine of trespass *ab initio* applies.

8. Trespass by remaining on land

Where a licence to enter and stay on land or premises is terminated or its purpose comes to an end, a trespass is committed if the person so licensed does not leave. Therefore, a hotel guest or football spectator must leave the hotel or stadium when the holiday or game is *finished* or if, as a result of misbehaviour, they are *asked to leave*. If they do not do so after a reasonable time, they become trespassers. *Reasonable force* may be used to eject the trespasser in such circumstances.

A person, such as a tenant, who is in lawful possession of the land, does not become a trespasser if he refuses to leave when requested. He may, however, be liable in an action for ejectment.

9. Trespass by placing things on land

This form of trespass may be committed by placing a physical structure, item or substance on the land or allowing such to come into contact with the land; e.g. throwing rocks onto the land, hammering nails into or leaning ladders against a wall. In *McDonald* v. *Associated Fuels* [1954] it was held to be trespass to blow carbon monoxide gas into a house.

In such circumstances, there will also be a *continuing trespass*, as long as the structure, item or substance remains. A series of successive actions may be maintained on a day to day basis until the trespass ceases. The damages are assessed in each case, up to the date of the action, unless they are awarded in lieu of an injunction. The continuing nature of the trespass also means that subsequent possessors of the land may sue while it continues, and subsequent purchases of the structure, item or substance may similarly be sued for its continuing presence.

A continuing trespass is also committed and the same rules apply where the offending thing is there by permission and is not removed when permission is withdrawn. A continuing trespass is not however committed where a past and completed trespass happens to have continuing consequences, e.g. where a hole is dug and simply left. Although the consequences (the existence of the hole) continue, this is a single and not continuing trespass unless other items, such as rubbish or a spade, are on the land.

TRESPASS BENEATH AND ABOVE THE SURFACE

The general rule is that the possessor of land also possesses the soil beneath, and the column of air above the land. If would appear to follow that an entry beneath or above the surface at any depth or height amounts to a trespass. This will often be the case. In *Willcox* v. *Kettel* [1937], the intrusion by 50 centimetres of a concrete foundation was held to be a trespass. In *Kelsen* v. *Imperial Tobacco Co. Ltd* [1957], an advertising sign obtruding by 20 centimetres was held to be a trespass. The general rule does, however, require some qualification in its application to incursions both *beneath* and *above* the surface.

10. Beneath the surface

Firstly, the owner or possessor of the surface may not be the owner or possessor of the sub-soil because ownership or possession has been severed, e.g. by granting of mining rights. If this is the case it is clearly not a trespass to work the area which one either owns or is permitted to work.

Secondly, it is unclear as to whether a surface owner can claim in relation to areas below the surface which, although never severed from the surface, he can neither control, gain access to or make use of. In an American case, *Edwards* v. *Sims* [1929], the plaintiff successfully claimed a share in the profits from a cave exploited as a tourist attraction, the entrance to which was on the defendant's land, but which ran 107 metres below the plaintiff's land. However Logan J dissented, saying, 'No man can bring up from the depth of the earth the Stygian darkness and make it serve his purposes, unless he has the entrance to it.'

In another American case, *Boehringer* v. *Montalto* [1931], the sewer commission was held to be entitled to maintain a sewer 46 metres below another person's land as it had 'effective control' over it.

11. Above the surface

The idea expressed by the maxim *cujus est solum ejus est usque ad coelum* that an occupier has control of the air space at any height above his land, cannot be taken too literally. Most of the decided cases have involved artificial projections, attached to the ground, e.g. *Kelsen* v. *Imperial Tobacco Company* above; *Gifford* v. *Dent* [1926] where a sign protruded by 142 centimetres over the plaintiff's land; *Wandsworth Board of Works* v. *United Telephone Co.* (1884), where it was held that subject to any statutory rights of the Post Office to erect telegraph or telephone lines, it would be trespass if a wire crossed someone's property at any height. In contrast, it was held in *Lemmon* v. *Webb* [1894], that overhanging branches of artificially planted trees amounted to nuisance and not trespass.

In *Bernstein* v. *Skyviews* [1978], Griffiths J reviewed the authorities and said that as a general principle the rights of an owner to the air space above his land should be restricted to such height as is necessary for the ordinary enjoyment of the land and the structures on it. Above this height he should have no greater rights than anyone else. He went on to hold that a plane which flew hundreds of feet above the plaintiff's land to take pictures had not interfered with the plaintiff's enjoyment of his land, and did not constitute a trespass. *See also Anchor Brewhouse Developments Ltd* v. *Berkley House Docklands Developments Ltd* [1987] and *London and Manchester Assurance Co. Ltd* v. *O. and H. Construction Ltd* [1989].

The plaintiff's enjoyment may be interfered with by a transient incursion. In *Ellis* v. *Loftus Iron Co.* (1874), it was held to be trespass where a horse on one side of a fence bit and kicked a mare on the other side. In a Tasmanian case *Davies* v. *Bennison* [1927], the defendant shot a cat on the plaintiff's roof. The incursion of the bullet was held to be trespass, damages being recoverable for this as well as for the value of the cat.

12. Trespass by aircraft

Section 76 (1) of the Civil Aviation Act 1982 provides that: 'No action shall lie in respect of trespass or . . . nuisance, by reason only of the flight of an aircraft over any property at a height above the ground which having regard to wind, weather and all the circumstances of the case is reasonable, or the ordinary incidents of such flight.'

The Act, however, also provides that damages are recoverable, *without proof of negligence*, for damage caused to persons or property by taking off or landing of an aircraft, or by things or persons falling from an aircraft. The Act, however, does *not* apply to aircraft on Her Majesty's service.

TITLE TO SUE

13. The importance of possession

A right to sue in trespass only rests in a person with *actual* possession of the land and the right to possession must be *immediate* and *exclusive*. The former requirement would disallow a landlord during the course of a lease or a purchaser before title has passed, from suing in trespass. A landlord could however maintain an alternative action if he could show damage to his reversionary interest in the land. In *Baxter* v. *Taylor* (1832) the defendant unloaded stones upon the plaintiff's land which at the time was occupied by the plaintiff's tenant. It was held that the landlord could not sue in trespass as he did not have actual and immediate possession of the land. Further as there was no damage to his reversionary interest, no other action was available.

The requirement that possession be exclusive prevents a person who merely has use of the land without any legal or equitable interest from maintaining a trespass action. These people would include lodgers, boarders, hotel guests, and persons with seats on public transport or in a cinema. If a person is able to show a legal or equitable interest, e.g. a fishing or timber cutting right, then an action in trespass may be maintained against strangers who directly interfere with that right.

Where there are competing claims to possession the situation is resolved by one party showing the better title to possess. If a party has an immediate right of entry he is taken to have had the right of possession since the date his right of entry accrued and is able to sue for trespasses committed since that date. This is known as the doctrine of *trespass by relation*, the possession of the plaintiff being related back to the date when he first acquired right of entry. It means that a tenant could sue for a trespass committed between the granting of a lease and his entry to the property. Similarly, a landlord may sue for trespass committed between the termination of the lease and his re-entry.

14. Establishing right of possession

As trespass is a tort against possession, it follows that, in order to succeed in his action, a plaintiff must establish his right of possession.

(a) An owner *not in possession* cannot sue except for permanent damage to his *reversionary interest*: *see* e.g. *Baxter* v. *Taylor* (1832).

(b) Possession, to give a right of action in trespass, must be *exclusive*. Thus, e.g. a guest or servant cannot sue for trespass to his room, as he lacks such exclusive possession.

(c) Possession is not confined to actual physical possession. It includes possession through servants or agents; and it may be *constructive*, e.g. where one leaves his house unoccupied for a long time but intends to return. In *Wuta-Ofei* v. *Danquah* [1961], the plaintiff acquired land in Ghana, which she did not physically occupy, but marked with pillars according to custom. Some years later the defendant built on the land. It was held that the plaintiff could succeed in trespass, 'the slightest amount of possession' being sufficient.

(d) A purchaser of *standing crops* acquires a right to bring an action for trespass for damage to them, although not in possession. In *Wellaway* v. *Courtier* [1918], the defendant's sheep ate growing turnips which the plaintiff had bought from the farmer in occupation of the land. It was held that the plaintiff could bring an action for trespass because, although not in occupation, he had *the exclusive right of possession* of the crop.

(e) If there is *more than one possessor*, e.g. A owns the subsoil and B occupies the surface, each can sue for trespass to his portion. But tenants in common and joint tenants cannot sue in trespass *inter se*.

TRESPASS *AB INITIO*

If a person enters land or premises of another in the exercise of a right conferred by law, but subsequently does some wrongful act there, then, subject to the conditions set out below, his original (lawful) entry will be regarded as a trespass, for which the occupier may recover damages additional to those for the wrongful act. The conditions which must obtain are:

(a) The entry must be in pursuance of a *right conferred by common or statute law*, e.g. not merely by leave of the occupier under contract.

(b) The wrongful act must be a misfeasance, not merely a nonfeasance, i.e. a *positive* wrongful act as distinct from a mere *omission* or *failure* to act. In *The Six Carpenters Case* (1610), six carpenters refused to pay for wine they had drunk in an inn. It was held that they had abused their lawful right to enter a common inn, but were not trespassers *ab initio*, as their refusal to pay was a nonfeasance only.

(c) For the doctrine to apply, the (subsequent) wrongful act must make the defendant's presence *totally unjustifiable*. He will not be a trespasser *ab initio* if, despite the wrongful act, his presence is still legally justified. In *Elias* v. *Pasmore* [1934], police officers entered the plaintiff's premises to make a lawful arrest, but also wrongfully seized certain papers. It was held that they were not trespassers *ab initio*, their presence before and after the wrongful seizure being justified by their *duty* to arrest.

REMEDIES AND DEFENCES

15. Usual remedies

A plaintiff in trespass normally sues for damages, or for an injunction to prohibit or restrain the trespass, or both.

Other possible remedies are:

(a) *Ejectment.* Ejectment is the historical name for the action to recover land. Originally available only to leaseholders, it was extended to freeholders by elaborate fictions (abolished in 1852) involving Messrs R. Roe and J. Doe. The main thing to note about the modern action is that the onus is entirely on the plaintiff claiming possession to show a *better title* than the person *in possession,* i.e. the plaintiff cannot rely merely on the *weakness of the defendant's title.* Furthermore, the plaintiff must be *out of possession* when the action is brought, and must show entitlement to *immediate* possession.

(b) *Action for mesne profits.* This is an action by a plaintiff claiming possession for damage suffered by being kept out of possession, e.g. for rent and the costs of the action.

(c) *Joint action.* The action for mesne profits may be joined with that for possession; indeed, since the action for mesne profits is an action for *trespass,* it can be brought separately only by a plaintiff in possession.

(d) *Action for an account.* When a person profits by using the land of another, e.g. by working mines, an action for an account may be the appropriate remedy.

16. Defences

It will be a good defence to an action in trespass for the defendant to show that he entered the plaintiff's land:

(a) *By authority of law.* This might include a power of search under the Police and Criminal Evidence Act 1984 or in pursuance of a right of access under the National Parks and Access to the Countryside Act 1949. Other examples include the right of a police officer to enter premises to prevent a breach of the peace or of a person to enter premises to abate a nuisance.

(b) *By licence. (Entry by licence.)* The classic definition of *licence* is that of Sir Frederick Pollock: '. . . that consent which, without passing any interest in the property to which it relates, merely prevents the act for which consent is given from being wrongful'. There are two types of licence, the first being *licence without consideration* which is a *bare* licence (i.e. one for which no valuable consideration was given) and may be revoked at will. The second is *licence by contract.* A contractual licence *not coupled with an interest* is revocable at will, subject to an action for breach; but there are exceptions:

(*i*) Where construction clearly reveals that the parties *meant* the licence to be irrevocable.

(*ii*) Where the licence was granted for a *specific purpose* and a *limited time.* In this case it is irrevocable until the purpose has been accomplished.

In *Jones & Sons Ltd* v. *Tankerville* [1909], an injunction was granted to prevent the revocation of a licence to fell and remove timber which had been sold to the plaintiff. *See also Winter Garden Theatre* v. *Millenium Productions* [1948] and *Hurst* v. *Picture Theatres* [1916]. In the former case Lord Greene MR said (*obiter*) that 'it is the settled practice of the Courts of Equity to do what they can by an injunction to preserve the sanctity of a bargain'. It is not clear what the position is where there is not time to get an injunction or the plaintiff seeks damages only.

Remaining after revocation, i.e. to remain on the land after one's right of entry has ended, is a trespass; therefore the licensee becomes a trespasser immediately on revocation. However, he must be given *reasonable* time to remove himself and his property, *see* **9** above. *Executed licences* cannot be revoked, e.g. X may revoke Y's licence to dump rubbish on X's land, but cannot by doing so oblige Y to remove rubbish already dumped.

A *licence* coupled with an *interest* is a *grant*, and irrevocable for although permission to enter is merely a right *in personam*, it confers a right *in rem* – which will be protected by equity – to do something after entry. Thus as Vaughan CJ said in *Thomas* v. *Sorrel* (1672), a man may have a bare licence to enter land to hunt, but a *grant* to carry away the deer.

(c) *To retake goods*. It is a good defence that the defendant entered the land to retake his goods placed there by the plaintiff.

(d) *To prevent danger to life*. An act which would otherwise be a trespass may be justified if done to avert danger to life. In *Esso Petroleum Co. Ltd* v. *Southport Corp.* [1956], oil jettisoned from a tanker was washed up on the Corporation's foreshore and it was held that there was no trespass, as the *crew's lives* were in danger.

Prior to 1992 a property owner had no right to enter another party's land against that person's will in order to make repairs to his own property, even if the state of the property amounted to a danger to the public. As a result, buildings adjoining the property of another person became impossible to maintain if the other party refused entry. The Access to Neighbouring Land Act 1992 now provides a procedure whereby application can be made to the court for an access order which, when granted, will override a neighbouring landowner's refusal of consent. Such an order will permit entry to 'buildings and other structures' where the works are seen by the Court to be necessary for the preservation of the whole or part of the applicant's property and cannot be carried out or would be substantially more difficult to carry out if entry upon the neighbouring land were refused. The Court may impose conditions upon the order if it sees fit.

As discussed above (*see* **4**), it is no defence to a voluntary trespass to plead that one is not aware that the land belongs to another, although to claim accidental trespass may be a good defence (*see* **6**).

Progress test 11

1. What are the essential elements of trespass to land?

2. Explain trespass by abuse of authority.

3. Who has a title to sue in trespass?

4. What remedies are open to a plaintiff in a trespass action?

5. Explain the effect of the Access to Neighbouring Land Act 1992.

12

TRESPASS TO THE PERSON

Trespass to the person may consist of:

(a) Assault and battery

(b) False imprisonment.

Assault and battery are two distinct torts although in practical situations they are often both committed by the same act or series of acts. An assault may be committed by simply *threatening* violence but for a battery to be committed the defendant has to go on and carry out some positive application of force. The requirements for each are described below.

ASSAULT AND BATTERY

1. Assault

Assault involves doing something which induces in another reasonable fear and apprehension of immediate violence. Thus, it would be an assault to point a gun or wield a stick at someone. Whether or not an assault is committed depends on the emotions which are aroused in the other party.

Stalking, the label given to the persistent harassment of an individual by following them, nuisance telephone calls, waiting outside their home, etc., has recently been held in the criminal courts to amount to assault. In *R.* v. *Burstow* [1996] the Court of Appeal Criminal Division held that a 'stalker' could be convicted of unlawfully and maliciously inflicting grievous bodily harm, contrary to section 20 of the Offences Against the Person Act 1861, even where he had not applied physical violence directly or indirectly to the body of the victim.

Behaviour which merely annoys the other person will not amount to an assault, but that which causes reasonable fear and apprehension of immediate violence will. Actions of the defendant which cause long-term psychological harm, by breaking the 'nerve' of the victim by 'stalking' her, is likely to be viewed by the courts as an assault, although it falls outside the definition of an 'apprehension of immediate violence': *see Burns* v. *Adzani* [1995]. The law of nuisance can be used to deal with situations of harassment: *see Khorasandjian* v. *Bush* [1993] at p. 143 above.

Fleming says, in his *Introduction to the Law of Torts*, that assault 'remains the only instance in English jurisprudence of a mere offensive sensation unaccompanied by any outward psychosomatic symptoms, let alone external trauma, giving a cause of action for damages'. It remains an assault, therefore, to threaten an act which you cannot or do not intend to do, e.g. to point a gun which you know not to be loaded, at a person who believes it to be loaded. On the same principle, however, it is not an assault to make threats which the other person does not know of, e.g. to point a gun at someone behind their back since, if a man is not aware that he is being threatened, it cannot induce in him fear and apprehension.

The apprehension of violence will not be reasonable, however, in the following situations:

(a) Where the threat is so qualified that the fear of immediate violence is dispelled. In *Turberville* v. *Savage* (1669), where the defendant laid his hand on his sword and said, 'If it were not assize-time, I would not take such language from you'. This was not an assault. A threat, however, is not qualified by offering not to carry it through if an unjustified order is carried out, e.g. to say 'Leave now or I'll kill you' or 'Your money or your life' is an assault.

(b) Where the threat cannot, at least at present, reasonably be carried out, e.g. to shake one's fist at someone from a distance or to swipe with a sword or stick when obviously out of range.

In *Thomas* v. *N.U.M.* [1986] violent and abusive language and threats directed at strike-breaking miners by 60 or 70 mineworkers picketing a colliery in the course of a strike was held not to constitute an assault. The requirement of imminence could not be satisfied as the pickets were being restrained by police and the strike breakers were being bussed into the colliery.

There is some doubt whether words are sufficient to constitute an assault, although it has been said that: 'Words may . . . give colour to an act that might otherwise be inoffensive, as where a man follows up an immoral suggestion to a woman by menacingly advancing towards her' (Fleming, *Introduction to the Law of Torts*).

Passive obstruction does not amount to an assault, e.g. where as in *Innes* v. *Wylie* (1844), the defendant acts 'like a door or wall'. The plaintiff in such circumstances is justified in using reasonable force to enable him to go about his business.

2. Battery

Battery involves the unlawful application of force to the person of another. The obvious instance would be A physically striking B. However, battery extends to situations where water is thrown at someone, *see Pursell* v. *Horn* (1832); a chair is pulled from under a person causing him to fall, *see Hooper* v. *Reeve* (1817); an object is wrested from a person, *see Green* v. *Goddard* (1704); or a person is spat on, *see R.* v. *Cotesworth* (1704). There need be no hostile intention or actual harm caused as long as the act takes place without consent or lawful authority, e.g. it could be battery to touch someone without their consent or fingerprint someone without legal authority. It was held in *T.* v. *T.* [1988] that surgical treatment, although not hostile, constitutes a battery if carried out without consent. Recent case examples of claims based upon the tort of battery include sexual abuse (*Stubbings* v. *Webb* [1993]) and a challenge to the failure to prosecute for murder (*Halford* v. *Brookes* [1992]).

The plaintiff *need not be aware* of the battery when it occurs, e.g. he may be asleep or under the influence of drugs. This is in contrast with assault where it is the plaintiff's awareness of the threat and consequent fear which is the crux of the tort.

A certain amount of physical contact is consequential in normal social intercourse and there is normally implied consent to the person who taps another on the shoulder to attract his attention. It has been said that there is no liability in assault for 'the jostler, the back-slapper and the handshaker' (Lord Devlin, *Samples of Lawmaking*).

3. Assault and battery

(a) Assault and battery may be distinguished in this way. Battery is the *application of unlawful force* to the person of another, assault is the putting of any person in *reasonable fear of immediate battery*.

(b) An act may be an assault although the defendant lacked the power to inflict violence, e.g. the defendant points a gun which he, but *not the plaintiff*, knows to be unloaded.

(c) An act will not be an assault unless it causes *reasonable fear of immediate violence*. There is no assault where, e.g., the plaintiff could not see the threatening action, but merely learnt of it afterwards. Similarly, if the defendant was so far distant from the plaintiff that he could not inflict an *immediate* battery, there is no assault. In *R.* v. *Burstow* [1996] the Court of Appeal Criminal Division held that a 'stalker' could be convicted of unlawfully and maliciously inflicting grievous bodily harm, contrary to section 20 of the Offences Against the Person Act 1861, even where he had not applied physical violence directly or indirectly to the body of the victim (*see* **1** above).

(d) It is not certain whether a plaintiff in assault and battery must show intention or negligence by the defendant. Battery derives from *trespass*, not *case*, so that its incidence depends on whether the injury was *direct*, not whether it was accompanied by *intention* or *negligence*. It was held in *Fowler* v. *Lanning* [1959] that proof of intention or negligence is essential to success in trespass to the person; but in view of the fact that *Fowler* v. *Lanning* was settled at first instance, and its approval by the Court of Appeal in *Cooper* v. *Letang* [1964] was merely *obiter*, the point cannot be regarded as finally settled.

(e) An assault is also a criminal offence. Indeed it is provided by ss. 44 and 45 of the Offences Against the Person Act 1861 that summary criminal proceedings operate as a bar to civil proceedings being taken on the same grounds.

FALSE IMPRISONMENT

4. The scope and nature of false imprisonment

(a) False imprisonment consists of *wrongful deprivation of personal liberty in any form*, and not necessarily by force or incarceration. For instance it will amount to false imprisonment to cast someone adrift on a boat.

An arrest by a policeman or store detective may amount to false imprisonment when procured by an implied threat of force, e.g. by the showing of a warrant. Williams J remarked in *Bird* v. *Jones* [1845], that, 'In such cases ... though little may be said, much is meant and perfectly understood.'

In *Warner* v. *Riddiford* [1858], the defendant, after dismissing the plaintiff as resident manager of a beer-house, prevented his going upstairs to collect his belongings. It was held that this amounted to false imprisonment. The Ministry of Defence's power to compel service in the armed forces can amount to false imprisonment: see *Prichard* v. *Ministry of Defence* [1995]. An unlawful arrest constitutes false imprisonment as does preventing someone from leaving: *see Davidson* v. *C.C. North Wales Police* [1994].

(b) *The deprivation must be complete.* It is not false imprisonment if the plaintiff had any *reasonable* means of leaving, e.g. if his path was barred in one direction, but not in another. In *Bird* v. *Jones* [1845], the defendants blocked one side of Hammersmith Bridge to form a grandstand for a boat race, thus preventing the plaintiff's passage. The plaintiff remained in the enclosure for some time, and refused to cross by the opposite path. It was held there was no false imprisonment as he had reasonable means of leaving. It would be *unreasonable* restraint if, e.g., a person was physically free to leave, but had been deprived of his clothes, or if the only means of escape was dangerous or inconvenient, e.g. by having to jump from a height or into water.

(c) Mere failure to facilitate the egress of persons on one's premises is not in itself imprisonment. The test is whether a plaintiff, who requires the assistance of the defendants in order to release himself from a particular place, has the right to leave at the time when he asks to do so. This will normally be determined by the terms of the contract or licence which requires or permits the plaintiff to be in that place. So, for example, in *Herd* v. *Weardale Steel, Coke & Coal Co.* [1915], a miner, in breach of his contract of service, demanded to be taken out of the mine. The defendants denied him use of the lift, thereby detaining him against his will. It was held that *volenti non fit injuria* applied, and there was no false imprisonment.

The practice of clamping cars which have been parked on the premises of owners which operate a clamping policy has been before the courts on a number of occasions recently. In *Total Car Park Management* v. *Fink* [1994], an unreported decision, the issue turned on the contractual terms in operation at a pay-and-display car park. In *Arthur* v. *Anchor* [1995], a key issue was whether or not the actions of the owner when clamping the defendant's car were lawful and whether or not the defendant acted within his rights to forcibly remove the clamp. The Court of Appeal held that by parking in the car park the defendant had voluntarily accepted the risk that his car might be clamped, he had also accepted the risk that the car would remain clamped until the fine was paid – he had therefore consented to both (otherwise tortious acts) clamping and detaining the vehicle.

(d) The plaintiff need not know he is restrained. A person may be falsely imprisoned *without* his knowledge. In *Meering* v. *Grahame White Aviation Co. Ltd* (1920), an employee of the respondent company, who was suspected of theft, agreed to wait in a room with two security officers. He was not told he was free to leave, although in fact he was. There was held to be false imprisonment. Atkin LJ said that, 'A person can be in imprisonment while he is asleep, while he is in a state of drunkenness, while he is unconscious and while he is a lunatic. So a man might in fact, to my mind, be imprisoned by having the key of a door turned against him so that he is imprisoned in a room in fact although he does not know that the key has been turned'. This principle has been confirmed by the House of Lords in *Murray* v. *Ministry of Defence* [1988]; in that case Lord Griffiths mentioned that, in the absence of knowledge of the imprisonment and of any harm, the plaintiff can usually only expect to be awarded minimal damages.

The fact that the plaintiff in a false imprisonment action does not have to be aware of the restraint was reaffirmed by Ralph Gibson LJ in *Weldon* v. *Home Office* [1992], where he opined:

'It is clear that the policy of the law is jealously to protect personal liberty. Thus, it appears that, if a man is without justification confined in a room, it would be no defence to show that, if he had not been locked in, he would not in fact have had occasion to leave the room during the period of time over which he was so confined, although . . . that would not be relevant to damages. The wrong done is the infringement of the right to the ability to leave and go elsewhere. Further, it would appear to follow that, if a man should be under some restraint not to leave a particular place for a period of time, for example because he does not have the means to leave, or because he has contracted to stay there to guard the place, or because, as a soldier or policeman, he has been ordered to remain there, he could, nevertheless, claim damages for false imprisonment if, without justification, he should be imprisoned within that place. The immediate and wholly unrestricted freedom and ability to go somewhere else are not, therefore, a precondition for asserting a claim in false imprisonment.'

The Court of Appeal proceeded to decide in *Weldon* that, even though a prisoner was serving a sentence which justified his detention in prison (*see* s. 12 Prison Act 1952), it was possible for him to be falsely imprisoned within the confines of that prison – e.g. when a prison officer intentionally and unjustifiably sends a prisoner to his cell at a time when, under the regime operated by the prison, the prisoner is entitled to 'associate' with other inmates. This may be based upon the idea that the prisoner enjoys a 'residual liberty' within the prison. Ralph Gibson LJ took the view that bad faith would need to be proven on the part of the prison officer in order to found an action for false imprisonment in such circumstances.

In *R.* v. *Deputy Governor of Parkhurst Prison ex parte Hague* [1990] it was asserted that, apart from a case where a prisoner was kept in intolerable conditions, an action for false imprisonment would not lie against the prison authorities because of the general power justifying imprisonment under s. 12 Prison Act 1952. The view that conditions of imprisonment could be so bad as to render an otherwise lawful imprisonment unlawful – whilst accepted in *Weldon* and *ex parte Hague* – had previously been approved in the Court of Appeal decision in *Middleweek* v. *Chief Constable of the Merseyside Police*, a previously unreported 1985 case since reported in 1990.

In a composite appeal to the House of Lords in *Hague* v. *Deputy Governor of Parkhurst Prison* [1991] and *Weldon* v. *Home Office* [1992], it was decided by their Lordships that a prisoner lawfully committed to prison under s. 12(1) of the Prison Act 1952 has no residual liberty vis-a-vis the governor of the prison which can be protected by private law remedies, since while in prison he has no liberty to be in any place other than where the prison regime requires him to be and therefore he has no liberty capable of deprivation by the prison regime which could constitute the tort of false imprisonment.

(e) A person who enters a police station on his own initiative, or by invitation of police officers, will be falsely imprisoned if detained *against his will* except by lawful arrest, e.g. by a false pretence that he is not free to go.

5. False imprisonment and malicious prosecution distinguished

The appropriate remedy against one who procures a court judgment which leads to imprisonment is *malicious prosecution* and not false imprisonment. So if A is wrongfully arrested and detained by B and brought before a magistrate who remands him in custody, he must pursue a malicious prosecution action for the period *after* the judgment and a false imprisonment action for the period *prior* to the judgment.

DEFENCES

6. Self-defence

(a) A person may use *reasonable*, i.e. necessary and *proportionate*, force to defend himself or *any other person* against unlawful violence. Note, however, that *necessary* and *proportionate* are not synonymous and force may be disproportionate although necessary. Thus, *trivial* violence cannot be warded off by a *fatal* blow, even though it could not be repelled in any other way; but 'if you are attacked with a deadly weapon you can defend yourself with a deadly weapon': *see Turner* v. *MGM Pictures Ltd* [1950], *per* Lord Oaksey. What is necessary in the circumstances is a question of fact and will depend on the nature of the assault, the type of weapons used and possibly the violent reputation of the assailant. So, for instance, it is not necessary to respond to a verbal threat by drawing a lethal weapon such as a gun or a knife. On the other hand if a person is being subjected to a vicious attack without a weapon he may use one if he reasonably believes this to be the only way to protect himself.

(b) It is not necessary, in order to justify violent self-defence, to warn of one's intention to use it. Furthermore the defender, if in reasonable fear of immediate battery, may lawfully strike the first blow. In the *Chaplain of Gray's Inn* case it was said that, 'I am not bound to wait until the other has given a blow, for perhaps it will come too late afterwards.' This might justify striking the first blow or inflicting a wound where A sees B reaching into his pocket for what could be a lethal weapon – particularly if B has a violent reputation.

7. Preservation of public peace

What would otherwise be a trespass to the person may be justified if done to support the law or maintain the peace. The onus is on the defendant to prove that he acted for those reasons.

(a) *Lawful arrest*. Force may be justified if used to effect a lawful arrest. The rules are as follows:

(1) Any person may arrest without warrant for a breach of the peace *committed in his presence*, or if he reasonably anticipates a *renewal* of such a breach. There must be actual disturbance of the public peace, with general alarm and excitement, and imprisonment will not be justified where the defendant is simply annoyed or insulted, as in the case of *Bryan* v. *Robinson* [1960], which involved smiling and beckoning by Soho hostesses. A *police officer* may forcibly arrest someone without warrant if he reasonably apprehends an imminent breach of the peace. He may also assault a person in such circumstances. In *Humphreys* v. *Connor* (1864), a policeman was held to be justified in removing an orange lily from a protestant lady because he reasonably apprehended that it would lead to a breach of the peace. In cases of unlawful assembly or riot *any subject* has a duty to use force – even fatal force – as is *reasonably necessary* to restore the peace.
(2) Any subject has the right to arrest with reasonable force for an arrestable offence, for treason, or to preserve life; but the onus is on the arrester to show *reasonable and probable* cause.
(3) A constable can justify an arrest with reasonable force by showing *reasonable suspicion* of an arrestable offence. A private person can justify such an arrest only by showing that the arrestable offence was *committed*. This rather anomalous rule has been called a 'dangerous trap for the public-spirited citizen' (Salmond and Heuston, *On the Law of Torts*). It means that such a citizen's liability for false imprisonment depends on the success of the prosecution, whereas a constable's liability depends only on his ability to show his reasonable suspicion of an offence. In *Wills* v. *Bowley* [1983], the House of Lords held (by a bare majority) that if the defendant can prove an honest suspicion based on reasonable grounds, this will suffice. The suspicion must be more than a mere hunch and should be able to be justified to an objective bystander. Under s. 25 of the Police and Criminal Evidence Act 1984, a constable may arrest for a non-arrestable offence without warrant where one of the general arrest conditions laid down is satisfied. These general arrest conditions are:

- The suspect's name and address are not known and cannot be ascertained by the police officer.

175

- The police officer has reasonable grounds for believing that the name and address supplied by the suspect are false.
- Arrest is reasonably thought necessary to prevent suspects from causing:
    physical harm to themselves or others
    loss or damage to property
    an offence against public decency, or
    an unlawful obstruction of the highway.
- Arrest is reasonably thought necessary for the protection of a child or other vulnerable person from the suspect. Under s. 28 of the Act the constable must give the true reason for the arrest whether or not it is obvious. Where some difficulty is encountered, e.g. deafness or a language barrier, he is only expected to take reasonable steps and not to search high and low for an interpreter.

An arrest which is justified in law but which is conducted with the use of undue force will not give rise to the tort of false imprisonment: *Simpson* v. *Chief Constable of South Yorkshire Police* [1991]. It may, however, give rise to a claim for battery.

(b) *Other justifiable force.* A private person may lawfully use force in the following circumstances:
- (*i*) to arrest a person escaping from lawful custody
- (*ii*) to arrest a mentally deranged person endangering himself or others
- (*iii*) in aid of police or other law officers performing their duties.

8. After the arrest

If a person is arrested he must be either handed over to the police (if arrested by a private citizen) or brought before a magistrate within a reasonable time. In *John Lewis* v. *Tims* [1952], only a managing director or general manager of the store was entitled, by the store regulations, to initiate a prosecution. The respondent was arrested on suspicion of theft by the shop's employees and detained in the office for a short time until the requisite authority was obtained. The House of Lords held that the store was not liable for false imprisonment simply because the respondent had not been taken to the police or brought in front of a magistrate immediately. Lord Porter said, 'There are advantages in refusing to give private detectives a free hand and leaving the determination of whether to prosecute or not to a superior official.'

9. Prevention of trespass

An occupier of land (i.e. one having exclusive possession) may use reasonable force to repel, eject or control a trespasser. In *Harrison* v. *Duke of Rutland* [1893], the defendant owned the soil of a highway which traversed his grouse moor. The plaintiff remained for some time on the highway for the purpose of diverting grouse from the butts. The defendant's servant restrained him with minimum force. It was held that the plaintiff's unreasonable use of the highway made him a trespasser, and the forcible restraint was justified.

Before force is used, the intruder must be asked and afforded a reasonable opportunity to leave, unless he has already used force in the course of entry or attempted entry. In *Green* v. *Goddard* (1704), it was said that, 'I need not request him to be gone, but may lay hands on him immediately for it is but returning violence with violence. So if one comes forcibly and takes away my goods, I may oppose him without any more ado, for there is no time to make a request.' The level of force should not exceed what is necessary to effect a forcible removal. In *Collins* v. *Renison* (1754), throwing a trespasser off a ladder was held to be not justifiable.

10. Consent of the plaintiff

On general principles, it is a good defence that the plaintiff consented to the trespass; but consent to personal violence (especially if unilateral) is difficult to establish. Obvious examples of consent are where a patient gives either express or implied (by holding out a limb to be treated) consent to medical treatment or a medical examination; where a landowner acquiesces in trespass to his land; or where a sportsman is taken to give implied consent to the risks ordinarily incidental to participation in that sport. In the latter case however, there is no consent to the use of unwarranted force in breach of the rules of the particular sport. Consent may also be vitiated if obtained by threatened or actual force, sedation or deceit. Examples include a patient who had refused consent for a spinal injection, later given consent when under heavy sedation, *see Beausoleil* v. *Communaute* [1964], and a choir master seducing a young pupil, having persuaded her that this would improve her voice, *see R.* v. *Williams* [1923]. The case of *Chatterton* v. *Gerson* [1981] illustrates that although a patient could be taken to have consented to an operation by having broadly understood its general nature, this might not prevent the doctor from being negligent in not giving a more full explanation which might have deterred the patient from consenting in the first place. The doctor might not be liable for *trespass* to the person, but he could be liable in *negligence* if the patient suffers injury, *see* Chapter 3. Further, in *Sidaway* v. *Bethlem Royal Hospital Governors* [1985], it was held that failure to explain fully inherent risks in an operation could in some circumstance vitiate the patient's consent. An adult patient has an absolute right to refuse consent to treatment, even if she/he will suffer serious injury and die: *see Airedale NHS Trust* v. *Bland* [1993] (HL).

The issue of consent arose in a different context in the case of *F.* v. *West Berkshire Health Authority (Mental Health Act Commission intervening)* [1989]. In that case the House of Lords had to consider the legality of a sterilisation operation which it was proposed to carry out on F., an adult woman whose mental capacity was such that F. was unable to consent to the operation. The view taken by the trial judge and of the Court of Appeal was that such an operation was in F.'s best interests; this was not challenged in the appeal to the House of Lords. A declaration had been granted by the trial judge that the sterilisation of F. would not be an unlawful act by reason only of the absence of F.'s consent. An appeal to the Court of Appeal was unsuccessful and a further appeal to the House of Lords was dismissed. The House of Lords did, however, amend the declaration so that it read: 'The operation . . . proposed to be performed on the plaintiff being in the existing circumstances in her best interests can lawfully be performed on her despite her inability to consent to it.' It was also ordered that if there was a material change in the existing circumstances before the operation took place, any party could apply to the court for such further or other declaration or order as might be just.

The House of Lords (Lord Griffiths dissenting on this point) did not think that it was mandatory as a matter of law in the case of sterilisation operations to obtain a declaration from the court that the operation was lawful, but as a matter of practice such a declaration should be sought. The case is important for Lord Brandon and Lord Goff's opinions on the broader issues of consent. The defence of consent is also of importance in the area of sports; see e.g. Condon v. Basi [1985]. See also Arthur v. Anker [1995] re car clamping.

11. Reasonable chastisement

(a) It is no trespass for a *parent* to administer *reasonable* chastisement to his child under eighteen. At common law, parental authority was traditionally treated as delegated to schoolteachers, who may therefore also administer reasonable chastisement or punishment. The modern view appears to be that teachers have an independent authority, see Ramsay v. Larsen [1964], which is not restricted to the physical confines of the school. In R. v. Newport [1929], a schoolmaster was held to be justified in caning a boy caught smoking in the street, contrary to school rules during term time. If a school authority is held vicariously liable for a teacher who goes beyond reasonable chastisement, they may seek indemnity against the teacher: see Ryan v. Fildes [1938]. This may act as a significant deterrent to the use of excessive force. For a European dimension to the right of schools to administer punishment to pupils see Costello-Roberts v. U.K. [1993]

(b) The master of a ship may arrest or imprison with reasonable force if he *reasonably* believes it necessary to preserve order or safeguard passengers. In Hook v. Cunard Steamship Co. Ltd [1953], the captain of The Queen Mary imprisoned the plaintiff (a steward) on suspicion of his having indecently assaulted a child passenger. In was held that the plaintiff could succeed for false imprisonment, the captain having failed to establish that his action was reasonably necessary to preserve order and safety as opposed to simply being a means of placating a passenger.

12. Inevitable accident

It appears to be established that inevitable accident is a good defence in trespass: see Stanley v. Powell [1891] and NCB v. Evans [1951]. In the former case the plaintiff was shot accidentally when the defendant shot at a pheasant, the pellet ricocheting from a tree. Note, however, that these decisions have been heavily criticised, and that the point has not been submitted to the House of Lords.

A particular point of difficulty is that later decisions (e.g. Fowler v. Lanning) have extended this idea by saying that negligence now requires to be proved in trespass to the person. This blurring of the distinction between the torts of trespass and negligence gives rise to several difficulties:

(a) Instead of the defendant in a trespass action having to prove he was not negligent, the plaintiff may now be required to prove that he was.

(b) Trespass does not require proof of damage where negligence does.

(c) It is unclear whether the contributory negligence defence can be raised in a trespass action.

13. Statutory authority

Statute may give authorisation for a medical examination or test which would otherwise amount to a battery, e.g. ss. 2 and 3 of the Road Safety Act 1967 authorise breath tests.

14. Other defences

The defences of contributory negligence, illegality and *volenti non fit injuria* are also available as defences to battery following the decision of the Court of Appeal in *Murphy* v. *Culhane* [1977].

Progress test 12

1. What is the distinction between assault and battery?

2. What is the significance, if any, of the case of *R.* v. *Burstow* [1996]?

3. What are the essential elements of false imprisonment?

4. To what extent is preservation of the public peace a defence in trespass to the person?

5. When is reasonable chastisement a defence in trespass to the person?

6. When is consent a defence in trespass to the person?

13

TRESPASS TO GOODS

The common law traditionally recognised a number of actions in tort for injury or interference to goods, the main examples being trespass to goods, conversion, detinue and replevin. There could also be an action in negligence if breach of a duty of care had resulted in damage to goods.

TORTS (INTERFERENCE WITH GOODS) ACT 1977

This Act created a new form of tortious liability called *wrongful interference with goods*. This is defined in s. 1 as including conversion, trespass to goods, negligence in so far as it results in damage to goods and (subject to s. 2) any tort so far as it results in an interest in goods or to damage to goods. Section 2 abolished the ancient tort of detinue. Consequently, although wrongful interference with goods is a *new tort*, liability under it depends on whether there would have been liability under any of the old common law torts (with the exception of detinue). It is therefore necessary to examine these torts, in particular trespass to goods and conversion.

TRESPASS TO GOODS

1. Definition and scope

(a) *Definition*. Trespass to chattels consists of a *direct* and unlawful injury to, or interference with, *goods* in the possession of another.

(b) *Direct interference*. Trespass to chattels is actionable *per se*, i.e. proof of the direct and unlawful application of force suffices, and it is unnecessary to prove damage. The type of conduct covered ranges from actual destruction or damaging of goods, through use of goods, to simply moving goods from one place to another. For example, in *Kirk* v. *Gregory* (1876), a deceased person's executor moved rings belonging to the former from one room to another because he mistakenly but genuinely believed that they were at risk from revellers in the house. The executor was held liable for trespass to the rings when they were lost. The moving of goods may also amount to conversion. Other situations where trespass to goods would be committed without any actual damage are, for example, where private documents are shown to an unauthorised person, *see* *Thurston* v. *Charles* (1905), or where a tape recording is erased.

Direct application of force does not necessarily involve physical contact, e.g. it is a trespass to drive away cattle, to propel a stone or vehicle against goods belonging to the plaintiff, or to train a dog to steal golf balls: *see Manton* v. *Brocklebank* [1923]. In the latter example, although there is physical contact by the dog, there is none by the defendant until, perhaps, later if and when the dog actually brings the balls to his master.

The tort is also committed by a defendant who subjects an animal to direct and unlawful injury or interference, e.g. where a dog is beaten, *see Wright* v. *Ramscot* [1667], or racing pigeons are shot, *see Hamps* v. *Darby* [1948].

2. Police powers of search

The Police and Criminal Evidence Act 1984, ss. 8–22 grants police officers wide powers of entry, search and seizure. If these powers are exceeded, the tort of trespass to goods may be committed. For example, s. 16(8) limits the extent of a search to such as is required in pursuance of the warrant. It would, for example, be trespass to goods to dismantle a vacuum cleaner in the search for a stolen TV. It would not, however, constitute trespass if the search warrant was to search for illegal drugs or stolen documents, items which could feasibly be concealed in a vacuum cleaner.

3. Requirement of possession

Only the person in possession of the goods at the time of the alleged trespass can bring the action. In *Armory* v. *Delamirie* (1721), a boy found a jewel, which he gave to a goldsmith to be valued. The goldsmith refused to return the jewel, and the boy sued him in conversion. It was held that the boy, as possessor of title to the goods, could maintain the action. In *The 'Winkfield'* (1902), the *Winkfield* negligently sank a mailship. The Postmaster General sued the *Winkfield's* owners in respect of the lost mail. It was held that the PG, although not the owner of the mail, could nevertheless sue as *bailee in possession*. It was stated by Collins MR that, 'As between bailee and stranger, possession gives title.' An owner of goods who takes them from a bailee will therefore be liable for trespass to the goods. It is no defence for the defendant to show that a third party has a better title to the goods than the plaintiff: *see* s. 8 Torts (Interference with Goods) Act 1977.

Possession normally means personal *physical custody* by the possessor. However, a master has legal possession of goods in the *custody of his servant, except* where the servant receives them from a stranger and withholds them from the master's possession. An *executor* or *administrator* is treated as having possession of the deceased's goods between his death and the grant of probate or letters of administration. A *trustee not in possession* is also treated as having possession for the purpose of bringing an action for trespass against third parties.

4. Proof of intention or negligence necessary

The plaintiff in an action for trespass to goods must prove intention or negligence by the defendant. This was not always so, but it has been established at least since the decision of the Court of Appeal in *NCB* v. *Evans* [1951] that inevitable accident is a good defence in trespass to goods. The application of this rule may also be seen in the context of highway accidents. Where accidental damage results to the property of an adjoining occupier (e.g. a car or animal) there will only be liability if *negligence is established*.

It is no defence for the defendant to claim a mistaken belief that the goods trespassed belonged to him. The distinction between *mistake* and *inevitable accident* can be illustrated by example: if A, while passing B's car, slips on ice or is pushed so that he falls into the car causing damage, this is neither *intentional* nor *negligent*. It is an inevitable accident for which A is not responsible. If, however, A intentionally gets into B's car, in the *mistaken* but genuine belief that it is his own car, he has committed the tort of *trespass to goods*.

5. Defences

A defence to an action for trespass to goods would be to show that:

(a) There was no direct or unlawful interference or injury, e.g. the interference or injury was lawful in pursuance of a police search warrant or in levying lawful distress for rent (*see* **2** above); *or*

(b) The plaintiff did not have actual possession at the time of the alleged trespass, e.g. where a car-hire firm alleges trespass to goods against A who steals the car from B, during the period of his contract of hire; *or*

(c) There was no intention or negligence on the part of the defendant.

(d) An alternative defence is to show that the trespass was committed in order to avert *immediate danger* to persons or property. The onus is on the defendant to show:

    (*i*) that the danger was real and imminent; and

    (*ii*) that he acted reasonably in the circumstances.

A farmer may, therefore, fire at dogs who are chasing his sheep, *see Goodway* v. *Beecher* [1951], or attacking breeding pheasants, *see Miles* v. *Hutchings* [1903]. In *Hamps* v. *Darby* [1948], however, it was held that a farmer was not justified in shooting pigeons unless he had first tried to scare them away from his crops with an initial warning shot.

CONVERSION

6. Definition and scope

Conversion consists of a wilful and wrongful interference with the goods of one entitled to possession of them, in such a way as to deny his right to that possession, or in a manner inconsistent with such right. Such interference may take place without actually taking possession of the goods, if in some way the right of the plaintiff to the goods is denied, e.g. in *Bryanston Leasings Ltd* v.

Principality Finance Ltd [1977], where a vehicle's log book was intentionally not returned.

The interference must be wilful and wrongful. If the defendant's conduct is merely negligent, it will not amount to conversion. In *Ashby* v. *Tolhurst* [1937], the defendant's car-park attendant negligently allowed a stranger to remove the plaintiff's car. There was held to be no conversion by the car-park proprietor, as his servant had not wilfully and wrongfully interfered with the plaintiff's goods, nor acted inconsistently with his title to them. However, this rule must be understood in the context of two important riders:

(a) Section 2(2) of the Torts (Interference with Goods) Act 1977 provides that an action lies where a bailee, in breach of his duty to his bailor, allows goods to be lost or destroyed.

(b) As with trespass to goods, an act is no less intentional because it is carried out in the mistaken belief that one is entitled to do it. So, subject to **(a)** above, it will not be conversion to allow negligently another's goods to be transferred, lost or destroyed, e.g. where A carelessly allows B to take C's goods.

It may, however, be conversion to deliver or dispose of goods in the mistaken belief that one is entitled to do so, e.g. where A is B's agent and sells on B's behalf what are, unknown to him, stolen goods, or where A's contract of sale to B is void for mistake, B sells to C who sells to D.

It is not conversion, however, for a person with whom goods have been deposited to return them to the person who gave them to him in the first place, unless he obtains notice of the plaintiff's title in the intervening period. In *Hollins* v. *Fowler* (1875), Blackburn J says that 'A warehouseman with goods that have been deposited is guilty of no conversion by keeping them or restoring them to the person who deposited them with him, though that person turns out to have no authority from the true owner.' If a person, such as a carrier or warehouseman, delivers goods to a third party he is not guilty of conversion if his state of knowledge was such that he believed himself merely to be transferring possession of the goods and not title. The rule is justified in that it encourages businessmen to be circumspect, requiring 'brokers at their peril to buy from the right person, not merely to have some perfectly good reason for buying from the wrong person'.

7. Types of conversion

Conversion may be committed in the following ways:

(a) *By wrongfully taking the goods.* To amount to conversion, the taking must be accompanied by an *intention to exercise temporary or permanent dominion* over the goods, otherwise it merely amounts to trespass to the goods; *see Foulds* v. *Willoughby* (1841), where the plaintiff's horses were removed by the defendant from his (the defendants's) ferry boat, whereby the plaintiff lost possession of the horses. It was held that the plaintiff could not succeed in conversion as the defendant's act, being accompanied by an intention to exercise dominion, was not conversion, but merely trespass *de bonis asportatis*. An example of exercising temporary dominion sufficient to constitute conversion would be taking a car for a joy ride or, as in the New Zealand case *Wellington C.* v. *Singh* [1971], wrongfully impounding a car.

(b) *By wrongfully detaining the goods.* Detention constitutes conversion only if accompanied by an intention to keep the goods from the person entitled to possession of them. Thus it is not conversion if the finder of the chattel merely refrains from returning it to the person entitled to possession, or if a bailee of goods, in the absence of any demand for their return, fails to return them at the end of the period of bailment. For conversion to be committed there must be *some positive denial of possession to the person entitled to it,* e.g. by refusing to surrender the chattel to him on demand. There need be no demand by the plaintiff if the conduct of the defendant manifests an intention to deprive the plaintiff of his possession. In *Philpott* v. *Kelley* (1835), it was held to be conversion for the defendant to bottle a pipe of wine with which he had been entrusted.

(c) *By wrongfully destroying goods.* Destruction amounts to conversion if (*i*) one person wilfully destroys the chattel of another; (*ii*) the chattel either ceases to exist or changes its identity as, e.g., when yarn is made into cloth or apples into cider. Mere *damage* cannot be conversion, although it may be trespass. The destruction must be wilful and not merely negligent as where, e.g., A carelessly wrecks a car which he has borrowed from B. If, however, A hires a car from B and negligently causes it to be destroyed, he will be liable in conversion under the special provision in s. 2(2) of the Torts (Interference with Goods) Act 1977, which makes a bailee liable in conversion for destruction of goods in breach of his duty to his bailor (*see* Conversion, above)

(d) *By wrongfully disposing of the goods.* Conversion by wrongful disposition consists of dealing with chattels so as to confer a good title to them on someone other than the person originally entitled to it, to his detriment. Thus, since the Hire Purchase Act 1964, if a person with a motor car on hire purchase sells it to another without revealing that it is on hire purchase, the buyer gets a good title adverse to the hirer, and the seller commits conversion.

(e) *By wrongfully delivering the goods.* Conversion by wrongful delivery occurs when one denies possession of goods to the person lawfully entitled to it, by wrongfully delivering them to another. In *Hollins* v. *Fowler* (1875), after complicated dealings, cotton lawfully belonging to F came into the hands of H, a broker. H, genuinely but mistakenly, believing that he had a good title to the cotton, delivered it to a client, who spun it into yarn. It was held that H had converted the cotton.

8. Conversion of documents

The *value* of a cheque is not a chattel, and therefore incapable of conversion. The difficulty is avoided by regarding the cheque itself, i.e. the piece of paper, as the converted chattel: *see Lloyds Bank* v. *Chartered Bank* [1929]. Note that this rule is not confined to negotiable instruments but may be extended to cover modern tokens like credit cards, cheque cards and book tokens.

TITLE TO SUE

9. Importance of possession

The plaintiff must be entitled to possession of the goods, although he need not have actual possession. Conversion consists of a wilful and wrongful interference with the goods of one entitled to possession of them, in such a way as to deny his right to that possession, or in a manner inconsistent with such right. In *North Central Wagon and Finance Co. Ltd* v. *Graham* [1950], C instructed the defendant G to sell his (C's) car, in breach of a hire-purchase agreement, thus entitling the finance company to terminate the hiring. When G sold the car the company sued him for conversion. It was held that they could succeed, as they became entitled to immediate possession of the car as soon as C broke the hire-purchase agreement. In a simple bailment, e.g. where A lends his car to his friend B, either A or B may sue in conversion. B's right derives from his actual possession and A's from his right to immediate possession.

10. The finder of an article

A finder owes a duty to the true owner to take reasonable care of it and return it if possible. If the true owner cannot be found the finder has a title to sue in conversion as against all others, e.g. in *Parker* v. *BAB* [1982], a person finding a gold bracelet on the floor of an airport lounge was held to be entitled to keep it: *see also Armory* v. *Delamirie* at **3** *above*. Another instance is *Bridges* v. *Hawkesworth* (1851), where the plaintiff found some banknotes on the floor of a shop, and gave them to the proprietor for him to return to the true owner. The latter was never discovered, and it was held that the finder of goods in a shop open to the public has a good title against everyone but the true owner.

It seems that if the article is attached to or under the surface, the owner of the land, as opposed to the finder, is entitled to it. This is based on the assumption that an owner or occupier intends to exercise control over things attached to or under the surface. In *Elwes* v. *Brigg Gas Co.* (1886), the defendants leased land, under the surface of which they discovered a prehistoric boat. As occupiers, the Gas Co. were held to have a good title as against the owners.

REMEDIES AND DEFENCES

11. Remedies

The main remedies are provided for in s. 3 of the 1977 Act which gives three alternatives:

(a) Recovery of the *value* of the goods *and* damages for detention

(b) Return of the goods or recovery of the value of the goods *and* damages for detention

(c) Return of the goods and damages for detention.

Remedy **(a)** is particularly appropriate where the plaintiff cannot claim return of the goods, e.g. because they have been sold to a third party who has obtained good title. The return of the goods contemplated by **(b)** and **(c)** is known as specific restitution. The Court has discretion, under the 1977 Act and Order 45, rule 4 of the Supreme Court Rules, in deciding whether or not to grant restitution (subject to the exception in s. 10 of the Contempt of Court Act 1987 relating to documents containing confidential information). Where the article is of no special value or interest to the plaintiff the court may consider it fair simply to award damages. If the court does order restitution and the defendant, while in possession, has enhanced the value of the property, the plaintiff will be required to make a fair allowance in respect of this. Just as the plaintiff is not entitled to insist on restitution, he cannot insist on damages in circumstances where he considers this would be more beneficial: *see USA* v. *Dollfus Mieg* [1952].

12. Effectual defences

(a) A defendant in conversion may traverse, e.g. aver that he had mere custody of the goods.

(b) He may show that the plaintiff had *no or insufficient possession* to maintain an action for conversion, e.g. that he was an owner out of possession, or that his right to possession was not immediate.

13. Ineffectual defences

(a) *Mistake.* Mistake is no defence, on general principles.

(b) *Plaintiff's default.* The general rule is that the plaintiff's negligence is no defence in conversion, unless it amounted to a breach of duty of care owed to the defendant.

(c) *Damage too remote.* It is immaterial that the defendant did not intend to deprive the plaintiff of his goods, or that such was not the natural or probable result of his act: *see Hiort* v. *Bott* (1874). However, an involuntary bailee commits conversion only if his wrongful dealing with the goods was also negligent: *see Elvin and Powell Ltd* v. *Plummer Roddis Ltd* (1933).

(d) *Defendant acted for another.* A person may be liable in conversion although he wrongfully interfered with the goods merely as the servant or agent of another, if he knows he is affecting title and not just possession. In *Consolidated Co.* v. *Curtis* [1892], a lady assigned furniture to the plaintiffs by bill of sale, but subsequently instructed the defendants (auctioneers) to sell the furniture – which they did, in ignorance of the assignment. It was held that the defendants were liable in conversion, as they knowingly affected the title to the goods.

(e) *Contributory negligence.* The Torts (Interference with Goods) Act 1977, s. 1(1) provides that contributory negligence is not a defence in proceedings founded on conversion or intentional trespass. Note, however, that the defence will apply where negligence is involved.

FURTHER EFFECTS OF THE 1977 ACT

In addition to the effects mentioned above, the Act also provides the following:

(a) Section 10 removes the former immunity at common law of co-owner who sold or disposed of (to a third party) property or goods owned in common, without the authority of his fellow owners, against an action by them in respect of the unauthorised sale or disposition. Co-ownership is no longer a defence to such an action.

(b) Section 7 provides that a defendant can no longer be required to pay more than the full value of the goods. Previously, at common law when a plaintiff out of possession relied on his right to possession, which was held by another (even wrongfully), the defendant might be liable both to the true owner and the possessor. The broad effect of the section is that those entitled to recover must account among themselves for no more than the full value of the goods, paid by the defendant.

RECAPTION AND REPLEVIN

14. Recaption

At common law a person may retake, with the minimum necessary force, goods of which he was wrongfully deprived. For this purpose he may peaceably enter upon the land of one who took the goods.

15. Replevin

This lies where goods have been wrongfully taken or detained by way of distress for rent – although it is not, in theory, confined to such a case. The object of replevin, which is now practically obsolescent, was to secure return of the goods pending the trial of the action.

Progress test 13

1. What are the main elements of trespass to goods?

2. What defences are open to a defendant in an action for trespass to goods?

3. How may conversions be committed?

4. Who has title to sue in conversion?

14

DEFAMATION

THE NATURE OF DEFAMATION

1. Introduction

The law of defamation has recently undergone scrutiny and change in the form of the enactment of the Defamation Act 1996. It had previously been an amalgam of principles of common law and legislation in the form of the Defamation Act 1952. The Neill Committee reviewed the law of defamation and reported back to the Lord Chancellor in 1991; over a gestation period of some four years these in part took the form of the Defamation Bill, which was enacted in the summer of 1996, receiving the Royal Assent in July 1996.

The 1996 Act adds to the legislative framework in three particular areas:

Defences
Procedure
Evidence.

In essence the Defamation Act 1996 makes limited changes to the substantive law (principally in respect of defences), and to adjectival aspects of the law of defamation (the introduction of a fast-track procedure and an amendment to the limitation period); additionally it legislates on evidential issues. These changes are in large part designed to expedite proceedings, save court time and reduce the cost of proceedings.

These reforms are not as thorough-going as some had anticipated; radical reforms such as taking the award of damages away from the jury and leaving them to the judge have been omitted from the legislation. The issue of the level of damages has been a thorn in the flesh of the judiciary: *see Tolstoy Miloslavsky* v. *United Kingdom* (1995).

The appropriate place to start a consideration of the law of defamation is the fundamental principles set out in the common law. The tort of defamation involves the making of a false and defamatory statement about another without lawful justification.

2. Injury to reputation

A defamatory statement is one which *injures the reputation* of the plaintiff by its tendency to 'lower him in the estimation of right-thinking members of society' or to cause right-thinking members of society to 'shun or avoid' him: *Sim* v. *Stretch* [1936], *per* Lord Atkin, perhaps because it brings him 'into hatred contempt or ridicule', e.g. because it alleges criminality, dishonesty or cruelty. This statement need not, however, impute misconduct or moral turpitude, e.g. a statement may be defamatory which shows the plaintiff as merely ridiculous. Nor need defamation consist of connected words or sentences, but may be e.g. carvings, paintings, or gestures. There is also no need to show that anyone believed the statement. In *Hough* v. *London Express* [1940], Goddard LJ said: 'If words are used which impute discreditable conduct to my friend, he has been defamed to me, although I do not believe the imputation, and may even know that it is untrue'. The plaintiff in question must be a legal person. This excludes claims by relatives or the estate of a dead person but allows claims by companies or municipal corporations in respect of statements alleging, for example, dishonesty or mismanagement of affairs.

It does not, however, include public authorities following the decision of the House of Lords in *Derbyshire County Council* v. *Times Newspapers Ltd.* [1993]. The reasoning behind this decision is that it is against the public interest for such bodies, in this case a local authority, to be allowed to bring proceedings for defamation. It was said in *Derbyshire* to be of the highest importance that the affairs of public bodies should be subject to scrutiny. It is in any event open to individual officers or members of an authority to use the tort to protect their reputations.

3. 'Right-thinking members of society'

The meaning of the phrase was considered in *Byrne* v. *Dean* [1937], where it was alleged that a lampoon was defamatory because it accused the plaintiff of 'sneaking' to the police about unlawful gambling in his club. It was held that the action of the club committee in allowing the lampoon to remain on the notice board did not constitute defamation, as members of society would not be right-thinking if they thought it defamatory to say that a man had discharged his public duty to help suppress crime. However, in objectively assessing the views of this group it seems that their views need not always be reasonable. So a statement causing the plaintiff to be 'shunned or avoided' due to prevailing prejudices may be defamatory. So that, although it may be more reasonable to have sympathy for a woman one hears has been raped, the courts have held that the reality is that she could be shunned or avoided: *see Yousoupoff* v. *MGM Pictures Ltd* (1934). The reason for taking people's prejudices into account has been given by Fleming as: 'A person's standing in the community, taking people as they are with their prejudices and conventional standards, is just as likely to be impaired by an attribution of misfortune as of contemptible conduct. In this matter it is to shut one's eye to realities to indulge in nice distinctions.' For a more recent case example *see Scuse* v. *Granada Television* [1993].

HISTORICAL DISTINCTION BETWEEN THE TWO FORMS OF DEFAMATION – LIBEL AND SLANDER

The differences between the two forms are as follows:

4. Libel

(a) The defamation is in a *permanent* form. This includes defamation in the course of:

- *Films.* In *Yousoupoff* v. *MGM Pictures Ltd* (1934), the defendants implied in a film that the Princess Y had been raped by Rasputin. It was held that this was libel. To say a woman had been raped would tend to make her shunned and avoided, even though she was morally blameless (*see* 3).
- *Broadcasting.* The Defamation Act 1952, s. 1, provides that 'for the purposes of the law of libel and slander, the broadcasting of words by means of wireless telegraphy shall be treated as publication in permanent form.' Broadcasting technologies have now moved on to include not only wireless and television but also the Internet and other accessible media. Broadcasting for general reception by either radio or television is libel: *see* the Broadcasting Act 1990, ss. 166 and 201.
- *Theatre production.* The Theatres Act 1968, s. 4 provides that words published during the course of a play should similarly be treated as publication in a permanent form.

(b) It is actionable *per se*, i.e. without proof of damage.

(c) It may be a crime, e.g. seditious or obscene libel.

5. Slander

(a) The defamation is in a non-permanent form, e.g. in the course of a speech.

(b) It is actionable only on proof of special damage, i.e. an actual pecuniary loss which the plaintiff can identify and value. The distinction between libel and slander particularly as it relates to the need to prove damage is arbitrary and illogical. Suppose a speaker in Hyde Park makes a statement defamatory of X (a slander) but which causes X no pecuniary loss. In such circumstances X has no course of action in defamation against the speaker. If, however, the statement is published by a newspaper (a libel) X may sue the newspaper in defamation.

(c) It cannot be a crime.

Although the distinction between libel and slander is *not necessarily* that between written and spoken defamation, it is usually so in point of fact.

6. Slander sometimes actionable *per se*

In the following four instances slander is actionable without proof of special damage.

(a) Imputing that the plaintiff has committed a crime not punishable by fine alone. The essential feature is the tendency to make others *shun* the plaintiff, *not* his being exposed to criminal prosecution.

(b) Imputing that the plaintiff has an *existing* contagious or infectious disease (e.g. HIV or AIDS) which would cause others to *shun* him.

(c) Imputing that a female has committed adultery or is not chaste: *see* Slander of Women Act 1891.

(d) Making statements about the plaintiff, 'calculated to disparage' him 'in any office, profession, calling, trade or business held or carried on by him at the time of the publication': *see* the Defamation Act 1952, s. 2

This section altered the common law rule that such a statement was not actionable unless it amounted to a *charge against* the plaintiff in respect of his profession, etc. It is now sufficient to show that the words were 'calculated to disparage', whether or not spoken of the plaintiff 'in the way of' his profession, etc. Thus before the Act it would not have been actionable.to say a solicitor was dishonest *except* in respect to a client; now the mere imputation of dishonesty would suffice in itself.

7. The limits of defamation

Defamation should be distinguished from the following:

(a) *Mere vulgar abuse* – which injures a man's dignity only, not his reputation. In *Penfold* v. *Westcote* (1806), the defendant said 'You blackguard, rascal, scoundrel, Penfold, you are a thief.' It was held that 'blackguard', etc. was mere abuse, but was defamatory in conjunction with 'thief'.

(b) *Injurious falsehood*. A statement is not defamatory unless it injures the plaintiff's reputation; e.g. a statement which injures his business but not his personal reputation is actionable (if at all) as *injurious falsehood*.

STANDARD OF PROOF

The plaintiff must prove:

(a) That the statement was *defamatory*.

(b) That the statement *referred* to the plaintiff.

(c) That the statement was *published*.

8. That the statement was defamatory

The test is not the nature of the defendant's intention but the *meaning* which would be *imputed by reasonable persons*. Innocent intention is not of itself a defence.

9. Functions of judge and jury

(a) The judge's function is to decide *as a matter of law* whether the statement is *reasonably capable* of bearing the defamatory meaning alleged by the plaintiff. If not so satisfied, he withholds the case from the jury. In order to enable the judge to rule in this matter, the plaintiff must give adequate particulars. *See Allsop* v. *Church of England Newspapers Ltd* [1972] and *DDSA Pharmaceuticals Ltd* v. *Times Newspapers Ltd* [1972]. See also s. 7 of the Defamation Act 1996 which states:

> 'In defamation proceedings the court shall not be asked to rule whether a statement is arguably capable, as opposed to capable, of bearing a particular meaning or meanings attributed to it.'

The purpose of this section is to save costs which could otherwise be wasted through futile submissions on particular interpretations of the meaning to be attributed to words/statements.

(b) The jury's function is to decide *as a matter of fact* whether the statement complained of is defamatory: *see Capital & Counties Bank Ltd* v. *George Henty & Sons* (1882) and *Aspro Travel* v. *Owners Abroad Group* [1995].

The words must be interpreted in their context. The plaintiff cannot select apparently libellous statements if the passage taken as a whole is not defamatory: *see Charleston* v. *News Group Newspapers* [1995].

10. Innuendo

(a) *Effect of innuendo*. An apparently innocent statement may nevertheless be defamatory if it contains an innuendo (defined by the OED as 'an oblique hint, allusive remark, usually deprecatory'). The essence of innuendo is that a statement is made, whether written, or by means of a drawing, painting or sculpture etc., which may be construed as totally innocent until it transpires that, from extrinsic evidence or reading between the lines, that the subject of the statement is being defamed, e.g. to refer to a woman as 'Mrs X' is innocent without the benefit of the knowledge that X is married to someone else: *see Cassidy* v. *Daily Mirror Newspapers* [1929].

(b) *Special pleading necessary*. An innuendo must be specially pleaded, i.e. the plaintiff must state and prove the grounds (with supporting evidence, e.g. his special knowledge) on which he alleges that the apparently innocent remark is defamatory. He must prove the meaning he himself attributes to the words.

(c) *Surrounding circumstances*. An innuendo may arise, not from the words, but from the facts and circumstances surrounding the publication. In *Tolley* v. *Fry* [1931], it was implied in a cartoon forming part of an advertisement that a famous amateur golfer had, by consenting to the use of his name, compromised his amateur status. In fact, he had not consented, and knew nothing of the advertisement until it appeared. There was held to be libel by innuendo.

In *Bookbinder* v. *Tebbit* [1989] the alleged slander was made at a political meeting. The Court of Appeal stated that the meaning to be attached to the defendant's words could be affected by, *inter alia*, the form of the question to which the words formed an answer or the general course of the speech in issue.

(d) *Objective test of innuendo.* It is not of itself a defence that the defendant did not know of the facts or circumstances turning the seemingly innocent statement into an innuendo if the innuendo would have been inferred by reasonable persons.

Again, however, an offer of amends may be made under the Defamation Act 1996 (*see* **34**).

(e) *Innuendo plea.* Innuendo can be pleaded additionally to a plea that the statement is defamatory in its ordinary meaning. In *Hayward* v. *Thompson* [1981] CA, the plaintiff alleged defamation by two articles in consecutive issues of a Sunday newspaper. In the first he was referred to as 'a wealthy benefactor of the Liberal Party' but in the second he was referred to by name. The defendants appealed against the trial judge's ruling that the jury could take account of the second article in order to decide whether the first article *was* admissible to show identification and innuendo in the first.

(f) *Innuendo and subsequent knowledge.* In *Grappelli* v. *Derek Block (Holdings) Ltd* [1981], the Court of Appeal considered the then unsettled question of whether innuendo could be established on the basis of facts which became known only after the publication of matter which was innocent at the time of its publication. In rejecting that proposition, Lord Denning MR cited words used in the judgment in the New Zealand case of *Simmons Pty* v. *Riddell* [1941]: 'Previous cases do not lay down that a writer of innocent matter can by reason of certain facts coming into existence subsequent to publication of his innocent matter become liable in damages for libel.' In *Grappelli* v. *Derek Block (Holdings) Ltd* [1981] CA, the famous violinist, Stephane Grappelli, cancelled a series of concerts arranged by his agents (the defendants) because he (Mr Grappelli) had not authorised the arrangement. The agents told the theatre managements involved that the cancellations arose because Mr Grappelli was seriously ill and unlikely to tour again. This was untrue. The agents then arranged a further series of concerts on dates and in places close to those originally arranged. Mr Grappelli alleged that this constituted an innuendo that he had given what he knew to be a false reason for cancelling the originally proposed concerts. The defendants denied this on the grounds that the main extrinsic fact (that Mr Grappelli was not ill) was not known to theatre managements and the general public when the notice of cancellation was published. It was held that there was no case in defamation to answer although the plaintiff succeeded in his action for injurious falsehood. *See* 7:**16**.

11. Physical relationship

Defamation (direct or by innuendo) may take the form of the mere physical relationship of objects. In *Monson* v. *Tussauds Ltd* [1894], the defendants placed an effigy of the plaintiff, against whom a charge of murder was 'not proven', close to those of convicted murderers. It was held that there was a *prima facie* libel, although an interlocutory injunction was not granted.

12. That the statement referred to the plaintiff

The court can dismiss the action in interlocutory proceedings where no reasonable person could believe that the statement referred to the plaintiff. The judge may withdraw the case from the jury on the same grounds. The reference need not be *express* but may be *latent*: see *Hayward* v. *Thompson* (**10** above). It is not necessary to show that the defendant intended to refer to the plaintiff, or even that the defendant knew of the plaintiff's existence. The test is: would a person to whom the statement was published *reasonably think* it referred to the plaintiff?

In *Hulton & Co.* v. *Jones* [1910], a newspaper article named a supposedly fictitious 'Artemus Jones' as having a mistress in France. The real Artemus Jones proved that persons reasonably believed that the reference was to him. This was held to be a libel. In *Cassidy* v. *Daily Mirror Newspapers Ltd* [1929], the defendants published a photograph of a prominent person with a lady. The caption said they had just become engaged. The defendants did not know that the plaintiff was already married to the prominent person and had made no attempt to find out whether he was married at all. It was held that the defendants were liable in defamation to Mrs Cassidy (the plaintiff) as reasonable persons would have taken the innuendo that she had been living with a man to whom she was not married. The electronic publication of a computer game (grafting the images of two well known t.v. personalities on to the bodies of persons in a pornographic episode), stills of which were reproduced in a newspaper with a caption clearly referring to the plaintiffs, *see Charleston* v. *News Group Newspapers* [1995].

The fact that the statement is true of A does not mean it cannot be defamatory of B. Again, the test is whether reasonable persons might understand the statement to refer to B. In *Newstead* v. *London Express Newspapers Ltd* [1940], the defendants reported on a bigamy trial, the accused being named as 'Harold Newstead, 30 year old Camberwell man'. This was a correct account of the trial of a barman of that name and extrinsic evidence was admissible to determine how reasonable persons would have understood the statement. In *Morgan* v. *Odhams Press* [1971], a kennel maid told a journalist about the doping of greyhounds. Subsequently she stayed with the plaintiff in his flat in Willesden, where she was seen by six people. The defendants published an article in which it was said that the girl had been kidnapped by a doping gang and kept at Finchley. The article did not mention the plaintiff by name or description. It was held that it was not necessary that there should be a 'key or pointer' indicating the plaintiff; extrinsic evidence could be brought to show that the six people in the flat might think the words complained of referred to the plaintiff.

13. Defamation of a class

(a) *A class cannot be defamed as such*, but it may be so small and well defined that what is said of the class necessarily refers to any or every member of it.

(b) *The class must be clearly defined.* The plaintiff may be defamed, although not specifically identified, if the class to which he belongs – and which is defamed – is so small and clearly defined that reasonable persons would take the words complained of as referring to the plaintiff. The larger and more ill defined the class, the greater the difficulty of showing the plaintiff was referred to. For example, to refer to all the lawyers as crooks is too vague to be defamatory of specific people. In *Knupffer* v. *London Express Newspapers Ltd* [1944], allegedly defamatory imputations were made against a group of twenty-four foreign refugees. There was evidence that the reference was thought to be to their leader. It was held that there was no libel as reasonable persons would not have thought so.

14. That the statement was published

To be published, a statement must be made known to at least one person other than the person defamed. Publication need not be to the public at large. Publication only to the party defamed suffices in criminal but not civil libel, because of the tendency to cause a breach of the peace. The following are examples of published and unpublished statements:

(a) Communications of husbands and wives *inter se* do not constitute publication, *see Wennhak* v. *Morgan* (1888), but a statement by a third person to one spouse about the other is publication, *see Wenman* v. *Ash* [1853].

(b) A defamation may be published by dictation, e.g. to a secretary, but this is probably slander only. If the communication is privileged the dictation, or other attendant circumstance, is also privileged.

(c) It is not publication when a printer returns the printed version of a manuscript to its author: *see Eglangtime Inn Ltd* v. *Smith* [1948].

(d) Failure to remove defamatory matter from one's premises may amount to publication, unless removal would be very difficult or impossible: *see Byrne* v. *Deane* [1937].

(e) A statement is not published unless understood. A person to whom an allegedly defamatory statement is published must understand:
(*i*) its meaning; and
(*ii*) that it refers to the plaintiff. In *Sadgrove* v. *Hole* [1901], the defendant sent A a postcard containing a statement defamatory of B, but with no mention of B's name. As A did not know that it referred to B it was held that there had not been sufficient publication.

(f) *Re* publication – *see Slipper* v. *BBC* [1991].

15. Publication sometimes presumed

Publication is presumed, and the burden of disproof thrown on the defendant, in the following cases:

(a) when a letter or postcard is posted

(b) when a document is printed

(c) when a fax is sent.

16. Dissemination

Every repetition is a separate and distinct publication which creates a new cause of action. Thus the proprietor, editor, publisher and printer may all be sued for libel in a newspaper, and in some circumstances a person (e.g. a newsagent) may be liable who does no more than offer the offending publication for sale. The originator of defamatory matter who authorises others to repeat it remains liable, jointly and severally, with those others. Furthermore, the liability of the origina-tor remains *strict*, i.e. innocent intention or lack of negligence is no defence.

An unintentional publication may be defamatory if made negligently, e.g. where dissemination is unnecessarily widespread: *see White* v. *Stone* [1939], where defamatory matter spoken by a man to his wife was overheard by a third person. However, unintentional dissemination to a third person will not be negligent if the disseminator had no reason to anticipate the third person's receiving it: *see Powell* v. *Gelston* [1916].

Publication to the defendant's own employees in the ordinary course of business is *prima facie* sufficient to create liability; but 'if a business communica-tion is privileged . . . the privilege covers all . . . treatment of the communication . . . in accordance with the usual and reasonable course of business': *see Edmonson* v. *Birch & Co. Ltd* [1907]. Dictation to a shorthand typist has been said to be 'reasonable and usual': *Osborn* v. *Boulter* [1930].

17. Innocent dissemination

Dissemination will not amount to actionable publication if the defendant **(a)** did not know, and **(b)** was not negligent in failing to discover, that the matter in question was defamatory.

In *Emmens* v. *Pottle* (1885), the defendant newsvendor widely disseminated defamatory matter. It was held there was no publication, as there was neither knowledge nor negligence in the defendant. An analogous case, *Bottomley* v. *Woolworth & Co. Ltd* (1932), involved innocent dissemination by the sale of magazines in Woolworth stores.

The cases above should be contrasted with *Vizetelly* v. *Mudie's Select Library Ltd* [1900] and *Sun Life Assurance* v. *W.H. Smith & Son Ltd* (1934), in which the defendants were held to have published libels through negligence in failing to discover defamatory matter in publications which they circulated.

The scope of innocent dissemination has been broadened by Section 1 of the Defamation Act 1996. Section 1(1) provides:

'In defamation proceedings a person has a defence if he shows that –

(a)   he was not the author, editor or publisher of the statement complained of,

(b)   he took reasonable care in relation to its publication, and

(c)   he did not know, and had no reason to believe, that what he did caused or
        contributed to the publication of a defamatory statement.'

Section 1(2) defines each of author, editor and publisher for the purposes of
section 1(1). Section 1(3) is a saving provision, setting out specific circumstances
where a person is not considered to be author, editor or publisher of a statement.
Section 1(4) considers the position of employees and agents of an author, editor
or publisher.

Section 1(5) provides:

'In determining for the purposes of this section whether a person took reasonable
care, or had reason to believe that what he did caused or contributed to the
publication of a defamatory statement, regard shall be had to –

(a)   the extent of his responsibility for the content of the statement or the decision to
        publish it,
(b)   the nature of the circumstances of the publication, and
(c)   the previous conduct or character of the author, editor or publisher'.

The relevance of this provision is particularly pertinent to those organisations
which provide the Internet to subscribers; it offers them a degree of protection
previously unavailable.

DEFENCES

A defendant in a defamation action may:

(a) deny that the matter is defamatory

(b) deny publication: s. 1 of the Defamation Act 1996 (above)

18. Other defences

The following defences are also available:

Justification.
Fair comment.
Privilege – absolute and qualified: Defamation Act 1996.
Offer of amends: Defamation Act 1996.
Apology: Libel Act 1843.
Consent.

19. Justification

Justification consists of proof that the allegedly defamatory matter was true.
Justification is a dangerous defence, because if it fails, *heavier damages* will
probably be awarded. On the other hand if the defendant's statements are true,
the defence will avail, even if he did not believe them to be true or made them
with malice.

(a) *Onus of proof.* Justification must be specially pleaded by the *defendant* who *must prove* the statement was true. The plaintiff does not require to establish its falsity.

(b) *Substantial truth suffices.* It is sufficient to prove the substantial truth of the statement, i.e. a minor inaccuracy will not vitiate the defence. Whether the inaccuracy was minor is a matter of fact for the jury – which is almost always present at a defamation action. In *Alexander* v. *North Eastern Railway Co.* (1865), the plaintiff having been convicted of travelling on a train without a ticket, it was stated that he had been fined one pound and jailed for three weeks. In fact a two week sentence was the penalty for defaulting on payment of the fine. This was held not to be sufficiently inaccurate to defeat the defence of justification.

(c) *Effect of Defamation Act 1952.* Section 5 provides that justification will not fail merely because the truth of one of several charges is not established – if, having regard to the other charges, it did no material injury to the plaintiff's reputation: *see Polly Peck (Holdings) plc* v. *Trelford* [1986].

(d) *Defendant's motive irrelevant.* The defence of justification, if otherwise good, will not fail because the defendant acted from a malicious or improper motive. However, an honest and reasonable but mistaken belief in the truth of the statement will not suffice to support justification.

(e) *Justification in criminal libel.* In criminal libel justification is a good defence if publication was for the public good – Libel Act 1843, s. 6. At common law, truth was no defence.

(f) *Rehabilitation of Offenders Act 1974.* Section 8 provides that where the plaintiff was defamed by the raising against him of a 'spent' conviction (as defined by the Act) proof of the truth of the allegation will not avail as a defence if the statement was published with malice.

20. Rumour, suspicion, innuendo and abuse

(a) Proof of the existence of a rumour or suspicion is insufficient; its truth must be proved.

(b) One who repeats a statement must prove its truth; proof of accurate repetition is insufficient.

(c) Mere abuse or invective incidental to the main charge need not be justified.

(d) If the words are held capable of bearing an innuendo, the truth of the innuendo must be proved.

(e) The defendant may justify part of the alleged defamation, provided it is severable from the rest of the statement.

21. Fair comment

Fair comment is comment honestly made on a matter of public interest. This criterion requires closer examination.

22. Comment

The defendant must prove that the statement was comment, i.e. one of *opinion, not fact*. If the statement consists of facts, justification is the appropriate defence. In *London Artists Ltd* v. *Littler* [1969], the defendant, a well-known impresario, was presenting a play in the West End. Four of the leading actors, through their agent, London Artists Ltd, simultaneously gave notice to leave the cast. The defendant, in a letter published in the press, alleged a conspiracy to bring the run of the play to an end. When sued for libel, he raised the defence of fair comment. It was held that the matter was one of public interest but the defence failed because the allegation of conspiracy was, in the circumstances, a statement of fact, not of opinion, and therefore not 'comment'.

In *Telnikoff* v. *Matusevitch* [1992] the House of Lords considered the approach which a trial judge should take where the defence of fair comment is raised. The House of Lords affirmed that it was a function of the jury to determine whether particular statements amount to assertions of fact or are comment. This decision was held to turn, as a matter of construction, on the document in question; reference cannot be made to the items on which the comment was based. Any publication will therefore be judged on its own terms. This rule is however subject to two important exceptions. First, it is permissible to comment on untrue statements published under the protection of privilege provided the report is a fair and accurate report of the statements: *Brent Walker Group plc* v. *Time Out Ltd* [1991]; secondly under section 6 of the Defamation Act 1952 (see below).

Fact and comment are difficult to separate. Because of this, the plea is sometimes couched in the form: 'In so far as the words complained of are statements of fact they are true in substance and in fact; and in so far as they consist of comment they are fair comment on a matter of public interest.' This, the *rolled-up* plea, is a plea of fair comment, not justification. The facts are proved merely to lay a foundation for the defence of fair comment. Furthermore, the Rules of Court provide that the plaintiff is entitled to be informed of the facts on which the defendant intends to rely.

The effects of factual inaccuracy are as follows: the Defamation Act 1952, s. 6 altered the previous position, where the slightest inaccuracy in the facts stated defeated fair comment. Section 6 provides that, where a statement consists partly of fact and partly of comment, the defence of fair comment 'shall not fail by reason only that the truth of every allegation of fact is not proved' if the expression of opinion is nevertheless fair, having regard to the facts which are proved.

23. Fairness

Although the comment must be fair, i.e. the honestly held opinion of the defendant, 'fair comment does not mean moderate comment'. The opinion of the court or the jury must not be substituted for that of the defendant: *see McQuire* v. *Western Morning News* [1903]. The test is: 'Was this an opinion, however exaggerated, obstinate or prejudiced, which was honestly held by the writer?': *see Silken* v. *Beaverbrook Newspapers Ltd* [1958], *per* Diplock J.

24. Honesty of statement

The defendant must have made the comment in good faith, believing in its truth and without malicious distortion. In *Merivale* v. *Carson* [1887], a false statement was made that a play contained an incident of adultery. It was held that the plea of fair comment was excluded. A *malicious motive* will exclude the plea of fair comment. In *Thomas* v. *Bradbury Agnew & Co. Ltd* [1906], the writer of a review made untrue allegations of fact, and harboured personal spite against the author. It was held that the comment was distorted by malice and therefore not fair. However, it should be emphasised that because a comment is unreasonable this does not mean it is malicious and incapable of being fair comment: *see* the judgment of Lord Porter in *Turner* v. *MGM Pictures* [1950]. This is not to say that the extreme perversity or unreasonableness of a comment made, for example, by a film critic would not provide evidence of lack of good faith and/or malicious motive.

An attack on the plaintiff's moral character, because it consists essentially of allegations of fact about the plaintiff's character, cannot be fair comment. Justification is the appropriate defence. In *Campbell* v. *Spottiswoode* (1863), it was alleged that the plaintiff's statement that he wished to spread the gospel in China was a hypocritical pretence to increase the sales of his newspaper. This was held not to be fair comment, but an attack on character. Cockburn CJ said: 'A writer in a public paper may comment on the conduct of public men in the strongest terms; but, if he imputes dishonesty, he must be prepared to justify'.

25. Public interest

The basis of the defence of fair comment is the necessity for free and fair comment on matters of public interest.

(a) *Comment on private matters excluded.* The defence is not available where the comment was on purely private matters. However, *public interest* is widely defined. It includes: the conduct of public men; the administration of public institutions; and even the affairs of private businesses which affect the public at large, or a section of it. The public interest in question may be restricted to a particular locality and have only an indirect effect on the rest of the country: *see Purcell* v. *Sowler* (1877).

(b) *Voluntary submission to comment.* The defence applies to activities which are voluntarily submitted to comment, e.g. acting, writing, painting, sculpture, music, and works of criticism. Advertisements, circulars and public speeches are also included.

26. Functions of judge and jury

(a) The judge decides the following as matters of law:
    (*i*) Whether the words used are capable of being statements of fact.
    (*ii*) Whether the subject, in law, is open to comment.
    (*iii*) Whether there is reasonable evidence to go to the jury that the comment was not fair.

(b) If the judge decides these in the affirmative, the issue of unfairness goes to the jury. Note that, contrary to the general modern practice in civil actions, a jury is almost always present in defamation cases.

27. Privilege

(a) A privileged communication may be defined as one in respect of which the law holds that the public interest in free speech overrides, wholly or conditionally, the private right to an untarnished reputation.

(b) Privilege is of two kinds. It may be:
    (*i*) *Absolute* – not actionable under any circumstances; or
    (*ii*) *Qualified* – actionable only on proof of express malice.

28. Absolute privilege

The following classes of statement are absolutely privileged.

(a) Those made in either House of Parliament. This stems from the Bill of Rights 1689, which stated: 'The freedom of speech and debates or proceedings in Parliament ought not to be impeached or questioned in any court or place out of Parliament.' It is undecided whether a letter from an MP to a Minister enjoys absolute privilege as a 'proceeding in Parliament'. For an example *see Prebble* v. *Television New Zealand Ltd* [1994] which, although a decision of the Privy Council, is of strong persuasive authority.

(b) Reports of parliamentary proceedings published by order of either House, or their re-publication in full (Parliamentary Papers Act 1849). Such re-publications were not privileged at common law: *see Stockdale* v. *Hansard* [1839].

(c) *Judicial proceedings.* Statements made by judges, advocates, jurors, witnesses or parties:
    (*i*)   in the course of judicial proceedings, civil or military; or
    (*ii*) with reference to such proceedings.
This extends to tribunals exercising judicial (as distinct from merely administrative) functions. In *Addis* v. *Crocker* [1961], an order of the Disciplinary Committee of the Law Society sitting in private was held absolutely privileged.

It does not extend however to licensing courts as in *Royal Aquarium Society* v. *Parkinson* [1892], where London County Council was *not a court* when hearing certain licensing applications, therefore statements by its members were not privileged. Neither are restrictive practices proceedings before the Commission of the EC, as this is an administrative not judicial procedure.

It does however extend to statements made by a witness to a party or his solicitor before (but with reference to) the trial, *see Watson* v. *McEwen* [1905], and statements inadmissible as evidence, if made with reference to the proceedings.

In *Brent Walker Group plc and Another* v. *Time Out Ltd and Another* [1991] the defendants wrote and published in a well-known weekly magazine an article about George Walker, the high-profile chairman of a public company which owned and operated casinos. The article was critical of Mr Walker's character and reputation, made reference to his alleged involvement in serious criminal activities in the 1950s, in particular his conviction for theft in 1956 and his sentence of two year's imprisonment, and questioned the Gaming Board's approval of the plaintiff company's gaming operations.

The plaintiff company and its chairman brought an action against the defendants for libel. The defendants pleaded fair comment on a matter of public interest and in their defence set out particulars of the facts on which they relied, which included privileged but unproven evidence by a police officer during the 1956 criminal trial. The plaintiffs applied to have those statements struck out of the defence. This was refused by the Master, the plaintiffs appealed and the judge allowed the appeal and struck out the statements complained of, on the ground that in order to sustain the defence of fair comment in relation to privileged but unproven statements it was not enough for the defendants to show that the witness statements relied on were made on a privileged occasion (i.e. in the case of a criminal trial), they also had to prove that their publication gave a fair and accurate report of these proceedings. The defendants appealed to the Court of Appeal.

The Court of Appeal held that where a defendant raised the defence of fair comment in libel proceedings brought in respect of an article written or published by him and sought to base his defence on unproven statements made on a privileged occasion, the defendant had to show not only that his comment was fair but also that he had given a fair and accurate report of the occasion on which the privileged statements were made if he was to establish a defence. Accordingly, in order to establish the defence of fair comment based on statements made by a witness in judicial proceedings, the defendants had to meet the additional requirement of showing that the publication gave a fair and accurate report of the proceedings. Since the defendants had failed to meet the additional requirement their appeal was dismissed and the order striking out the statements complained of was upheld.

This privilege extends to other tribunals recognised by law provided they are exercising functions equivalent to those of an established Court: see s. 14(3) Defamation Act 1996. This has been held to include, for example, courts-martial. It will not however include bodies exercising merely administrative functions, e.g. complaints to social security adjudication officers: *Purdew and Purdew* v. *Seress Smith* [1993].

(d) *Officers of State*. A statement is absolutely privileged if made by one officer of State to another in the course of official duty. *See Chatterton* v. *Secretary of State for India* [1895], which involved a communication by a Minister to the Under-Secretary of State for India, to enable him to answer a parliamentary question. It was held to be privileged.

The following have been held to be 'officers of State': a Military Officer reporting to his superiors; a Minister communicating with an official; and a High Commissioner reporting to the Prime Minister. A police officer reporting to his superior, however, is not. Statements made in Great Britain by officials of foreign governments are probably protected by *diplomatic* privilege.

(e) *Husband and wife*. Statements made by one spouse to the other are absolutely privileged; but not statements by one spouse to a third party about the other.

29. Qualified privilege

(a) For a statement to enjoy qualified privilege there must be:
  (*i*) a legal, moral or social duty to make it on one side *and*
  (*ii*) a corresponding interest to receive it on the other.

Both these conditions must be satisfied. In *Adam* v. *Ward* [1917], Lord Atkinson said: 'This reciprocity is essential'. *See Watt* v. *Longsdon* [1930], which established that the reciprocal duty and interest are *essential in all cases* of qualified privilege, not only those in which the allegedly defamatory statement was made in discharge of a duty. In this case, W and L were members of the same firm. A (also a member of the firm) wrote to L, making defamatory statements about W's morals and behaviour. L showed the letter (a) to the Chairman of the firm; (b) to W's wife. It was held that the publication to the Chairman was privileged, as there was a reciprocal duty to make it and a reciprocal interest to receive it; but publication to W's wife was not privileged; she had an *interest* to receive the information but L had *no duty* to show her the letter.

In *Bryanston Finance Ltd* v. *De Vries* [1975], the two co-defendants were in dispute with the Chairman of a company. They enlisted the help of two clerks in drafting a document which they sent to the Chairman, threatening to expose his alleged malpractices unless he settled their claim for conspiracy. The Chairman obtained an interim injunction to prevent publication and the question arose as to whether the publication of the document to the two clerks was privileged. It was held that as the plaintiff Chairman had no common interest with its authors to receive the document, its publication to him was not privileged and neither was its publication to the two clerks.

The judge decides whether the duty exists. The test of what constitutes a moral or social duty seems to be an objective one: 'Would the great mass of right-minded men . . . have considered it their duty . . . to make the communication?': *see Watt* v. *Longsdon* [1930] *per* Green LJ. The burden of proving to the jury that, as a matter of fact, the defendant was malicious is on the plaintiff: *see* e.g. *Fraser* v. *Mirza* (1993).

(b) *Extent of the privilege.* The following statements enjoy qualified privilege: those made (*i*) in discharging a duty; (*ii*) in protecting an interest; (*iii*) in reports of parliamentary, judicial and certain other public proceedings. In *Tsikata* v. *Newspaper Publishing plc* [1996] the Court of Appeal held that qualified privilege does not cease merely because the newspaper report for which it is claimed was not published contemporaneously with the events which the report described.

It is not absolutely settled whether professional communications between solicitor and client enjoy qualified or absolute privilege, but the better opinion seems to be that it is qualified only.

30. Discharging a duty

A purely voluntary or gratuitous defamatory statement will *not* be privileged unless the relationship of the maker and recipient was such as to *create a duty* in the maker to speak on his own initiative. Examples include: communication from servant to master about the master's interests: *see Lawless* v. *Anglo-Egyptian*

Cotton Co. [1869]; communications from host to guest about a servant's dishonesty: *see Stuart* v. *Bell* [1891]; and statements in good faith by members of public bodies in pursuance of their duties: *see Andrew* v. *Nott-Bower* [1895].

It is a necessary extension of the duty/interest relationship that a statement may enjoy qualified privilege if the maker and recipient have a *common interest* in its being made about the plaintiff. *Nevill* v. *Fine Arts & General Insurance Co.* [1897] involved a communication by an insurance company to its policy holders about one of its agents. It was held to be privileged because of common interest in the finance of the company. *Winstanley* v. *Bampton* [1943] concerned a complaint by tradesmen to a commanding officer about an officer's unpaid bills. It was held to be privileged because of common interest in the financial probity of HM officers. In *Botterill* v. *Whytehead* (1879), however, a general interest in church architecture did not constitute a common interest between a clergyman and the parishioners of a church with which he had no connection.

The existence of the common interest is a *matter of law* for the judge. A mere honest belief in its existence is not enough. There is no established test, but the interest must be *common*, e.g. there is a common interest between X and Y in the case of mere gratuitous meddling by one in the affairs of the other.

31. Protecting an interest

A statement enjoys qualified privilege, even if there is no duty to make it, if made to protect a *lawful interest*, e.g. the person, property or reputation of its maker. Again, *reciprocity* is essential; there must be an interest to be protected and a duty to protect it. In *Somerville* v. *Hawkins* [1851], a master warned his servants about the character of a fellow servant. It was held to be privileged as master and servants had a common interest in the matter, and there was a duty to protect the servants. In *Quartz Hill Gold Mining Co.* v. *Beall* (1882), it was held that publications *inter se* of members or shareholders of an enterprise have qualified privilege if made in defence or furtherance of their common interest.

So far as public interest is concerned, the interest to be protected may be that of the public at large in the honest and efficient discharge of public duties; and the reciprocal duty of an individual may be to disclose breaches of such duty. Thus, charges of misconduct against public officials will be privileged only if made to an individual such as a Member of Parliament, or the official's superior, with a *corresponding interest* to receive them – the privilege would be exceeded and lost by publication, for instance, to a *newspaper*.

Note, however, that the Defamation Act 1952, s. 10 provides that a defamatory statement made by, or on behalf of, a candidate at an election is not privileged merely because it refers to an issue in the election.

32. Reports of parliamentary, judicial and public proceedings

Reports of statements should not be confused with the *statements themselves*, e.g. by a judge in court or an MP in the House – which are *absolutely* privileged. By way of example *see Rost* v. *Edwards* [1990]. Absolute privilege has been extended by s. 14 of the Defamation Act 1996 to reports of the European Court of Justice and the European Court of Human Rights. Section 14 of the Defamation Act 1996 provides:

14(1)   A fair and accurate report of proceedings in public before a court to which this section applies, if published contemporaneously with the proceedings, is absolutely privileged.

14(2)   A report of proceedings which by an order of the court, or as a consequence of any statutory provision, is required to be postponed shall be treated as published contemporaneously if it is published as soon as practicable after publication is permitted.

14(3)   This section applies to –

(a)   Any court in the United Kingdom
(b)   The European Court of Justice or any court attached to that court
(c)   The European Court of Human Rights
(d)   Any international criminal tribunal established by the Security Council of the United Nations or by any international agreement to which the United Kingdom is a party.

In paragraph (a) 'court' includes any tribunal or body exercising the judicial power of the State.

Section 14 of the Defamation Act 1996 extends qualified privilege to reports set out in Schedule I, Parts I and II. Reports protected by qualified privilege in Part I are those that do not require any explanation or contradiction, while Part II sets out those statements privileged subject to publication of an explanation or contradiction if required. It should be noted that the Schedule to the Defamation Act 1952 was only concerned with newspapers.

33.   Solicitor and client

Professional communications between solicitor and client possess qualified privilege on the grounds that the interests of *justice* demand it. The communication must be made by or to the solicitor in his professional capacity, e.g. not merely as a personal friend, and must be relevant to the relationship of solicitor and client, having regard to the business in hand. It seems now to be generally agreed that this privilege is *qualified*; but the point is not absolutely settled as the Court of Appeal has treated it (on separate occasions) as both absolute and qualified; and in *Minter* v. *Priest* [1930], the House of Lords expressly reserved its opinion.

34.   Offer of amends: Defamation Act 1996

This defence is now provided for by sections 2, 3 and 4 of the Defamation Act 1996, which provide:

'2.—(1)   A person who has published a statement alleged to be defamatory of another may offer to make amends under this section.

(2)   The offer may be in relation to the statement generally or in relation to a specific defamatory meaning which the person making the offer accepts that the statement conveys ('a qualified offer').

(3)   An offer to make amends –

(a)   must be in writing,
(b)   must be expressed to be an offer to make amends under section 2 of the Defamation Act 1996, and
(c)   must state whether it is a qualified offer and, if so, set out the defamatory meaning in relation to which it is made.

(4)   An offer to make amends under this section is an offer –

(a)   to make a suitable correction of the statement complained of and a sufficient apology to the aggrieved party,
(b)   to publish the correction and apology in a manner that is reasonable and practicable in the circumstances, and
(c)   to pay to the aggrieved party such compensation (if any), and such costs, as may be agreed or determined to be payable.

The fact that the offer is accompanied by an offer to take specific steps does not affect the fact that an offer to make amends under this section is an offer to do all the things mentioned in paragraphs (a) to (c).

(5)   An offer to make amends under this section may not be made by a person after serving a defence in defamation proceedings brought against him by the aggrieved party in respect of the publication in question.

(6)   An offer to make amends under this section may be withdrawn before it is accepted; and a renewal of an offer which has been withdrawn shall be treated as a new offer.

3.—(1)   If an offer to make amends under section 2 is accepted by the aggrieved party, the following provisions apply.

(2)   The party accepting the offer may not bring or continue defamation proceedings in respect of the publication concerned against the person making the offer, but he is entitled to enforce the offer to make amends, as follows.

(3)   If the parties agree on the steps to be taken in fulfilment of the offer, the aggrieved party may apply to the court for an order that the other party fulfil his offer by taking the steps agreed.

(4)   If the parties do not agree on the steps to be taken by way of correction, apology and publication, the party who made the offer may take such steps as he thinks appropriate, and may in particular –

(a)   make the correction and apology by a statement in open court in terms approved by the court, and
(b)   give an undertaking to the court as to the manner of their publication.

(5)   If the parties do not agree on the amount to be paid by way of compensation, it shall be determined by the court on the same principles as damages in defamation proceedings.

The court shall take account of any steps taken in fulfilment of the offer and (so far as not agreed between the parties) of the suitability of the correction, the sufficiency of the apology and whether the manner of their publication was reasonable in the circumstances, and may reduce or increase the amount of compensation accordingly.

(6) If the parties do not agree on the amount to be paid by way of costs, it shall be determined by the court on the same principles as costs awarded in court proceedings.

(7) The acceptance of an offer by one person to make amends does not affect any cause of action against another person in respect of the same publication, subject as follows.

(8) In England and Wales or Northern Ireland, for the purposes of the Civil Liability (Contribution) Act 1978 –

(a) the amount of compensation paid under the offer shall be treated as paid in bona fide settlement or compromise of the claim; and
(b) where another person is liable in respect of the same damage (whether jointly or otherwise), the person whose offer to make amends was accepted is not required to pay by virtue of any contribution under section 1 of that Act a greater amount than the amount of the compensation payable in pursuance of the offer.

(9) In Scotland –

(a) subsection (2) of section 3 of the Law Reform (Miscellaneous Provisions) (Scotland) Act 1940 (right of one joint wrongdoer as respects another to recover contribution towards damages) applies in relation to compensation paid under an offer to make amends as it applies in relation to damages in an action to which that section applies; and
(b) where another person is liable in respect of the same damage (whether jointly or otherwise), the person whose offer to make amends was accepted is not required to pay by virtue of any contribution under section 3(2) of that Act a greater amount than the amount of compensation payable in pursuance of the offer.

(10) Proceedings under this section shall be heard and determined without a jury.

4.—(1) If an offer to make amends under section 2, duly made and not withdrawn, is not accepted by the aggrieved party, the following provisions apply.

(2) The fact that the offer was made is a defence (subject to subsection (3)) to defamation proceedings in respect of the publication in question by that party against the person making the offer.
A qualified offer is only a defence in respect of the meaning to which the offer related.

(3) There is no such defence if the person by whom the offer was made knew or had reason to believe that the statement complained of –

(a) referred to the aggrieved party or was likely to be understood as referring to him, and
(b) was both false and defamatory of that party;

but it shall be presumed until the contrary is shown that he did not know and had no reason to believe that was the case.

(4) The person who made the offer need not rely on it by way of defence, but if he does he may not rely on any other defence.

If the offer was a qualified offer, this applies only in respect of the meaning to which the offer related.

(5) The offer may be relied on in mitigation of damages whether or not it was relied on as a defence.'

The offer to make amends itself is:

(a) to make a suitable correction and apology

(b) to publish the correction and apology in a manner which is both reasonable and practicable

(c) to pay the complaining party compensation and costs.

There is no requirement, as previously under s. 4 of the Defamation Act 1952, that the offer should be 'as soon as practicable'. A further break from the past is the provision for payment of compensation. From a practical point of view the old defence under s. 4 of the 1952 Act was little used. The new defence will prove a viable alternative.

The offer of amends, if not accepted, can operate as a defence but if it is relied on as a defence, no other defences may be pleaded. This may be a deterrent to defendants. If not accepted and not relied on as a defence, it can still be relied on as mitigation.

It should be noted, from a procedural and evidential perspective, that there is a presumption in favour of the defendant, that the publication was innocent.

35. Apology: Libel Act 1843

Apology was no defence at common law. The Libel Act 1843, however, provides that:

(a) In the case of a libel in a newspaper, where there has been no actual malice or gross negligence, it is a defence that the defendant apologised at the earliest opportunity, and paid monies into court by way of amends.

(b) The defendant having offered an apology at the earliest opportunity may be pleaded in mitigation of damages.

The act is seldom invoked, as failure increases the damages by the amount paid into court.

36. Consent

It is a defence that the plaintiff gave *express* or *implied consent* to the allegedly defamatory publication, e.g. by saying 'repeat that in front of witnesses'.

EVIDENTIAL MATTERS

Sections 7, 12 and 13 of the Defamation Act 1996 deal with evidential matters.

Section 7 provides that a court will not be asked to rule whether a statement is arguably capable, as opposed to being capable, of bearing the meaning attributed to it.

Section 12 deals with the issue of evidence of convictions as proof of commission of an offence. Under s. 12, evidence of a conviction will no longer be conclusive proof of the commission of the offence except in relation to a conviction of the plaintiff. This does not apply to the witnesses for the plaintiff.

Evidence concerning proceedings in Parliament is dealt with by s. 13. Under s. 13, for the first time, a right of waiver is given to enable questions to be raised in relation to proceedings in Parliament. The waiver does not affect the absolute privilege which attaches to statements made in the Houses of Parliament.

DAMAGES

The main function of the tort of defamation is to compensate for loss of reputation. A series of exceptionally high awards by juries in libel cases led to concern about excessive levels of damage and extensive press coverage. A turning point came in the case of *Sutcliffe* v. *Pressdram Ltd* [1990] where an award of £600,000 was set aside by the Court of Appeal. Under the Courts and Legal Services Act 1990 the Court of Appeal now has power to substitute 'such sum as appears to be proper' for an amount awarded by a jury which is subsequently held to be 'excessive'. This power was used in the case of *Rantzen* v. *Mirror Group Newspapers* [1993] where an award of £250,000 was reduced to £110,000. The Court of Appeal in *Rantzen* looked at the award in the light of Article 10 of the European Convention on Human Rights in determining the question of whether the award was 'excessive'. Article 10 pronounces the right to freedom of expression, which can only be limited by restrictions or penalties 'as are prescribed by law and are necessary in a democratic society'. The Court looked at the word 'necessary' which it saw as meaning justified by pressing social need. Damages would therefore be 'excessive' when they exceeded a sum that was not 'necessary' in the eyes of a reasonable jury to compensate for injury to reputation. This decision has been seen as the turning point for the award of lower-level damages in defamation cases.

The Defamation Act 1996 does not make any provision to take the assessment of damages away from the jury in libel cases. Guidelines have been given by the Court of Appeal for juries in determining the measure of damages in *Elton John* v. *Mirror Group Newspapers* [1996] but these have been assiduously ignored subsequently, e.g. *Percy* v. *Mirror Group Newspapers* [1996].

The 1996 Act should still have a positive effect: it provides *inter alia* for a fast-track procedure, amendments to evidential and procedural matters designed to make trials less costly and speedier. The Act has also amended the defence of an offer to make amends.

PROCEDURAL CHANGES

37. Fast-track procedure

Sections 8, 9, 10 and 11 provide for a fast-track procedure. This enables a judge alone to deal with libel actions and grant relief, including damages up to £10,000.

This new procedure is to be welcomed, since many plaintiff's cannot meet the cost of a libel action. There is no Legal Aid and few people have the means to commence proceedings and run the risk of cost being awarded against them.

Under the fast-track provisions a judge may grant the following relief:

(a) a declaration that the statement was defamatory of the plaintiff

(b) an order that the defendants publish a suitable correction or apology

(c) an award of damages up to £10,000; and

(e) an order restraining further publication of the libel.

The judge has under this procedure power to determine the compensation and to decide on the content of the apology in the absence of agreement between the parties.

38. Limitation period

Under s. 5 of the Defamation Act 1996, the limitation period for libel actions and for actions for malicious falsehood is reduced to one year. This provision does not, however, exclude the exercise of the court's discretion to hear a case brought outside the limitation period.

Progress test 14

1. Who is a 'right-thinking member of society' in the context of defamation?

2. In what circumstances will an innuendo be defamatory?

3. Define publication of a statement in a defamation action. How has the Defamation Act 1996 had an impact on this?

4. Distinguish between the defences of justification and fair comment.

5. Consider the defences for absolute and qualified privilege in the context of defamation. How have these defences changed following the 1996 Act?

6. Of what significance if any are sections 8 to 11 of the Defamation Act 1996?

15

DEFENCES AND LIMITATION

GENERAL DEFENCES

There are a number of general defences which may be raised to any tort action. These must be distinguished from defences which are relevant only to specific torts, e.g. contributory negligence or qualified privilege.

1. *Volenti non fit injuria*

(a) A person cannot be heard to complain of an injury to the risk of which he *expressly* or *impliedly* consented; such an injury is not actionable as a tort. For example, a person on a public road impliedly consents to the risk of 'such mischief as reasonable care on the part of others cannot avoid': *Holmes* v. *Mather* (1875), *per* Bramwell B.

(b) In respect of negligence, the courts have adopted two distinct approaches to the defence:

(*i*) That the defendant's plea of consent amounts to a denial that he owed a duty of care; as in *Murray* v. *Harringay Arena Ltd* [1951], where a boy of six was injured at an ice-hockey match when the puck was hit into the spectators. The plea of negligence failed on the grounds that no duty of care is owed by organisers of sporting events to guard spectators against dangers normally incidental to the sport in question. *See also dicta* of Lord Diplock in *Wooldridge* v. *Sumner* [1963], cf. Edmund Davies LJ in *Wilks* v. *Cheltenham Home Guard Motor Cycle and Light Car Club* [1971].

(*ii*) That the defendant owed and broke a duty of care but that the plaintiff's assumption of the risk is a good defence. The preferable view is probably the former. This does not mean, however, that attendance at, or participation in, a sport constitutes a waiver of the duty of care owed towards one by the other participants. It is a question of fact in each case whether a duty exists and the rules of the game will be a factor in deciding whether reasonable care has been taken: *see Condon* v. *Basi* [1985].

2. Requirement of knowledge and consent

The test is not whether the plaintiff *knew* of the risk, but whether he *consented* to it. The maxim is *volenti non fit injuria* not *scienti non fit injuria*.

In *Smith* v. *Baker (Charles) & Sons* [1891], a workman in a quarry knew there was danger from a crane overhead. He had protested, but continued to work in the dangerous place. He was injured and sued his employers. It was held that his knowledge of the danger and continuing to work in spite of it did not make him a volunteer, as there was no *true consent* on his part.

An employee will rarely be held *volens* if, when he was injured, he was obeying his employer's instructions, except where the risk he ran was necessarily or ordinarily incidental to his work. In *Bowater* v. *Rowley Regis Corp.* [1944], it was said that '[*volenti non fit injuria*] can hardly ever be applicable where the act to which the servant is said to be *volens* arises out of his ordinary duty, unless the work for which he is engaged is one in which danger is necessarily involved', per Goddard LJ.

In *Dann* v. *Hamilton* [1939], a girl accepted a lift from a driver she knew was drunk, when she could have travelled by bus. It was held that these facts did not make her a volunteer, and she could succeed in negligence: *see also Nettleship* v. *Weston* [1971]. Extreme facts may, however, produce the opposite result.

In *Morris* v. *Murray* [1991] (CA) the plaintiff and defendant decided to go on a flight in the defendant's light aircraft having spent some considerable time drinking alcohol. The plaintiff drove the car to the airfield and assisted the defendant in refuelling and starting the aircraft. The defendant piloted the aircraft which crashed shortly after take-off killing the defendant and severely injuring the plaintiff. In an action for damages for the injuries which he sustained, the plaintiff brought against the deceased's personal representatives; the trial judge giving judgment for the plaintiff found that the defendants had succeeded in their plea of contributory negligence but not on the alternative plea of *volenti non fit injuria*.

On the defendant's appeal it was held by the Court of Appeal, allowing the appeal, that the plaintiff willingly embarked upon the flight, knowing that the defendant, who was piloting the aircraft, was so drunk as to be incapable of discharging a normal duty of care; that the danger in embarking upon the flight was both obvious and great and the plaintiff was not so drunk as to be incapable of appreciating the nature and extent of the risk. Accordingly, the plaintiff must be taken to have fully accepted the risk of serious injury and implicitly discharged the defendant from liability for negligence in relation to the flying of the aircraft; and that accordingly the maxim *volenti non fit injuria* applied as a defence to the plaintiff's claim.

In *Armstrong* v. *Cottrell* the Court of Appeal held that a 12 year old child should lose one third of her compensation for injuries suffered in a collision with a car whilst attempting to cross a busy main road. This was on the ground that someone of her age ought to be familiar with the basics of the Highway Code.

3. No licence in advance

It is suggested in *Dann* v. *Hamilton* that *volenti non fit injuria* will not avail where the act of the plaintiff relied on as consent preceded the alleged tort and is claimed as a *licence in advance* to commit it. This is based on the view that at this stage the plaintiff does not have full knowledge of the nature and extent of the risk and therefore cannot properly be said to have consented to it.

In more recent cases *volenti* has successfully been raised in circumstances suggesting that such a licence can be implied where there was a sufficient measure of prior agreement, although falling short of a contract between the plaintiff and the defendant. *See Buckpitt* v. *Oates* [1968] and *Bennett* v. *Tugwell* [1971] – both cases involving 'exempting' notices stuck on car dashboards which had the effect of making an injured passenger *volens*. Note, however, that the Road Traffic Act 1972, s. 143 makes insurance against liability to passengers compulsory: *see Pitts* v. *Hunt* [1990].

4. The rescue principle

A plaintiff will not be a volunteer:

(a) if, although knowing of the risk, he went to the rescue of a third party endangered by the defendant's negligence

(b) if, although knowing of the risk, he acted under a compelling legal or moral duty.

In *Baker* v. *T.E. Hopkins & Son Ltd* [1959], a doctor went down a well to help men overcome by fumes, and was killed. It was held that he was not *volens*. Ormerod LJ said that 'Dr B may well have had the knowledge of the risk he was running, but that is wholly different from saying that he freely and voluntarily took the risk . . . he acted under the compulsion of his instincts as a brave man and a doctor' (compelling moral duty). 'The doctrine [*volenti non fit injuria*] would not . . . apply in a case of attempted rescue when the act was the natural and foreseeable result of the negligence of the defendant' (third party endangered by defendant's negligence). In *Haynes* v. *Harwood* [1935], a policeman dashed from a police station and stopped runaway horses, thus averting serious danger to women and children. It was held that he freely undertook the risk, but was not *volens* because he acted under a legal and moral duty. He could recover damages from the owner of the horses.

5. Limitations of the rescue principle

Volenti non fit injuria would be a good defence where the plaintiff was injured through his own gratuitous act, when not engaged in a rescue. In *Cutler* v. *United Dairies (London) Ltd* [1933], C was injured while attempting to stop a horse on a quiet country road. He had not been asked to help and there was no danger to others. It was held that he was a volunteer. In *Sylvester* v. *Chapman Ltd* (1935), S was mauled by a leopard when he went inside a barrier to put out a cigarette end on the straw. It was held that he was a volunteer.

6. Illegality, public policy and their relationship with *volenti non fit injuria*

The Court of Appeal's decision in *Pitts* v. *Hunt and Another* [1990] raises a number of important issues, in particular the nature and relevance of illegal conduct as a bar to an action for personal injury.

In *Pitts* v. *Hunt and Another*, the plaintiff (aged 18) and a friend (aged 16) spent the evening drinking at a disco before setting off home on the friend's motor cycle with the plaintiff riding as a pillion passenger. The plaintiff was aware that the motor cyclist was neither licensed to ride a motor cycle nor insured. On the journey home the motor cyclist, encouraged by the plaintiff, rode the motor cycle in a fast, reckless and hazardous manner deliberately intending to frighten other road users and members of the public. The motor cycle hit an oncoming car and the plaintiff was severely injured. The motor cyclist, whose blood alcohol level was more than twice the legal limit for driving a motor vehicle, was killed. The plaintiff claimed damages in negligence against the personal representatives of the motor cyclist and against the driver of the oncoming car. The judge found that there had been no negligence on the part of the driver of the car and held that the plaintiff could not recover damages against the motor cyclist's estate because they were engaged in a joint illegal enterprise.

The judge further held that the claim would have been defeated by the defence of *volenti non fit injuria* but for the fact that s. 148(3) Road Traffic Act 1972, by providing that 'any agreement or understanding' between the driver and a passenger of a motor vehicle had no effect so far as it purported to negative or restrict the driver's liability to the passenger, precluded the defendants from relying on that defence in the context of a motor accident, and that, in any event, the plaintiff was 100 per cent contributorily negligent. The plaintiff appealed against the dismissal of his claim against the motor cyclist's estate. The Court of Appeal held:

(a) *Joint illegal enterprises.* Where one person is injured as a result of the actions of another while they are engaged in a joint illegal enterprise the issue whether the injured party is able to claim against the other person is to be determined not according to whether there was any moral turpitude involved in the joint illegal enterprise but whether the conduct of the person seeking to base his claim on the unlawful act and the character of the enterprise and the hazards necessarily inherent in its execution were such that it was impossible to determine the appropriate standard of care because the joint illegal purpose had displaced the ordinary standard of care.

On the facts, the plaintiff had played a full and active part in encouraging the motor cyclist to commit offences which, had an innocent third party been killed (e.g. another road user), would have amounted to manslaughter by the commission of a dangerous act. The plaintiff ought not to be permitted to recover damages for the injuries which he sustained arising out of the unlawful conduct. The reasoning behind this being founded upon (*i*) the application of the maxim *ex turpi causa non oritur actio*, (*ii*) public policy and (*iii*) that the circumstances of the case precluded the court from finding that the motor cyclist owed any duty of care to the plaintiff. The appeal was therefore dismissed.

(b) *Contributory negligence.* In the context of a plea of contributory negligence it is logically insupportable to find that the plaintiff was 100 per cent contributorily negligent. This is so because the premise on which s. 1 Law Reform (Contributory Negligence) Act 1945 operates is that there is fault on the part of both parties which has caused the damage and that the responsibility must be shared according to the apportionment of liability.

In *Barrett* v. *Ministry of Defence* [1995] the Court of Appeal took the view that 'To dilute self-responsibility and to blame one adult for another's lack of self-control is neither just nor reasonable and in the development of the law of negligence an increment too far'. In that case, a naval airman drank himself into a stupor and suffocated on his own vomit after his mates had taken him to his room and put him in his bunk. The trial judge ruled that the Ministry of Defence should have controlled the amount of drinking at the naval base and reduced damages by 25%. The Court of Appeal held that the Ministry of Defence was not liable for allowing the deceased to drink too much. The Court of Appeal accepted that his mates had failed to look after him properly once he had collapsed, and upheld the trial judge's decision subject to a reduction of 66%. Consider also the Court of Appeal's decision in *Morely* v. *United Friendly Insurance* [1993].

(c) *Volenti non fit injuria* – Section 148(3) Road Traffic Act 1972: the effect of s. 148(3) of the RTA 1972 is that it is not open to the driver of a motor vehicle to say that the fact that his passenger could be said to have willingly accepted a risk of negligence on the driver's part relieves the driver of liability for his negligence since the defence of *volenti non fit injuria* is precluded by s. 148(3) RTA 1972 in the context of a motor accident.

7. *Volenti non fit injuria* and contributory negligence contrasted

There should be no confusion with the defence of contributory negligence under the Law Reform (Contributory Negligence) Act 1945. A plaintiff who is not a volunteer (i.e. did not consent to the risk) may nevertheless have contributed negligence. The difference may be summed up as follows:

(a) In *volenti non fit injuria* the plaintiff truly consented to the risk to which he was exposed.

(b) In contributory negligence the defendant failed to take *reasonable care* for his own safety.

(c) The dividing line has never been precisely established, but the Law Reform (Contributory Negligence) Act 1945 marked a step in the process whereby the scope of *volenti non fit injuria* has been progressively *narrowed* during the last hundred years.

(d) Contributory negligence only applies, as its name suggests, to negligence actions – *volenti non fit injuria* applies in a broader context.

(e) The situation where a person may be said to be 100 per cent contributorily negligent is the point at which the two defences may logically meet. However, in *Pitts* v. *Hunt* [1990] the Court of Appeal took the view that 100 per cent contributory negligence is not sustainable (*see* p. 213).

8. Consent by contract

A person may contract to consent to a risk, but such a purported exemption will be construed strictly against the party claiming the benefit of it. Also, exemption may be prohibited by statute. Thus, the Public Passenger Vehicles Act 1981, s. 29, provides that no exemption from liability can be claimed in respect of death or injury incurred as a passenger in a public-service vehicle. The Unfair Contract Terms Act 1977 provides that:

(a) a contractual term purporting to exclude or restrict a business's liability for death or personal injury resulting from negligence is void, *see* s. 2(1); and

(b) a contractual term purporting to exclude or restrict a business's liability for other heads of loss must be fair and reasonable, *see* s. 2(2) and s. 11(3).

In *Johnstone* v. *Bloomsbury Area Health Authority* [1992] a junior doctor claimed compensation for damage to his health as a result of working long hours. He had contractually agreed to do this but it was suggested by the Court of Appeal that such terms which purported to make him *volens* were subject to the Unfair Contract Terms Act 1977.

9. Consent a question of fact

Exemption apart however, whether or not *volenti non fit injuria* applies is a question of *fact* to be decided in the light of the circumstances of *each case*. The test is: was there or was there not a *real* consent to run the risk?

10. Statutory authority

(a) *Statutory authority confers statutory indemnity*. It will be a good defence in tort that the alleged tortfeaso had statutory authority to do the act complained of. In such a case no compensation can be obtained unless it is provided for by the statute itself.

(b) The defence of statutory authority is of general application, but is particularly relevant to *nuisance*.

(c) Statutory authority may be *absolute* or *conditional*.

11. Absolute statutory authority

Absolute statutory authority confers immunity in respect of:

(a) the act itself

(b) all the *necessary consequences* of the act.

A consequence is necessary if it could not have been avoided by reasonable care and skill; but the 'onus of proving that the result is inevitable is on those who wish to escape liability': *see Manchester Corp.* v. *Farnworth* [1930], *per* Lord Dunedin.

The House of Lords laid down in *Geddis* v. *Proprietors of Bann Reservoir* (1878), *per* Lord Blackburn, that it was 'thoroughly well established' that 'no action will lie for doing that which the legislature has authorised, if it be done without negligence . . . but an action does lie for doing that which the legislature has authorised, if it be done negligently'. This definition was adopted in the more modern cases of *Longhurst* v. *Metropolitan Water Board* [1948] and *Marriage* v. *East Norfolk Rivers Catchment Board* [1950]. In *Vaughan* v. *Taff Vale Railway Co.* (1860), the defendants had statutory authority to run steam locomotives. Damage was caused by sparks from one of their locomotives. It was held that as the engines had been manufactured with all *reasonable skill and care*, and it was impossible entirely to prevent the escape of sparks, the statutory indemnity extended to the damage done by the sparks.

Note, however, the emission of sparks would have been an actionable nuisance at common law, but this was overridden by the statutory authority.

In *Pride of Derby etc. Angling Association* v. *British Celanese Ltd* [1953], the Derby Corporation were the second defendants. They admitted polluting the plaintiff's fishery but claimed statutory indemnity under the Derby Corporation Act 1901 which imposed on them a duty to provide a sewerage system. It was held that a true construction of the Act revealed that it *did not* empower the defendants to commit a nuisance in the discharge of their statutory duty.

The position outlined above has been reiterated by the House of Lords in *Allen* v. *Gulf Oil Refining Ltd* [1981]. The Gulf Oil Company relied on the Gulf Oil Refining Act 1965 for immunity in respect of vibrations, noise and smell caused in extending a refinery. The Court of Appeal held that the Act conferred no such statutory authority, but the House of Lords, following *Manchester Corporation* v. *Farnworth*, held that the Act conferred immunity for the inevitable consequences of the work – otherwise the purpose of the Act (to enable the construction and operation of a refinery) would be nullified. There would however be a remedy for any nuisance exceeding the inevitable, and the onus of *proving inevitability* would be on the company.

In *Tate & Lyle Ltd* v. *GLC* [1983], the defendants acting under statutory authority erected ferry terminals on the Thames. Due to the design adopted, excessive silting of the river bed was caused. This obstructed the public right of navigation and caused damage to be suffered by the plaintiffs. There was an alternative design which would have avoided these consequences. The House of Lords held, therefore, that as these consequences were not the inevitable result of the exercise of the statutory authority, the defendants were liable to the plaintiffs.

12. Conditional statutory authority

This confers authority to do an act only if it can be done without interference with private rights.

13. The statute must be construed in each case

Whether statutory authority is conditional or absolute depends on the construction of the statute.

In *Metropolitan Asylum District* v. *Hill* (1881), a statute empowered a local authority to erect a smallpox hospital. It was held that the statute gave conditional authority only. The local authority was restrained from erecting the hospital where it would cause danger to residents.

14. Imperative and permissive authority

In general, if the statutory power is *imperative*, the authority will be *absolute*: but authority which is merely *permissive* is *prima facie conditional* – for there is a rebuttable presumption that the legislature did not intend to take away private rights without compensation. The burden of proof is on the party asserting that Parliament did intend to take away private rights without compensation. Authority to do a particular act is *prima facie conditional*; but authority to execute a project involving various acts and activities is *prima facie absolute*. The court will more readily hold that authority is absolute if the statute provides for compensation for persons adversely affected.

15. The requirement of good faith

An authority upon whom statutory power is conferred must act in good faith and within the scope of the power: see *Marriage* v. *East Norfolk Rivers Catchment Board* [1950].

16. Powers and duties

A statute which confers a *power* does not (necessarily) impose a *duty*. If the power is merely permissive, no action will lie for failure to exercise it, or for doing so inadequately. In *Smith* v. *Cawdle Fenn Commissioners* [1938], drainage commissioners exercised their permissive power to build an embankment. It was too low to protect the plaintiff's land. It was held that he could not succeed in his action for negligence. The defendants could not be liable for doing negligently what they were not obliged to do at all. He who exercises a power, however, has a duty not to add to the damage that would have accrued if he had done nothing: see *East Suffolk Rivers Catchment Board* v. *Kent* [1941].

NECESSITY, INEVITABILITY AND ACTS OF GOD

17. The rules governing necessity

The following are the main rules governing the defence of necessity:

(a) *Avoidance of greater evil*. The necessity of doing an otherwise tortious act may be good defence even where damage was done intentionally if it can be proved to have been done to *avoid a greater evil* – to the Realm; to a third party; or to the defendant himself. In *The Case of the King's Prerogative in Saltpetre* (1606), it was a good defence that it was necessary for the Crown or a subject to trespass on the land of another in order to take measures (e.g. erect fortifications) for the defence of the Realm. In *Cope* v. *Sharpe* [1912], a gamekeeper, in order to save his master's young birds, set fire to the heather of an adjoining landowner. It was held that no trespass had been committed. Despite the fact that the birds would not have been harmed had the heather not been fired, it was reasonable in the circumstances for the gamekeeper to think his action necessary to avert a greater evil.

A further example would be where an emergency arose in the course of treatment to which a patient had consented. If the doctor gave further treatment in response to the emergency without obtaining the patient's consent, he would probably be able to defend an action for trespass to the person by alleging necessity.

(b) *Life and property*. A different scale of values applies to the saving of life than to the saving of property. 'The two are beyond comparison and the necessity for saving life has at all times been considered a proper ground for inflicting such damage as may be necessary to another's property.' *See* Lord Devlin in *Esso Petroleum Co. Ltd* v. *Southport Corp.* [1956]. For other case examples *see F.* v. *West Berkshire Health Authority* [1989]; *Re T (adult: refusal of medical treatment)* [1992] and *Re S (adult: refusal of medical treatment)* [1992].

(c) *Destruction of animals*. When property is in real danger, necessity will be a good defence to an action for the destruction of animals, e.g. in *Hamps* v. *Darby* [1948], a homing pigeon; and in *Goodway* v. *Beecher* [1951], a dog. However, the courts do not favour the defence of necessity. In *Andreae* v. *Selfridge & Co. Ltd* [1937], the court rejected the defence of necessity of carrying on noisy building operations in order to save time and money.

18. Effect of defendant's negligence

The defence of necessity is not available if the defendant's predicament is due to his own negligence. Thus in *Esso Petroleum Co. Ltd* v. *Southport Corp.* [1956], the Esso Company could not have succeeded with the defence of necessity if the ship had gone aground through negligence.

19. Inevitable accident

It is a good defence that an accident was one which could not have been avoided by any care, precaution or forethought that a reasonable man could have taken in the circumstances of the case. In *Stanley* v. *Powell* [1891] the plaintiff and defendant were both members of a shooting party. The plaintiff was wounded by a pellet which had been fired in a proper manner by the defendant, but had glanced off a tree almost at right angles. It was held that the accident was inevitable and the defendant not liable.

In *National Coal Board* v. *Evans* [1951], the Court of Appeal held that inevitable accident was a good defence to an action for trespass to chattels. The colliery company which preceded the NCB had buried an electric cable in the County Council's land. This fact was unknown to, and could not have been reasonably discovered by, either the Council or its contractor. The contractor damaged the cable while excavating the land. It was held that the accident arose mainly from the wrongful act of the plaintiff's predecessors in burying cables on another's land. Therefore the defendants were without fault and could escape liability through the defence of inevitable accident.

Note, however, inevitable accident is probably not a defence to a claim under the rule in *Rylands* v. *Fletcher*, for which (it seems) only the more stringent defence of Act of God would suffice, *see* **20**.

20. Human forethought excluded, i.e. Act of God

This defence applies only to accidents or injuries which no human care or forethought could have avoided, and in which there was *no human intervention*.

Nichols v. *Marsland* (1876) was an action under the rule in *Rylands* v. *Fletcher*. The defendant constructed a series of artificial pools by damming a natural stream. The pools were well constructed and adequate in all normal circumstances. However, they were destroyed by a storm of quite exceptional violence, with resultant damage to the plaintiff's bridges. It was held that no one had been negligent and the accident was due entirely to an Act of God (*see* 9:12).

21. Limitations of the defence

Act of God is a defence of very limited application, imposing a heavy onus on the defendant. There are *dicta* in a number of cases to the effect that heavy rainfall and violent snowstorms were not Acts of God, i.e. the resultant damage could have been avoided by human care and forethought. The following points should also be noted:

(a) An accident is not an Act of God unless it is the direct result of natural causes *without* human intervention, although this does not mean that human activity must have been completely absent. The direct and immediate cause of the accident must be looked at to determine whether it was caused by Act of God or act of man. Thus, an aeroplane may be destroyed in the air by Act of God notwithstanding that it could not have been in the air except by human action.

(b) An act need not necessarily be violent or exceptional to be an Act of God. The test is: could harm have been prevented by human care? For example, if an accident is caused by the sudden death of a lorry driver from a disease he did not know he had or against the effects of which he could not have guarded, it will be an Act of God: *see Ryan* v. *Youngs* [1938]. This would not be so if, for instance, the driver was a diagnosed diabetic who had neglected to take his treatment.

PLAINTIFF A WRONGDOER

22. Plaintiff acting unlawfully

Can a plaintiff succeed if, at the time of the allegedly tortious act, he was himself acting unlawfully? Unlawfulness and illegality of purpose were considered in the cases of *Pitts* v. *Hunt* [1990] (*see* **6** above) and *Kirkham* v. *Chief Constable of Greater Manchester Police* [1990].

23. Plaintiff's injury and conduct directly connected

It will be otherwise, however, if the harm suffered by the plaintiff was directly connected with his own unlawful conduct, then 'plaintiff a wrongdoer' may be a defence. In *National Coal Board* v. *England* [1954], it was said that a wrongdoer would not be debarred from suing 'unless some unlawful act or conduct on his own part is connected with the harm suffered by him as part of the same transaction'.

24. Common unlawful purpose

No cause of action may arise between persons who had engaged in a common unlawful purpose: *see Pitts* v. *Hunt* [1990].

25. Limitations of the defence

(a) 'Plaintiff a wrongdoer' ought not to be equated with *ex turpi causa non oritur actio* (a base cause cannot found an action). This maxim belongs to the realm of *contract* and probably has no application in tort. A contract is by definition a joint activity, in which the unlawful conduct of each party will be directly connected with the harm done him by the other, but this is not necessarily so in tort.

(b) 'Plaintiff a wrongdoer' should not be confused with *volenti non fit injuria*, contributory negligence, or remoteness of damage, none of which depend primarily upon the allegation that the plaintiff was acting *unlawfully*. It has been suggested that there is no need to recognise the defence of 'plaintiff a wrongdoer' because in the exceptional cases in which it might be applicable, the fact would always bring the defence within one of the three categories mentioned.

TORTS COMMITTED ABROAD

26. Foreign torts actionable in Great Britain

A tort committed abroad will be actionable in Great Britain only if the following conditions apply:

(a) The wrong must have been actionable as a tort if committed in England.

(b) It must have been unjustifiable by the law of the country where it was committed, but need not be classified as a tort in that country. For example, our courts would regard a wrong as 'unjustifiable' if it gave rise to criminal liability in the country of commission, although merely tortious here.

In *Diamond* v. *Bank of London & Montreal Ltd* [1979] CA, the plaintiff, a sugar broker, relied on the confirmation of the defendant bank (in Nassau) as to the bona fides of vendors of sugar in the USA. The vendors did not, in fact, possess the sugar which the broker intended to buy and which was the subject of his enquiry. The broker sued for fraudulent misrepresentation by the defendant bank and for loss of commission on the aborted business. The Court of Appeal considered the question of whether the allegedly fraudulent misrepresentation by the bank in Nassau would constitute a tort committed within the jurisdiction for which a writ could be served out of the jurisdiction, in accordance with RSC Order 11. It was held that the tort took place in England because it was here that the plaintiff decided to accept the (non-existent) sugar, the case being on all fours with *Entores Ltd* v. *Miles Far East Corp.* [1955], where a contract was concluded in England on receipt of a telex from Holland. However, the Court of Appeal exercised its discretion to refuse leave to serve the writ out of the jurisdiction on the ground that the action was in any case prevented by the Statute of Frauds Amendment Act 1828 (Lord Tenterden's Act). Our courts will not entertain a civil action concerning rights over, or trespass against, *foreign land*.

27. Defences

When an action brought here is based on a wrong committed abroad, the defendant may raise *any defence available here* although it would not be available in the country of commission: *see Phillips* v. *Eyre* (1870). 'Two conditions must be fulfilled. First, the wrong must be of such a character that it would have been actionable if committed in England . . . secondly, the act must not have been justifiable by the law of the place where it was done;': *per* Willes J, in *The Halley* (1868). In this case an English and a Dutch ship collided in Dutch waters because of the negligence of the pilot of the English ship. By Dutch law **(a)** the ship was obliged to take a pilot; **(b)** the owners of a ship causing damage were liable in respect of it although the compulsory *pilot was in charge* at the time. This was not the case according to English law. It was held that the defendants were not liable since an English court will not enforce foreign municipal law in respect of an act not unlawful by English law. In *Machado* v. *Fontes* [1897], an action was brought here in respect of a libel published in Brazil. By Brazilian law libel was a crime but not a civil wrong. It was held that the court would hear the case as the wrong was *tortious* here and *unjustifiable* in Brazil. The rule as to foreign torts has been criticised on the ground that damages may be obtained here for an act which would give no right to damages in the country of commission.

LIMITATIONS OF ACTIONS

28. The Limitation Act 1980

This Act came into force on 1 May 1981 and repealed the Limitation Acts of 1939, 1963, and 1975. The 1980 Act is now the major statute governing limitation of actions. The following two points need to be remembered:

(a) Limitation is of great importance in practice; but as it is adjectival rather than substantive it can be dealt with only in barest outline in a book of this nature. Students who need a more extensive knowledge should read appropriate texts.

(b) The Fatal Accidents Acts have been considered in the Fatal Accidents Act 1976, which applies to deaths on or after 1 September 1976.

29. The general rule

The Limitation Act 1980 provides that an action in tort must be brought within six years of the date on which the right of action accrued. In the case of libel and slander, the action must be brought within three years.

30. Negligence, nuisance and breach of duty resulting in personal injury

Section 2 of the 1980 Act continues the previous rule that actions for negligence, nuisance and breach of duty (whether existing by virtue of a contract or any provision made by or under a statute or independently of any contract or any such provision) alleging personal injury, for which damages are claimed, must be brought within *three years* of the date at which the cause of action accrued, or the date of the plaintiff's knowledge, whichever is the later. Section 11(5) provides that if the person injured dies before the expiration of the three-year period (however calculated), the period applicable as respects the cause of action surviving for the benefit of his estate, by virtue of s. 1(2) of the Law Reform (Miscellaneous Provisions) Act 1934, shall be three years from the date of death; or the date of the personal representative's knowledge whichever is the later.

The phrase 'breach of duty' has recently been held not to include deliberate torts such as trespass: *Stubbings* v. *Webb* [1993]. In that case, the plaintiff claimed that she had been sexually abused as a child by her stepbrother and adoptive father. She claimed in battery when she was 35 years old on coming to appreciate the link between the abuse and ongoing psychiatric problems. The House of Lords held that her claim was subject to an absolute limitation period of six years.

31. Application to Fatal Accidents Act 1976

The Limitation Act 1980 provides in s. 12 that no action under the Fatal Accidents Act 1976 shall be brought after the expiration of *three years* from the date of death; or the date of knowledge of the person for whose benefit the action is brought, whichever is the later.

32. Date of knowledge

Section 14 of the 1980 Act provides that references to a person's date of knowledge are references to the date on which he first had knowledge of the following facts:

(a) that the injury was significant

(b) that the injury was attributable in whole or in part to an act or omission which is alleged to constitute negligence, nuisance or breach of duty

(c) the identity of the defendant; and

(d) if it is alleged that the act or omission was that of a person other than the defendant, the identity of that person and the additional facts supporting the bringing of an action against the defendant; and knowledge that any acts or omissions did or did not, as a matter of law, involve negligence, nuisance or breach of duty, is irrelevant.

33. Injury and knowledge

Subsections 2 and 3 of s. 14 expand on the meaning of *significant injury* and *knowledge*:

(a) *Subsection 2.* For the purposes of this section an injury is significant if the person whose date of knowledge is in question would reasonably have considered it sufficiently serious to justify his instituting proceedings for damages against a defendant who did not dispute liability and was able to satisfy a judgment. This subsection was considered by the Court of Appeal in *Dobbie* v. *Medway Health Authority* [1994]. The plaintiff suffered severe psychological illness after the removal of a lump in her left breast. A plea by the defendant health authority that, as the plaintiff's claim had arisen more than three years before issue of proceedings, her action was statute barred was accepted by the Court. It was held that when a prospective plaintiff knows that the personal injury on which his claim is later founded is capable of being attributed to something done or not done by the defendant whom he wishes to sue that knowledge is sufficient to cause time to run against him, notwithstanding that he does not then know that his injury was caused by the defendant's negligence and that he has a possible cause of action.

(b) *Subsection 3.* For the purposes of this section a person's knowledge includes knowledge which he might reasonably have been expected to acquire:

    (*i*) from facts observable or ascertainable by him; or

    (*ii*) from facts ascertainable by him with the help of medical or other appropriate expert advice which it is reasonable for him to seek; but a person shall not be fixed under this provision with knowledge of a fact ascertainable only with the help of expert advice so long as he has taken all reasonable steps to obtain (and, where appropriate, to act on) that advice.

34. Extension of time limits

Section 33 of the 1980 Act confers discretionary power on the courts to extend the time limits in respect of actions for personal injury or death, having regard to the circumstances of the case and in particular to a number of factors specified in subsections (a) to (f) of s. 33(3).

35. The offset of the Limitation Act 1980

This was to prevent the period running in personal injury cases until the plaintiff had the requisite knowledge. The Latent Damage Act 1986 provides a similar protection for potential plaintiffs in non-personal injury cases.

The Defamation Act 1996 by s. 5 makes amendments to the limitation period for defamation actions taking defamation and malicious falsehood actions outside the scope of s. 2 of the Limitation Act 1980 and reducing the limitation period to one year.

It should be noted that the trial judge still has discretion to hear a case brought outside the limitation period; this has not been specifically excluded by the 1996 Act.

36. Latent Damage Act 1986

This Act inserted two new sections (14A and 14B) into the 1980 Limitation Act. Section 14A provides a time limit for claims not involving personal injuries, of either *six years* from the date when the cause of action accrued or *three years* from when the plaintiff knew or ought to have known about the damage, whichever is the later. Section 14B provides an *overriding* time limit of *15 years* (known as *the long stop*) from the date of the defendant's breach of duty. The Act is only applicable to actions in tort: *see Iron Trades Mutual Insurance Co. Ltd* v. *JK Buckenham Ltd* [1990].

37. Fraud, concealment and mistake

Section 32 provides that where an action is based on the fraud of the defendant, or where the defendant has deliberately concealed any fact relevant to the cause of action, or the action is one for relief from the consequences of a mistake, time shall not begin to run until the plaintiff has discovered the fraud, concealment or mistake or could with reasonable diligence have done so. Note that by s. 32(2) deliberate commission of a breach of duty in circumstances in which it is unlikely to be discovered for some time, amounts to deliberate concealment of the facts involved in that breach of duty. A defendant would be thereby barred from taking advantage of the *long stop* provisions of the 1986 Act (*see* **36**).

38. Theft and previous conversion

Section 4 introduces a new provision in that if a chattel is stolen, the right of the person from whom it was stolen to bring an action in respect of the theft shall *not* be subject to the normal *six years* time limit. This shall apply even if the owner's title has been extinguished by the fact that a conversion of the chattel took place more than six years previously, if the theft in question preceded the conversion. However, if anyone purchases the stolen chattel in good faith neither the purchaser nor any conversion following it shall be regarded as related to the theft.

225

Progress test 15

1. Explain the defence of *volenti non fit injuria* and its distinction from contributory negligence.

2. Of what significance is the Court of Appeal's decision in *Pitts* v. *Hunt and Another* [1990]?

3. In what circumstances will the provisions of a statute excuse an act which would otherwise be tortious?

4. How is the defence of necessity established in tort?

5. Outline the provisions of the Limitation Act 1980 as they relate to actions in tort.

6. Explain the effect of the Latent Damage Act 1986 on limitation provisions in tort.

16

REMEDIES

Remedies are often classified as judicial and extra judicial. This chapter will deal only with the *judicial remedies* of damages, injunction and restitution of property.

TYPES OF DAMAGE

1. Damages classified

Damages may be classified in two groups: **(a)** general and special; **(b)** nominal, real/substantial, exemplary, contemptuous, aggravated.

2. General and special damages differentiated

(a) General damages are damages awarded because a tort has been committed from which the law presumes loss or injury to follow, e.g. the plaintiff's loss of the use of his private car after it has been damaged by the defendant's negligence.

(b) Special damages are awarded for injury or loss arising from the tort which is of a kind that the law does not presume to follow from it: e.g. loss of earnings; pain and suffering; hospital expenses. Special damages must be specially pleaded, and quantified in the pleadings.

Note carefully, however, that the definitions of general and special damages are not entirely self-contained and mutually exclusive, e.g. damages for pain and suffering in personal injury claims are *general*.

3. Nominal damages

Nominal damages are a small sum of money awarded, not as compensation, but solely because the plaintiff has proved that a tort has been committed against him, e.g. in a case of trespass to land involving no physical damage to the land or other loss to the plaintiff. It follows that nominal damages are confined to torts actionable *per se*. In *Constantine* v. *Imperial London Hotels Ltd* [1944], the famous West Indian cricketer was refused admittance to the defendant's hotel without reasonable cause, but suffered no special damage. It was held that the exclusion was tortious, and he could recover nominal damages of five guineas.

4. Real, substantial or ordinary damages

These are the general unliquidated damages awarded to compensate the successful plaintiff for the loss, injury or damage he has suffered and, as far as possible, to *restore* him to the *condition* he was in before the tort – *restitutio in integrum*. The quantum of damages is a question of fact, but the methods of assessment used by the courts are outside the scope of this book.

5. Exemplary damages

Exemplary damages (sometimes called *vindictive* or *punitive* damages) represent an addition to what is awarded as real damages, to compensate the plaintiff for what the court considers deplorable or outrageous conduct by the defendant, and (in effect) by way of punishment for it. Exemplary damages are sometimes criticised on the grounds that a civil court should have no concern with punishment. In *Rookes* v. *Barnard* [1964], the House of Lords laid it down that exemplary damages should be awarded only in the following types of cases:

(a) Where there is oppressive, arbitrary or unconstitutional action by the servants of the government (but not by private persons or corporations). See, by way of case example, *AB* v. *South West Water Services Ltd.* [1993] and *Arora* v. *Bradford City Council* [1991] (CA).

(b) Where the defendant's conduct (e.g. by deliberately and tortiously interfering with the plaintiff's trade) was calculated to gain him profit which might exceed the compensation payable to the plaintiff.

(c) Where a statute expressly provides for exemplary damages, e.g. the Reserve and Auxiliary Forces (Protection of Civil Interests) Act 1951, s. 13(2).

Note that these principles were re-affirmed by the House of Lords in *Cassell & Co. Ltd* v. *Broome* [1972], overruling the finding by the Court of Appeal that they had been given *per incuriam*. A review of this case was made by the Court of Appeal in *AB.* v. *South West Water Services Ltd* [1993]. It was held that a nationalised body was not performing a governmental function when conducting its main commercial activity and could not, therefore, fall within the first class of case outlined by Lord Devlin in *Rookes*. The Court further held that, as the intention in *Rookes* had been to restrict the awards of exemplary damages to those areas which were covered by previous authority, such awards could not be made in the absence of pre-1964 authority establishing the availability of exemplary damages for the particular tort. Exemplary damages would therefore be available in e.g. defamation, private nuisance and trespass but not in claims brought in public nuisance or negligence. This reflects the general view that awards of damages in cases of personal injury are designed to compensate rather than to punish.

6. Contemptuous damages

These are awarded to unmeritorious plaintiffs who are nevertheless entitled to succeed. They are the court's expression of its displeasure at a frivolous, vexatious or vindictive action. *See Dering* v. *Uris* [1964] and *Pamplin* v. *Express Newspapers Ltd* (1985), where in each case damages of 'the smallest coin in the realm' were awarded. A plaintiff awarded contemptuous damages is unlikely to be awarded costs.

7. Aggravated damages

These are the reciprocal of contemptuous damages, in that they represent an additional sum awarded to the plaintiff because the defendant's conduct was e.g. wilful or malicious. Aggravated damages differ from exemplary damages in that aggravated damages represent merely *additional compensation*, whereas exemplary damages contain a *punitive* and *deterrent* element.

8. Measure of damages

The function of damages is that, theoretically, they should *restore* the successful plaintiff to his *original condition – resitutio in integrum*. In practice, however, this is often impossible, e.g. where the plaintiff has lost a limb. It is therefore better to regard damages merely as monetary compensation (in so far as, in any given case, money can compensate) for the loss or injury suffered by the plaintiff. For the purposes of assessment, damages may be classified under the headings: **(a)** *damage to property*; **(b)** *injuries to the person*. The actual sum arrived at will be a question of *fact in each case*.

The Administration of Justice Act 1982 gives power to the courts to order interest to be paid on judgments for damages for personal injuries or death, for the period between the date when the cause of action arose and the date of the judgment, unless there is a special reason for not doing so. The heads under which interest is to be awarded were indicated by Lord Denning MR in *Jefford* v. *Gee* [1970].

DAMAGE TO PROPERTY

9. General damages

(a) *Trespass to land*. The damages awarded represent the loss actually suffered by the plaintiff, as represented by the decrease in the value of the land, not the cost of restoring the land to its original condition. Note, however, that damages can be recovered where the defendant derived benefit from wrongfully using the plaintiff's land thereby depriving him of its use, even though the land was not damaged: *see Whitwham* v. *Westminster Brymbo Coal & Coke Co.* [1896].

(b) *Mesne profits*. A plaintiff wrongfully excluded from his land can recover, in an action for mesne profits, the losses he suffered as a result of the exclusion. The action for mesne profits is usually joined with one for ejectment; but a plaintiff may also sue for mesne profits:
  (*i*) after regaining possession

(*ii*) without ejectment or repossession, if his interest in the land has already ended.

(c) *Damage to chattels*. A plaintiff is entitled to the market value of a chattel of which he has been permanently deprived; for a damaged chattel he can recover the full cost of restoring the damage; but he cannot recover from the defendant the cost of restoring damage done by someone else to a chattel which was also damaged by the defendant. In *Performance Cars Ltd* v. *Abraham* [1961], the plaintiff's car was damaged by someone other than the defendant and subsequently damaged by the defendant before repairs to the first damage had been done. It was held that the plaintiff could not recover from the defendant for repairs arising from the first accident.

(d) *Temporary deprivation of chattel*. A plaintiff thus deprived can recover:
    (*i*) for the loss of use of the chattel
    (*ii*) by way of special damages, for its repair and the cost of hiring a replacement (even if no replacement was actually hired), and for other expenses arising from the deprivation.

10. Conversion

(a) *Damages for conversion*. The *quantum* of damages for conversion and its assessment raise some special points, the more important of which may be summarised as follows:
    (*i*) A person with less than full legal ownership of a chattel (e.g. an agent or bailee) who had *actual possession* of a chattel may recover in an action for conversion the entire value of the chattel, and not merely the value of his interest.
    (*ii*) The amount the plaintiff recovers over and above his own interest he holds *on trust* for those entitled to it, and will be liable to them in an action for money had and received for their use. Clearly, however, if the defendant himself, or a third party to whom the defendant was responsible, is among those entitled to the surplus value, then the plaintiff's claim will be reduced by the amounts of such interests.

(b) *Assessment of damages for conversion*. The plaintiff may be entitled to recover:
    (*i*) the chattel itself – either in lieu of monetary damages, or merely by way of reduction of them
    (*ii*) the market value of the chattel at the time of the conversion
    (*iii*) if the chattel had no market value, the cost of its replacement
    (*iv*) damages for any other losses consequent on the conversion, which are not too remote.

(c) *No double satisfaction*. A plaintiff who obtains judgment for the value of property nevertheless retains his title to it, and may therefore, before satisfaction of the judgment, seize it or bring action (where appropriate) for its specific restitution. But he cannot exercise these rights in such a way as to obtain *both* the property and its value. Satisfaction of a judgment, either by return of the property or by paying its value, extinguishes all further rights of action in respect of the same conversion of the same property.

(d) *The Torts (Interference with Goods) Act 1977*, s. 3 deals with proceedings for wrongful interference against a person who is in possession or control of goods. The provisions of the section, which are based on the common law remedies for detinue, are, briefly:

(*i*) an order for restitution and payment for consequential damage

(*ii*) an order for delivery of the goods, but with the alternative of repaying damages

(*iii*) damages.

DAMAGES FOR PERSONAL INJURY

This is a difficult and complex matter, of which only the main points can be indicated here. The assessment of the actual amount of damages is a question of fact in each case. We have seen, however, that general damages are intended to effect *restitutio in integrum*, whereas special damages are awarded to compensate for injuries not presumed to follow the tort.

11. General damages

General damages for personal injuries may be awarded for loss of expectation of life; loss of amenities of life; and pain and suffering.

(a) *Loss of expectation of life.* This is an independent head of damages and was established in the following cases. In *Flint* v. *Lovell* [1935], the expectation of life of the elderly but active plaintiff was reduced to one year through the defendant's negligent driving. It was held that the plaintiff could recover, *inter alia*, for loss of expectation of life. In *Rose* v. *Ford* [1937], a girl died four days after being injured through the defendant's negligent driving. The Court of Appeal declined to award damages for loss of expectation of life for the benefit to the estate under the Law Reform (Miscellaneous Provisions) Act 1934. The House of Lords, however, awarded £1,000 as of right, under the Law Reform (Miscellaneous Provisions) Act 1934, s. 1, for loss of expectation of life.

The Law is now contained in the Administration of Justice Act 1982. Section 1(1) provides that in an action for personal injuries:

(*i*) no damages are recoverable in respect of any loss of expectation of life caused to the injured person by the injuries; *but*

(*ii*) if expectation of life has been reduced by the injuries, the court will take account of the plaintiff's awareness of this in assessing damages for pain and suffering.

(b) *Loss of amenities of life.* The extent of the loss is a question of *fact*, e.g. a young and active person suffers more under this head than an elderly and infirm one. In *Lim Poh Choo* v. *Camden Health Authority* [1980], a successful professional woman of 36 was held entitled to at least £20,000 when her life was totally transformed. It is immaterial to this type of award that the plaintiff is mentally incapable of *realising* his loss, or that he himself will not be able to *use the money*. In *West (H.) & Son Ltd* v. *Shephard* [1964], the defendant's negligence left the plaintiff partially unconscious, totally paralysed and requiring full time nursing. It was held that her 'grave and sombre deprivation' judged objectively entitled her to substantial compensation.

(c) *Pain and suffering.* Damages under this head are generally in personal injury claims. Where there is reasonable apprehension of prolonged suffering, even a large sum may be awarded in respect of the plaintiff's knowledge of his diminished expectation of life. Following the decision of the House of Lords in *Hicks* v. *Chief Constable of South Yorkshire* [1992] it seems likely that no award of damages for pain and suffering may be made in respect of the pain and suffering endured in the course of the person's death. The plaintiffs, personal representatives of two of the victims of the Hillsborough disaster, failed in that case to obtain damages as they were unable, on the facts of the case, to produce evidence that the victims had suffered physical injuries prior to the crushing that killed them. Reference should also be made to *Frost* v. *C.C. of South Yorkshire* [1996]: see p. 51. The settlement reached by the families of the child victims in the Beverley Allitt murders break new ground. In the *Hillsborough* case it was held by the House of Lords that only those relatives of the dead and injured who witnessed the disaster were entitled to compensation. The settlement in the *Allitt* case recognises that this limitation is open to challenge.

(d) *Damages for reduced working life.* Until recently it was unclear as to whether loss of earning power was a separate and distinct head of compensation from loss of expectation of life. In *Pickett* v. *British Rail Engineering* [1980], a 51-year-old vehicle builder's life expectation was reduced to one year after inhaling asbestos dust during his work. The House of Lords awarded his estate a sum for loss of earnings in respect of his eleven lost years of working life.

The Administration of Justice Act 1982, s. 4 now prohibits claims by a deceased person's estate for loss of earnings in respect of a period after his death. In the *Pickett* case, however, the claim was made by the injured party who died before the case was appealed to the House of Lords.

12. Effect of subsequent events on damages

The effect of subsequent events will differ according to whether the events are tortious or non-tortious.

(a) *Tortious events.* In assessing damages the court will take account of injuries to the plaintiff caused by a tortious event subsequent to the original tort, but will not reduce the amount unless the 'devaluation' of the plaintiff by the subsequent event is separate from the effects of the first injury. In *Baker* v. *Willoughby* [1970], the plaintiff succeeded in respect of a car accident which made his left leg useless. Between the accident and the trial he was innocently involved in a robbery, in which he was shot in the injured leg which had to be amputated. It was held that the plaintiff would continue to suffer for as long as he would have done had he not been shot, so his damages would not be reduced on appeal. The second tortfeasor is of course liable for any additional devaluation which he has caused to the plaintiff.

(b) *Non-tortious events.* The difference is illustrated by the following case: *Jobling* v. *Associated Dairies* [1981] HL. In 1973 the plaintiff injured his back through his employer's negligence, whereby his earning power was reduced by 50 per cent. In 1976 he was found to be suffering from a disease of the spinal cord which was entirely unconnected with the injury of 1973. As a result of the disease he was unable to work at all from its discovery in 1976. The trial judge (following *Baker* v. *Willoughby*) awarded a sum for 50 per cent loss of earnings from 1976. The Court of Appeal deleted that sum, on the grounds that the disease of 1976 did not arise from the defendant's tort of 1973 and therefore, the plaintiff's original injury having been subsumed in the later disease, the defendant's liability for his tort of 1973 ceased in 1976.

13. Special damages

Special damages for personal injuries are awarded for loss of earnings and for expenses.

(a) *Loss of earnings.* The plaintiff is entitled to claim his earnings, less income tax and national insurance contributions, for the period between the start of his incapacity and the actual or estimated date of his recovery or death. In *British Transport Commission* v. *Gourley* [1956], the respondent, a person of high earnings, was incapacitated by the appellant's negligence, and had been awarded £37,720 for loss of earnings. It was held that he was entitled only to recover his earnings after tax, and the award would therefore be reduced to £6,695. The following points are to be noted re loss of earnings:

(*i*) In assessing damages, account is taken of any benefits received under the Law Reform (Personal Injuries) Act 1948, s. 2. By s. 4 of the Fatal Accidents Act 1976, certain benefits are not taken into account: *see Stanley* v. *Saddique* [1991] and *Hayden* v. *Hayden* [1992].

(*ii*) Although income tax and national insurance contributions are deductible from damages, the proceeds of insurance policies are not, nor are pensions, payable at *discretion;* but pensions payable *as of right* are deductible. Interest (whether under a court order or not) on damages is excluded from income tax calculations (Income and Corporation Taxes Act 1988, s. 329).

(*iii*) Damages are not to be deducted for loss of earnings between the accident and the death: *see Murray* v. *Shutter* [1975].

(*iv*) Damages should be finally assessed, on established principles, as a global sum, not actuarially under each head: *see Fletcher* v. *Autocar and Transporters Ltd* [1968].

(*v*) Where the injured person continues in the employ of the defendant employer, account may be taken of the difficulty the plaintiff might experience in obtaining equally well-paid employment in the future: *see Moelinker* v. *A. Reyrolle & Co. Ltd* [1977].

(*vi*) Injury to a housewife which impairs her capacity to housekeep is to be treated as a separate head of special damages: *see Daly* v. *General Steam Navigation Co.* [1981] CA.

(b) *Expenses.* The plaintiff may recover by way of special damages all expenses actually and reasonably incurred before the trial. These include, e.g., those for lost or damaged clothing, loss of no-claims bonus, and for medical and nursing expenses. Note that, for the purpose of assessing expenses, no account is taken of benefits under the welfare state legislation. A claim may be made for expenses incurred by a third party on the plaintiff's behalf, e.g. a mother giving up work to care for her injured son. This will not, however, cover services voluntarily rendered from motives of affection or duty by a defendant tortfeasor in caring for a plaintiff who has been injured by the defendant's negligence following the decision of the House of Lords in *Hunt* v. *Severs* [1994].

(c) *Wells* v. *Wells* [1996]. In the cojoined appeals of *Wells* v. *Wells*, *Thomas* v. *Brighton Health Authority* and *Page* v. *Sheerness Steel Co. plc*, the damages in respect of future loss and expense had been calculated using a multiplier based on the return on Index-Linked Government Securities at 3 per cent a year, which had produced a much higher sum of damages for future loss and expense than would have been reached on the conventional approach using a multiplier based on a return of 4 to 5 per cent on the capital sum. Each defendant appealed. Hirst LJ giving the judgement of the Court of Appeal said that the plaintiff should not be placed in a better position than the prudent investor. The award of each plaintiff was substantially reduced (see also 'The shareholder under the Clapham omnibus', *Solicitors Journal*, 1996, vol. 140, p. 1044).

14. Damages Act 1996

The Damages Act 1996 makes significant changes in relation to damages for personal injury:

  (*i*) Section 1: Assumed rate of return on investment of damages.
  (*ii*) Section 2: Consent orders for periodical payments.
  (*iii*) Section 3: Provisional damages in fatal accident claims.
  (*iv*) Sections 4, 5 and 6: Structured settlements, including enhanced protection for annuitants.

These provisions will have significant impact on the conduct of litigation, the negotiation of settlements in personal injury cases and the long-term effectiveness of personal injury compensation.

REMOTENESS AND INTENTION MUTUALLY EXCLUSIVE

Damages in tort cannot be recovered if the wrong complained of is too remote, i.e. not sufficiently closely connected with the harm suffered by the plaintiff. However, damage is *never too remote if it was intended* by the defendant, and a person is presumed to intend the *natural and inevitable consequences* of his acts and omissions.

15. Remoteness of damage in negligence: effect of *The Wagon Mound*

Before *The Wagon Mound (Overseas Tankship (UK) Ltd* v. *Morts Dock & Engineering Co. Ltd* [1961]), the rule was that a defendant in negligence was liable for all the direct consequences of his act, notwithstanding that he could not reasonably foresee them. This was the effect of the decision in the case usually referred to as *Re Polemis* [1921], where through the negligence of the charterers' servants a plank fell into the hold of a ship, striking a spark, and igniting petrol vapour escaping from defective tins, the resultant fire destroying the ship. It was held that the loss of the ship was the direct consequence of the negligence of the servants of the charterers and the latter were therefore liable for it, although they could not reasonably have foreseen it.

In *The Wagon Mound*, as a result of this case, reasonable foreseeability was re-established as the test of remoteness of damage in negligence cases, and *Re Polemis* ceased to be good law. This seems to have been accepted by the House of Lords, *see Hughes* v. *Lord Advocate* [1963], and was specifically accepted by the Court of Appeal in *Doughty* v. *Turner Manufacturing Co. Ltd* [1964], despite the fact that *The Wagon Mound* was decided by the Judicial Committee of the Privy Council and is, therefore, of *persuasive authority* only. It does not appear to be finally decided whether the decision applies only to negligence, but the better opinion seems to be that this is the case.

The facts of *The Wagon Mound* are that appellants, charterers of the *Wagon Mound*, allowed oil to escape from her in Sydney harbour. The appellants could not reasonably have discovered that the oil might ignite when floating on the water but, in fact, it was ignited by sparks from welding operations on the respondent's wharf, to which considerable damage was caused. It was held that the appellants were not liable for this damage because they could not reasonably have foreseen it. Lord Simonds said that, '[Re Polemis] should no longer be regarded as good law. . . . Thus foreseeability becomes the effective test.'

Remoteness of damage in the tort of negligence is fully discussed in Chapter 4. It is, however, useful at this juncture to reflect on where the courts have recently drawn the boundary for the recovery of damages for nervous shock, particularly in the light of the Hillsborough Stadium disaster (*see* 2:**22**).

16. The requirement of reasonable foreseeability

This does not apply in the following cases:

(a) Torts of strict liability, e.g. *Rylands* v. *Fletcher*. However, in *Cambridge Water Co. Ltd.* v. *Eastern Counties Leather plc* [1994] the House of Lords held, by analogy to the law of nuisance, that it is a prerequisite of liability under *Rylands* that the type of damage which occurred was reasonably foreseeable to the defendant.

(b) Breaches of strict statutory duties, e.g. those imposed by the Factories Acts.

(c) Claims under, e.g., the Fatal Accidents Acts, where the question is simply whether the plaintiff is entitled to the compensation for which the Act provides.

(d) Actions for the tort of deceit.

(e) Where, although the damage was foreseeable, it is not of a type against which the defendant was under a duty to guard: *see Gorris* v. *Scott* (1974).

In these cases the test remains whether the damage was the direct consequence of the defendant's act or omission.

17. Extent and amount of damage irrelevant

The test of reasonable foreseeability applies to the type of damage caused, but not to its amount. Thus, provided the damage caused was of a type the defendant ought reasonably to have foreseen, he will be liable for it notwithstanding that its amount is larger than he could reasonably have foreseen. The following cases illustrate these points.

(a) In *Smith* v. *Leech Brain & Co. Ltd* [1961], an employee of the defendants was, through the latter's negligence, splashed by molten metal, as a result of which he subsequently contracted cancer, from which he died. It was held that the widow could recover damages under the Fatal Accidents Acts and the Law Reform (Miscellaneous Provisions) Act 1934, as the injury suffered by the deceased was reasonably foreseeable – although its consequences were not.

(b) In *Hughes* v. *Lord Advocate* [1963], Post Office workmen, having opened a manhole, left it covered by a tent, but with a gap between the bottom of the tent and the ground. Paraffin warning lamps were also left. Two young boys took a lamp and entered the tent, subsequently dropping the lamp into the manhole, causing an explosion which badly burned one of the boys. It was held that the workmen were negligent in thus leaving the manhole, as *children were known* to play nearby. The boy could recover damages because the accident was of a type reasonably foreseeable in the circumstances. The fact that it happened in an unforeseeable way was irrelevant.

(c) In *Doughty* v. *Turner Manufacturing Co. Ltd* [1964], the plaintiff, an employee in the defendant's factory, unintentionally knocked an asbestos cement cover into molten liquid at high temperature, thus causing an explosion, in consequence of which metal was thrown from the vat, injuring the plaintiff. It was held that the plaintiff could not succeed because, in the state of knowledge at the time, the explosion was not reasonably foreseeable. The explosion (which was the sole cause of the accident) was a phenomenon entirely different from the foreseeable splash caused by the cover entering the liquid. This rather restrictive view of foreseeability should be seen in the light of the judgment in *Owgo* v. *Taylor* (discussed above at 4:5).

18. Condition of the plaintiff

The general rule is that a tortfeasor must take his victim as he finds him, so that damage which occurs or is aggravated as a result of some condition of the plaintiff, unknown to the defendant at the time of the tort, is nevertheless foreseeable and therefore actionable.

In *Wieland* v. *Cyril Lord Carpets Ltd* [1969], the plaintiff was injured through the defendant's negligent driving, so that she was obliged to discard the bi-focal glasses she had worn for ten years and suffered a fall as a result. It was held that she could recover from the defendants in respect of the fall.

In *Malcolm* v. *Broadhurst* [1970], a husband and wife were injured by the defendant's negligent driving. A pre-existent nervous condition of the wife was made worse because of a personality change in the husband caused by the accident. It was held that the defendant was liable for the wife's consequential loss of earnings, as the psychological injury to her was foreseeable.

19. Condition of the plaintiff and act of a third party

The decision in *Robinson* v. *Post Office and Another* [1974] re-affirms the principle that a tortfeasor must take his victim as he finds him, so that, if the victim suffers from a condition from which it may reasonably be foreseen that some injury or harm may arise, negligence by a third party will not break the claim of causation so as to make the damage too remote. In *Robinson* v. *Post Office and Another*, the plaintiff's leg was cut when he slipped on an oily ladder provided by his employer. The treatment given by the plaintiff's doctor caused encephalitis and brain damage. It was held that the defendant could *reasonably foresee* that medical treatment would be necessary for injuries arising from his negligence and was therefore liable for any harm resulting from the *treatment given*.

CAUSATION ESSENTIAL FOR LIABILITY

We have seen that a man is responsible for the natural and probable consequences of his acts or omissions, but he will not be so liable unless his act or omission caused the plaintiff's injury. There will be no such causation if an independent *act*, or an act of a third party (*see Weld-Blundell* v. *Stephens* [1920]), or of the plaintiff himself (*see Cummings* (or *McWilliams*) v. *Sir Wm Arrol & Co. Ltd* [1962]) *intervened* so as to break the *chain of causation* and become an independent cause of the harm suffered by the plaintiff. However, now every such action breaks the chain of causation, for it may be a 'mere conduit pipe' through which injury is transmitted from defendant to plaintiff.

20. Intervening act defined

An intervening act, to break the chain of causation, must be 'extraneous' or 'extrinsic' to the extent that it so 'disturbs the sequence of events' as to divorce the tort of the defendant from the consequences suffered by the plaintiff: *see Lord* v. *Pacific Steam Navigation Co. Ltd (The Oropesa)* [1943], *per* Lord Wright. In *Owners of SS Temple Bar* v. *Owners of MV Guildford* [1956]), the *Guildford* and the *Temple Bar* collided. The *Guildford* refused the *Temple Bar's* offer of a tow, and waited several hours for a tug. However, she sank before she could be towed into harbour. It was held that the *Guildford* could recover damages in respect of the

Temple Bar's negligence, the decision of the *Guildford's* Master to await the tug being reasonable in the circumstances, and therefore not a *novus actus interveniens*.

This may be contrasted with *Harnett* v. *Bond* [1925], where the plaintiff was on leave from a mental hospital, the superintendent of which had a discretionary power to take the plaintiff back into confinement if his condition warranted it. The plaintiff called upon the commissioner in lunacy, who mistakenly believing him to be wrongly at large, detained him for some hours while the superintendent was summoned to take him back to the hospital, where he was detained for a further nine years. Eventually, when free the plaintiff sued the commissioner for false imprisonment. It was held that he could succeed in respect of the time he was detained in the commissioner's house, but not for the subsequent nine years, the superintendent's exercise of his discretion being a *novus actus interveniens*.

21. The intervening act may be inoperative

A *novus actus interveniens* does not necessarily absolve the defendant. In the following instances, the defendant remains liable despite the *novus actus interveniens*. The basis of this liability is that the *novus actus interveniens* was reasonably foreseeable by the defendant, and therefore inoperative.

(a) Where the intervening act is the natural and probable consequence of the tort. If the injury to the plaintiff was 'the very kind of thing which is likely to happen if the want of care which is alleged takes place', *see Haynes* v. *Harwood* [1935], *per* Green LJ, then the intervening act will not absolve the defendant, who will remain liable. In *Clay* v. *A J. Crump & Sons Ltd* [1964], the plaintiff was injured by the collapse of an unsafe wall, which an architect and demolition contractors had negligently allowed to remain standing. The plaintiff's employers, building contractors, in reliance on their two co-defendants, did not carefully inspect the wall, which any reasonable careful expert would have seen was unsafe. It was held that the demolition contractor's negligence was not a *novus actus interveniens* absolving the architect and building contractors; and the plaintiff's employers were in breach of their duty to provide a safe system of work. All three were liable to the plaintiff.

(b) Where the intervening act was that of the defendant himself. The defendant remains liable if: (*i*) he himself committed the intervening act; (*ii*) he authorised or instigated another to commit it.

(c) Where the intervener lacked *full tortious responsibility*. If the intervening act was that of e.g. a child, *see Bebee* v. *Sales* (1916), or a person whom the defendant had thrown into a state of sudden alarm, chain of causation is not broken and the defendant remains liable. In *Scott* v. *Shepherd* (1773), the defendant threw a lighted squib on to Yates's stall. Willis, a bystander, threw it on to Ryal's stall. Ryal threw it away, so that it struck the plaintiff and put out his eye. It was held that the defendant was liable; Willis and Ryal did not break the chain of causation, as they acted *instinctively for their own sake*.

(d) Where the intervening act was a legal or moral duty. In such a case, the chain of causation is unbroken, and the defendant remains liable: *see Baker* v. *T.E. Hopkins & Son Ltd* [1959] (*see* 15:4).

(e) Where the intervenor is *asserting* or *defending his rights* there is no *novus actus interveniens*, and the defendant remains liable: *see Clayards* v. *Dethick and Davis* [1848].

(f) Where the plaintiff acts to minimise danger. We have seen that the intervening act may be that of the plaintiff himself, but this will not be so where he was doing no more than discharge his duty to minimise the danger. This does not break the chain of causation and the defendant remains liable.

(g) Where the alleged intervention was contemporaneous with the tort. The *novus actus interveniens* must follow the tort it is alleged to nullify. If two contemporaneous but independent acts cause the same damage, one cannot be an intervening act so as to absolve from liability for the other.

For a full discussion of causation *see* Chapter 4.

22. Negligent valuations – quantum of damages

The House of Lords recent decision in *South Australia Asset Management Corporation* v. *York Montague* [1996] held that the negligent surveyor should only be responsible for the loss arising from the valuation being wrong and not for all of the loss which flowed from the negligent valuation. In effect this decision places a 'cap' on the damage which is recoverable, the correct measure of damage being the loss which is attributable to the inaccuracy of the information, and which was sustained by the plaintiff in entering into the transaction on the assumption that the valuation was accurate.

INJUNCTIONS AND RESTITUTION

23. Injunction a discretionary remedy

An injunction is an equitable remedy given at the discretion of the court. However, since the Supreme Court of Judicature (Consolidation) Act 1925 (now repealed and replaced by the Supreme Court Act 1981 s. 37), it can be granted by any division of the High Court, and may be given in addition to damages. Injunctions may also be granted by county courts.

24. Injunctions of four kinds

Note carefully, however, that they are not exclusive, i.e. prohibitory and mandatory injunctions may each be either interlocutory or perpetual.

(a) *Prohibitory injunctions* are granted to prohibit the doing of an act, e.g. closing a right of way or committing a trespass or nuisance.

(b) *Mandatory injunctions* are granted to compel the defendant to perform some act, e.g. to pull down a building which is obstructing the plaintiff's light.

(c) *Interlocutory injunctions* are granted summarily on the plaintiff's affidavit to prohibit the commission or continuance of some activity by the defendant, pending the hearing of the action. The plaintiff must satisfy the court: (*i*) that he has a triable case, and is probably entitled to relief; (*ii*) that a just settlement would be difficult or impossible unless the interlocutory injunction was granted. The *quia timet* action is a variant of that for an interlocutory injunction. It is granted to restrain the threatened commission of a tort, and is not necessarily followed by any further action. In deciding whether to grant an interlocutory injunction the court should first determine whether damages would be an adequate remedy. If so then an introductory injunction should be refused. If there is doubt as to the adequacy of damages the court asks whether the balance of convenience requires an injunction to be granted. This question is answered by deciding whether uncompensatable harm, and inconvenience, will be suffered to the plaintiff should the injunction be refused. These guidelines were laid down by the House of Lords in *American Cyanamid* v. *Ethicon Ltd* [1975].

(d) *Perpetual injunctions* are granted permanently to compel the defendant to, or prohibit him from, some action.

Note needs to be taken of the so-called *Mareva* injunction whereby a creditor may be restrained from removing assets out of the jurisdiction: *see Mareva Compania Naviera SA* v. *International Bulk Carriers* [1975].

25. Damages in lieu of injunction

The Supreme Court Act 1981 preserves the power of the High Court, originally given by the Chancery Amendment Act 1858, to award damages in lieu of an injunction. However, as the courts are generally unwilling to allow a defendant, in effect, to purchase a licence to continue his tortious activity, they will grant damages in lieu of an injunction only if the following conditions, laid down in *Shelfer* v. *City of London Electric Lighting Co.* [1895], *per* Smith LJ, are fulfilled:

(a) If the injury to the plaintiff's legal rights is small.

(b) If it is capable of being estimated in money.

(c) If it would be oppressive to the defendant to grant an injunction.

In *Sampson* v. *Hodson-Pressinger* [1981] CA, a tenant of a flat, whose agreement contained a covenant for quiet enjoyment, sued the main leaseholder of the block and the tenant of the flat above for nuisance arising from noise consequent upon faulty conversion work. The plaintiff claimed an injunction and damages. The county court awarded damages against one defendant but refused an injunction. The Court of Appeal was asked whether the award of damages could stand, as the plaintiff preferred it to do so and did not wish to press his claim for an injunction. It was held that although damages in place of an injunction would not normally be granted if the effect would be to legalise future nuisances, in this case the grant if damages was at the plaintiff's request and he accepted them in lieu of his right to complain of future nuisance.

The *onus is on the defendant* to establish special circumstances which justify the award of damages in lieu of an injunction: *see McKinnon Industries Ltd* v. *Walker* [1951].

26. An injunction may be suspended

The courts may suspend the operation of an injunction, e.g. to allow the defendant time to adjust his affairs so as to be able to comply with the injunction when it is reimposed.

27. Restitution of property

The court has a discretionary jurisdiction under the Judicature Act 1873 to order the specific restitution of property of which the plaintiff was tortiously dispossessed by the defendant. The following rules apply:

(a) Specific restitution will normally be ordered where the value of the chattel exceeds the damages recoverable by the plaintiff.

(b) The court will not order restitution of a chattel of no special interest or value to the plaintiff where damages would be adequate compensation.

(c) If the defendant, while tortiously in possession of the plaintiff's property, increased its value, the plaintiff can recover only its original value. *See* Torts (Interference with Goods) Act 1977, s. 6. Note also the *Anton Piller order*, under which the court may grant a power of entry and search: *see Anton Piller KG* v. *Manufacturing Processes Ltd* [1976].

Progress test 16

1. Outline the various types of damages which may be awarded in a tort action.

2. What damages are available for conversion?

3. Explain the significance of the decision in *The Wagon Mound* case.

4. When will an intervening act break the chain of causation?

5. What types of injunctions may be granted and when may damages be awarded in lieu of an injunction?

6. What impact if any has the *South Australia Asset Management Corporation* v. *York Montague* [1996] had on the calculation of damages in professional negligence claims arising from property valuations?

APPENDIX

DISCUSSION QUESTIONS

1. '. . . a person under a duty to take reasonable care to provide information on which someone else will decide upon a course of action is, if negligent, not generally regarded as responsible for all the consequences of that course of action. He is responsible only for the consequences of the information being wrong. A duty of care which imposes upon the informant responsibility for losses which would have occurred even if the information which he gave had been correct is not in my view fair and reasonable as between the parties. It is therefore inappropriate either as an implied term of a contract or as a tortious duty arising from the relationship between them'.

   per Lord Hoffmann, *South Australia Asset Management Corporation* v. *York Montague* [1996] 3 WLR at p. 95 (HL).
   Analyse Lord Hoffman's dictum with regard to the scope of duty of care in professional negligence actions.

2. Examine the duties owed by an employer to his employee with regard to injury to the employee and with respect to provision of references on termination of employment.

3. Jack is the manager of The Rovers Return, a public house. He is employed, together with his wife, Vera, to manage the pub. He invites a number of regulars at the pub to stay behind after licensing hours for a small informal party to celebrate his and Vera's wedding anniversary. Mike, one of the guests, leaves the flat above the pub via the external iron staircase at the rear of the premises to go and have a look at Jack's pigeons. Mike slips on the wet unlit staircase and sustains a fracture to his left thigh bone. Vera calls an ambulance which takes 20 minutes to arrive; in order to get Mike out of the rain and to make him more comfortable, Vera, Rita and Mavis move Mike, causing him an agonising compound fracture to his left thigh.

   Advise Mike as to any claims which he may have against Jack, Vera and the brewery which owns and manages The Rover's Return, for the injuries which he has sustained. Consider the defences, if any, which each potential defendant may have to Mike's claim.

4. Tony has been drinking heavily following an argument with a work colleague Claire. Tony is knocked down by Jim who is driving his car at 29 miles per hour, because he was not looking ahead and did not see Tony lurch into the road or that the traffic signal controlling the pedestrian crossing was red. Tony sustains a blow to his head and injuries to his chest and a fracture of his left leg; he is also knocked unconscious by the impact of Paddy's 4 × 4. Tony is rushed to St Margaret's Teaching Hospital, where he is attended by Virginia a junior doctor who is working her fourth consecutive night shift and who hasn't slept for 52 hours. Virginia realises that the injuries to Tony's chest may be serious and telephones Michael the A&E consultant surgeon at his home. Michael is holding a dinner party and refuses to attend Tony at the hospital reassuring Virginia that she can cope and that she does not need to drag him in. Michael outlines to Virginia the steps she should take, but omits to tell her that some patients may have a severe allergic reaction to the drugs used in the treatment which

he is proposing for Tony. Virginia follows the treatment regime outlined by Michael; however, within six hours of the treatment Tony suffers heart failure and dies. The autopsy shows that Tony had a severe allergic reaction to the drugs but that this alone would not have caused heart failure and that a contributing factor was the injuries which he sustained when struck by Jim's vehicle.

Consider what action(s) if any can be brought and by whom in relation to Tony's injuries and his death.

5. Bianca lives in a terraced house in an inner city suburb. About half a mile away is Parrot Wharf, an urban renewal project. The main structure at Parrot Wharf is a very high office block. Since the office block has been completed Bianca has not been able to get clear reception on BBC1 and ITV; she can get weak reception on BBC 2 and only slightly better reception on Channel 4. She cannot get any radio reception at all. Next door, to Bianca's house lives Ethel, she keeps a fierce dog called Willy. This dog barks each time Ethel locks him out and when she leaves the house, and for the duration of her absence Willy whines constantly. From a nearby house Pat runs a mini-cab business and across the way David has started to run a scrapyard using the land to the side of his house as a parking area for parking cars before he 'scraps' them on his drive.

Advise Bianca whether she has any potential claim(s) in tort. If so, against whom and on what basis?

6. 'Where a statute confers a private law right of action a breach of statutory duty howsoever caused will found the action. Where the statute authorises that to be done which will necessarily cause injury to someone no action will lie if the act is performed with reasonable care. If, on the other hand, the act is performed carelessly whereby unnecessary damage is caused a common law action will lie. This because the act would, but for the statute, be actionable at common law and the defence which the statute provides extends only to the careful performance of the act. The statute only authorises the invasion of private rights to the extent that the statutory powers are exercised with reasonable and proper regard for the holders of such rights. The careless performance of an authorised act, rather than amounting to breach of a new duty, simply ceases to be a defence to a common law right of action.'

per Lord Jauncey in *X. v. Bedfordshire County Council* [1995] 3 All E.R. 353 (HL).
Critically evaluate the above statement.

7. C is being stalked by a former girlfriend D. D sits outside the radio station where C is a D.J. with a big banner which reads 'I will always love you'. C's current girlfriend insists that C has a word with D about her ridiculous and humiliating behaviour. She suggests that C invites D to his flat one evening to try and settle things. C invites D to his flat, and begins to tell her that she must stop stalking him whereupon she takes a large knife from her Gucci handbag and says 'I will end it all here and now if I cannot have you'. Hearing what is going on from an adjacent room C's girlfriend storms into the room. D cuts C on his arm. She then places the knife at her own throat and says that if they call the police she will slash her throat. C rugby tackles D, and D sustains a broken collar-bone and bruising. C dials 999 and the emergency services arrive and take control of the situation.

Advise C what actions, if any, he may have in tort against D as well as any defences which D may raise.

INDEX

Psychiatric harm
  bystanders, 50
  damages, 46, 49–54
  duty of care, 13, 46–9
  foreseeability, 46–8, 49–50
  Hillsborough disaster, 49–51
  ME, 52–3
  omissions, 45
  Page v *Smith*, 52–4
  proximity, 46–7, 50, 51, 53
  remoteness, 75, 76
  rescue services, 47
  stalking, 169
  standard of care, 57
Public policy
  barristers, 34
  breach of statutory duty, 155, 158
  duty of care, 12, 13–14, 15, 32–3
  economic loss, 32–3
  false imprisonment, 33
  fire services, 42
  police, 32, 33
  prison officers, 40
  psychiatric harm, 52
  volenti non fit injuria, 213–15

Reasonableness
  breach of statutory duty, 156
  defamation, 191, 194, 195
  independent contractors, 84
  negligence, 8
  nuisance, 126–7, 135
  occupiers' liability, 81, 84, 86, 91
  standard of care, 55, 60
  warnings, 86
Reception, 187
References, 25, 28, 45
Rehabilitation of offenders, 198
Reliance
  duty of care, 12
  negligent misstatements, 27
  Hedley Byrne v *Heller*, 22, 23, 27
  volenti non fit injuria, 213
Remedies, 227–39. *See also* Damages,
    Injunctions
  restitution, 186
  trespass to goods, 185–6
  trespass to land, 166–7
Remoteness, 4, 65, 72–6
  breach of duty, 72
  causation, 72
  damages, 234–7
  'eggshell skull' rule, 75–6
  foreseeability, 72–6
  intention, 234–7
  psychiatric harm, 75, 76

  safe system of work, 76
  trespass to goods, 186
Replevin, 187
Res ipsa loquitur, 101–2, 109
Rescue services, 42, 47
Restitution, 186, 240–1
Rights of way, 81, 85, 90, 162
Road traffic offences, 3, 56, 154, 214

Safe system of work, 76, 105–6
Schools, 45–6, 178
Self-defence, 174–5
Slander of title and goods, 119–20
Solicitors
  beneficiaries, 29, 35
  defamation, 205
  duty of care, 29, 34–6
Sport
  insurance, 40–1
  standard of care, 63
  teachers, 40–1
  trespass to the person, 177
  volenti non fit injuria, 211
Stalking, 169
Standard of care, 6–7, 55–64
  breach of statutory duty, 157
  children, 64
  damages, 55
  driving offences, 56
  foreseeability, 56–7, 63
  knowledge, 58
  magnitude of risk, 58
  medical negligence, 36
  negligence, 9
  objective, 56–7
  occupiers' liability, 90
  precautions, 59–60
  prison service, 61–2
  professional, 60–3
  psychiatric harm, 57
  reasonableness, 55, 60
  sport, 63
  suicide, 62
  valuations, 61
Standard terms of contract, 5
Stress. *See* Psychiatric harm
Strict liability, 6, 137–51
  absolute, 137
  Acts of God, 143
  acts of strangers, 142–3
  animals, 144–9
  consent, 141
  consumer protection, 149–51
  damages, 142, 235
  default, 141–2
  defences, 141–4